Christology as Narrative Quest

Michael L. Cook, S.J.

A Michael Glazier Book
THE LITURGICAL PRESS
Collegeville, Minnesota

Cover design by David Manahan, O.S.B. "Jesus Encounters His Mother," oil painting, anonymous, 17th century, Quito, Ecuador.

A Michael Glazier Book published by The Liturgical Press

All abbreviations of periodical literature follow Siegfried M. Schwertner, *Theologische Realenzyklopädie: Abkürzungsverzeichnis,* 2nd rev. ed. (Berlin, N.Y.: Walter de Gruyter) 1994, with the exception of *JH/LT (Journal of Hispanic/Latino Theology)* and *NTR (New Theology Review).*

1	2	3	4	5	6	7	8

Library of Congress Cataloging-in-Publication Data

Cook, Michael L. (Michael LaVelle), 1936–
    Christology as narrative quest / Michael L. Cook.
        p.   cm.
    Includes bibliographical references and index.
    ISBN 0-8146-5854-7
    1. Jesus Christ—Person and offices—History of doctrines.
    2. Hermeneutics—Religious aspects—Christianity.   I. Title.
BT202.C673   1997
232—dc21   96-51701
                                                     CIP

For William G. Elliott, S.J.,
my novice master
who, into his second century,
was still teaching me
what it means to be a Jesuit.
And for all my brother Jesuits
with affection and gratitude
for "many years"
as companions in Christ.

Contents

Acknowledgements

This book would not have been possible without the support and encouragement of many people. While I can mention only a few here, I am deeply grateful to all. First, I wish to acknowledge Gonzaga University, especially in the person of the Academic Vice President Patrick J. Ford, S.J. who graciously granted me a sabbatical in 1993–1994. That year enabled me to finish a great deal of the research and writing. In that connection I wish to thank James Dallen, the chair of our department at that time, and my colleagues in the Religious Studies Department for their unfailing support and encouragement. Next I would like to thank Robert E. Manning, S.J., the Rector of the Jesuit community in Berkeley, as well as the community members themselves, for providing a comfortable and agreeable environment for me to live and work during the sabbatical. I also wish to thank the library staff at the Graduate Theological Union in Berkeley for their generous assistance in the use of the library resources. In a special way I would like to thank J. J. Mueller, S.J. of St. Louis University and Michael Downey of Bellarmine College, Louisville, the distinguished Flannery Professors at Gonzaga in successive years who graciously read through the entire manuscript. In addition, I would like to thank Linda M. Maloney, the Academic Editor at Liturgical Press whose diligence and acuity in editing the text have certainly made the text more readable. I also thank Donald E. Highberger, S.J., whose generous help was indispensable for producing the index. Finally I thank my brother Jesuits to whom this book is dedicated. They have been with me in good times and bad and I am most deeply grateful for their companionship on the journey.

Introduction

"The work of seeking a fresh image of Jesus in the life of a believing people has never ceased."[1] Jesus continues to energize the imagination. Were it not so we would not still be seeking to speak of him in such intense and personal ways almost two thousand years after his death. The question that underlies this book is one that concerns many in our contemporary world: has our image of Jesus, the way we experience and imagine him, shifted? And if so, is this a legitimate shift and does it remain in continuity with the human, historical Jesus of Nazareth who proclaimed the reign of God, suffered and died on the cross, and was raised into the glory of the Father? Indeed, do our contemporary ways of speaking about Jesus remain in continuity with the ways Christians have imagined him and brought him to expression throughout the centuries?

The fact is that every Christian, as believer, has a faith-image of Jesus, i.e., an image that arises out of and so assumes a relationship of faith. Such an image is normally the product of both personal experiences and historical tradition. An image is created and handed on by a community of faith and is appropriated both communally and individually according to particular lived experience within a given cultural context.

To understand what this means for our question we must first make some initial clarifications regarding (1) the power of imagination; (2) faith as "a life of the imagination;"[2] (3) theology as a hermeneutical enterprise that is traditional, creative, and contextual; and (4) doctrine, or "belief," understood not as mere opinion but as official formulations of the Christian faith in the multiple forms of Scripture, creed (including liturgy), and council. These initial clarifications will then make it possible for us to propose a plan of inquiry in terms of four key faith-images of Jesus that have had a paradigmatic impact on the Christian consciousness and to clarify the purpose and ultimate goal of the present work as a whole.

1. Initial Clarifications

The Power of the Imagination. Can we imagine, says Jonathan Schell, complete nuclear or ecological annihilation, "immersion in death" (Robert Jay Lifton), the absolute nothingness of extinction?—or, as Stephen Hawking puts it, the "big crunch" as the universe contracts to a singularity that parallels its origins? One end is evoked by the destructive power of human technology, the other by the immense and mysterious power of the cosmos. Both authors use their imaginations to reach for alternatives.

In discussing the technical and gruesome reality of nuclear weapons, Schell remarks: "It may be only by descending into this hell in imagination now that we can hope to escape descending into it in reality at some later time."[3] Although not excluding the possible religious dimension he appeals primarily to the alternative of human responsibility: not the continued dominance of reason over nature but the fundamental instinct of nature itself for the preservation of the species, which for humans comes to expression as creative love *(eros)*. This involves three "principles of life": respect for human beings, born and unborn; respect for the earth; respect for the power of creativity (whether conceived of as God or as Nature) that we can destroy but that, because it is the originating power of life, we cannot create or recreate once destroyed.[4] Our numbness and inertia in the face of threatened extinction is a failure of imagination. And it is imagination that can empower us to change our "modes of thinking" (Einstein): can we move beyond national sovereignty with its "vital interests" to embrace the human family, mother earth, and indeed the whole generative cosmos as one interactive and interlocking web of vital relationships?

Schell says that we *can* choose life not only for ourselves but especially for the future generations of humankind. While Schell focuses on "the fate of the earth," Hawking stretches our imagination to embrace the whole of the cosmos. In opposition to theories of a "singularity" (= "a point in space-time at which the space-time curvature becomes infinite") whether at the beginning of the universe ("big bang") or at the end ("big crunch"), he employs a quantum theory of gravity to propose what he calls the *"no boundary condition: The idea that the universe is finite but has no boundary (in imaginary time)."* If there is no boundary, then we do not need to set boundary conditions, whether by a theorem of singularity or God or new laws. "The universe would be completely self-contained and not affected by anything outside itself. It would neither be created nor destroyed. It would just BE."[5] Of course, as he says farther on, the real test of this theory, as of any scientific theory, is whether it makes predictions that agree with observation. "The no boundary proposal for the universe predicts the existence of a well-defined thermodynamic arrow of time because the universe must start off in a smooth and ordered state. And the reason we observe this thermodynamic arrow to agree with the cosmological arrow is that intelligent beings can exist only in the expanding phase. The contracting phase will be unsuitable because it has no strong thermodynamic arrow of time."[6]

It is not my intention to enter into the merits of such a proposal as a scientific theory (something beyond my competence), but as a theologian I do question the implied concept of God that is operative throughout. One is reminded of LaPlace's famous reply to Napoleon: I have no need of that hypothesis. The difficulty is that Hawking seems to conceive of God as a function of the beginning or end of the process. If there is no beginning or end, there is no need for God. The Hebraic-Christian imagination, on the other hand, empowers us to know God as alive, active, and present throughout the creative process. This is a God who is not merely at the boundaries or necessary to fill in the gaps in our scientific theories, but a God who is at the center of human life and experience, a personal God known in the imaginative power of narrative, i.e., the story we tell to make sense of the universe. In this story, however, it is God who is the primary "teller of the tale."

What is at play here is the power of the *ironic* imagination. Both Schell and Hawking reflect on the limits of birth and death. It should be emphasized that neither is speaking of individuals as such. Schell speaks of the "second death," that of the species as a whole that threatens the "loss of birth."[7] Hawking seeks to exclude the possibility of the infinite by positing a completely finite world with no boundaries, thus eliminating the need to talk about beginnings or endings. But such a "totalitarian world" excludes "infinite possibility" and with it "the free and creative imagination."[8] It is between birth and death, between the infinite and unending potential of life and the finality and decisive closure of death, that the ironic imagination comes into play. Sandra Schneiders offers a fine insight in her phrase "the paschal imagination." She is speaking of the world behind the New Testament that gave rise to the text and she sees the process as involving a move from historical experiences to their transformation in the power of the imagination:

> I have tried to show that what gave rise to the text was not simply the life of the actual earthly Jesus and the first Christian communities but the theological-spiritual imagination of the believing community, which transformed its historical experience into a dynamic image of Jesus the Christ as locus of divine revelation. The New Testament text is the product of that paschal imagination.[9]

In the course of her argument she analyzes the characteristics of images as produced by the "constructive imagination," i.e., "our capacity to construct our world" as distinct from imagination as merely reproductive, recalling past experiences through images, e.g., a walk in the woods, or as synthetic, combining images in one's mind that may or may not exist independently, such as a blue horse. Images like that of the "proclaimed Jesus" constructed by the paschal imagination are dynamic and tensive principles of interpretation that allow us to relate individual and partial experiences into a whole. They operate simultaneously in relation to past, present, and future, yet are open-ended so that the process of interpretation is a never-ending spiral. Finally, they are "loaded with affect" and so involve the whole person, not just the intellect or will, in their dynamism.[10] To this I would only add, especially when one speaks of the Hebraic-Christian faith, William Lynch's emphasis on the ironic whose "main task is to keep opposites together in a single act of the imagination."[11]

Irony depends on our imaginative capacity to see and experience the reality of our world or God or ourselves in new and unexpected ways that appear to the so-called "realist" or person of "common sense" as contradictory or absurd. "There is no more ironic scene in all the Gospel literature than the wise men from the East discovering the one who had been born king of the Jews 'seated on, the knees of *a peasant woman, a worker's wife* in a peasant worker's rustic hut'" (Matt 2:1-12).[12]

Faith as a Life of the Imagination. Faith is "a way of experiencing and imagining the world; or it is a world within which we experience or imagine."[13] At its most fundamental faith is the simple but profound human capacity to transcend oneself and to entrust oneself to another person. Religious faith specifies a relationship with God and Christian faith more specifically still with God in Christ, but such specifications take up into themselves in a transformative way the universal human experience of mutual empowerment through the simple act of trust. As such faith is not an epiphenomenon, something added to human experience, but is that which constitutes the very possibility of truly human experience. To trust someone demands a leap of the imagination beyond any possibility of empirical proof in the strict sense. Clearly I will not trust another person unless I have good grounds for doing so. Those grounds are the lived experience of a historical relationship: time, interests, background, experiences shared at various levels. But if a relationship is to move beyond the level of a simple acquaintance or generic friendliness there comes a moment, whether sudden or gradual, when one transcends the "evidence" and takes the risk of entrusting oneself to the other person. It is a risk, for one could be mistaken and the trust betrayed. Thus the imaginative leap involves at one and the same time unlimited possibilities of a new life together through mutual empowerment and life-threatening vulnerability.

This does not cease to be true in our relationship with God, especially as experienced in Christ. It is true that according to the doctrine of grace God first empowers us to have faith in a religious or Christian sense. But God's power is not coercive; it is an invitation that depends on our free human response. By such a response, in a very real sense, we empower God. We allow God to live in our hearts and so in our world and we express that life through images that are ironic. Indeed, it is the ironic imagination that allows us to see the infinite worth and dignity of each particular human person.

In speaking of specifically Christian faith Avery Dulles makes the valid point that we should not forget the particularity of such faith.[14] Faith in Christ means that we see everything in a different way. Christians read the Jewish Scriptures through the lens of faith in Christ. They view God as personally available in a sacramental way. They recognize as inseparable and indispensable a relationship to God in Christ and to one another as a community of faith. They view history not simply as coming to an end, whether through thermonuclear disaster or ecological destruction or contraction to a "singularity," but as an eschatological event in which God comes to us, a new and surprising "advent."[15] Above all they affirm the most ironic reality of all—that the eternal and triune Creator has become one of us in the person of Jesus, like us in all things except sin (Heb 4:15; 5:7-10). The irony of faith is the irony of Christ and "the irony of Christ is Christ himself."[16] Christian faith involves a particular relationship to one individual, Jesus of Nazareth, and so is profoundly rooted in the concrete particularity of history. Yet that individual is seen to embody the fullness of what it is to be human in relation to the divine and so to break the bonds of a world understood too narrowly as a self-contained reality. The ironic imagination opens us to infinite possibility. Christian faith, mediated as it always is by a community of believers/disciples, affirms the interconnectedness of all things: the cosmos, the earth, the human species, and the creative love of God.[17]

Theology as a Hermeneutical Enterprise. Theology, unlike a more "objective" and empirical study of religion, assumes the personal commitment of faith as constitutive of a community in which the gifts given to each are intended for the good of the whole "body" (Rom 12:4-5; 1 Cor 12:4-11, 12-31; Col 3:14-15; Eph 4:11-16). This community exists, in turn, not for its own sake but for the sake of the reign of God that reaches out to and includes the whole of creation. Theology, according to Anselm, is "faith seeking understanding." Robert Schreiter employs a very helpful analogy to differentiate faith, theology, and belief (doctrine). Taking a clue from the work of Noam Chomsky on the transformation of grammar he suggests that faith is analogous to language competence, theology to language performance, and the "loci of orthodoxy" (Scriptures, creeds, councils, etc.) to grammar, which mediates competence and performance.[18] We will focus on theology in this section and on belief or doctrine in the next.

Just as each of us is born into our native language and normally manifests surprising competence in the use of language at a very early age, so each Christian is through baptism born into the life of faith as described above. Just as in language we know that one is competent by the ability to form correct, well-formed sentences (grammar functions normatively here to describe in a set of rules what is or is not a well-formed sentence, but grammar can and does change through the creativity of new or exceptional performances), so theology can be understood as the "language of faith" on the level of performance. We will return to the normativity of orthodoxy as the "grammar of faith," but for the moment it is important to emphasize the creativity involved in the theological enterprise as expression of the living faith of the whole Christian community in each successive generation. In addition it must also be underlined that theology is too important to leave to the professional theologians alone. A great cathedral, an artistic painting or statue, a vibrant liturgical celebration, a dramatic enactment in a poem or play, a deeply moving story—all these and more are the ways Christians bring to expression the depths of their faith commitment.

We must broaden our understanding of who does theology and how. To do so it is helpful to look at some of the "paradigm shifts" that have taken place and that underlie the current debate between the teaching authority of the official magisterium and the responsibility of theologians as an academy of professionals. Schubert Ogden, following Thomas Kuhn, distinguishes two meanings of paradigm.

> In the first, relatively broader sense it refers to a "disciplinary matrix" which consists in "an entire constellation of beliefs, values, techniques and so on shared by the members of a given community." In the second, relatively stricter sense it refers to one of the types of items included in this disciplinary matrix—namely, "exemplars" or "concrete puzzle-solutions which, employed as models or examples, can replace explicit rules as a basis for the solution of the remaining puzzles of normal science."[19]

In line with the preparatory papers of the symposium he notes that the first is applicable in the theological context to the question of "a consensus (of a hermeneutical kind) about a certain theoretical-practical understanding of theology" and the second to "a consensus (of a material kind) about particular teachings, doctrines, dogmas." We are concerned with the first in this section and with the second in the next.

Other authors in the symposium, looking for still broader categories to account for shifts in theology, speak of "epochal shifts" or "conjunctural history" that embrace larger periods and are more comprehensive.[20] In a similar vein, though still employing the language of "shifting paradigms," John Thiel analyses the shift from the "classical paradigm" to the "romantic paradigm" in modern theology.[21] Following Robert Schreiter and later Stephen Bevans,[22] might we not now speak of yet another "paradigm shift," i.e., the contextual paradigm? Let us briefly consider each of these paradigms in theology, the first emphasizing more the traditional, the second the creative, and the third the contextual dimensions of contemporary theology.

The "classical paradigm," which according to Thiel covers the period from the twelfth century to the Enlightenment, placed primary emphasis on the tradition understood as the accepted "authorities" (Scriptures, creeds, and councils, patristic authors). The primary task of the theologian was to offer commentaries on the accepted sources that would clarify and illumine but never question what was deemed to come from God as the sole author of the truth of salvation. Therefore theological responsibility was seen in terms of an ecclesial role to maintain faithfulness to divine revelation through the authorities. Even when an individual theologian such as Thomas Aquinas employed originality and creativity it was intended not as a denial or criticism of the authorities in order to create a new theology but as an attempt to bring out more clearly the deeper intention of the authorities themselves.

The shift to the "romantic paradigm" in the nineteenth century was in part a reaction against and in part an appropriation of Enlightenment rationalism. The ideal of free critical investigation over against the predominance of extrinsic authorities, the appeal to evidence based on experience and observation in both science and history, the recognition of historical process and historical consciousness in the discovery of truth, the importance attached to the subject and to reliance on one's own sensibilities and talent all found their correlate in the personal creativity and originality of the theologian who now became an author (authority) patterned at times on the heroic identity of the romantic hero. This was not intended to deny but rather to emphasize the theologian's responsibility to the community of faith. The theologian does this, however, precisely as defender of the freedom of religious imagination and of openness to new possibilities so that the focus now is upon "imaginative construction" rather than "mimetic representation." The tension between freedom and fidelity has evoked a corresponding ambivalence in the official magisterium, which by Vatican II had at least recognized a certain division of labor between the pastoral responsibility of bishops to maintain the continuity of tradition through proclamation and the academic responsibility of theologians to explore new frontiers through research and study. These are not clearly drawn lines as all theologians should be pastoral and all bishops should be theologically astute. Nonetheless, it represents a certain practical necessity in the face of the growing complexity of doing responsible theology in the modern world.

But as many claim today, we live in a post-modern world. The individualism implicit in the romantic paradigm is being countered by a stronger emphasis on the feminist and ecological values of interconnectedness, mutuality, and relationship. The temptation to elitism and a certain overweening professionalism is being countered by appeals to the voice of the people, especially the poor and oppressed. The Eurocentric cast of modern theology is being countered by a profound recognition of cultural diversity as legitimate, necessary, and cherished. The abstract certainties of the academic establishment (in science and the humanities as well as in religion) are being challenged by a hermeneutics of suspicion that recognizes ideological bias, ambiguity, and radical limitation in all constructions of the human mind. And so another paradigm shift seems to be emerging in theology: the contextual paradigm.[23]

Robert Schreiter describes "local theology" as involving a constant dialectical interaction between three very complex realities: gospel, church (tradition), and culture.[24] Stephen Bevans says the same but teases out a fourth dynamic from what Schreiter subsumes under culture, namely social change. In both authors the important and decisive reality, often ignored in past theological constructions, is culture. In an important chapter on the study of culture, focusing on semiotic analysis (the sign-system of a given culture), Schreiter affirms that "the process of constructing local theologies begins with a study of the culture."[25] Bevans, citing Bernard Lonergan, agrees: "Theology, according to Lonergan, is what mediates between a cultural matrix and the significance and role of religion in that matrix. Theology, in other words, is the way religion makes sense within a particular culture."[26]

Bevans prefers "contextualization" to other terms such as "indigenization" or "inculturation" because it includes the other terms but opens out more to present realities: social, political, economic, etcetera. But the real issue is how one understands the interaction of gospel and tradition with culture and social change. Bevans follows Ian G. Barbour's analysis of models as constructions, ideal types, to be taken seriously but not literally.[27] "Models, in the same way as images and symbols, provide ways through which one knows reality in all its richness and complexity. Models provide a knowledge that is always partial or inadequate, but never false or merely subjective."[28] Understanding Barbour's use of "theoretical models" as organizing images that are descriptive and complementary he offers five models of contextual theology, no one of which is claimed to be better than any other, although certain ones can be said to function more adequately within certain concrete situations than others.[29] A brief summary of the five models will serve to illustrate the inescapability of the contextual paradigm for contemporary theology.

The "translation model" assumes that Christian identity is more important than cultural identity, which is ambivalent. There is a supracultural "core" of the gospel message that is unchanging, though dynamic, and must be "put into" particular cultural forms. The danger of this model would be to devalue particular cultures in favor of a universal and unchanging message. On the other hand the "anthropological model" puts the main emphasis on culture, that is, on authentic cultural identity that brings the gospel to expression from within the concrete, human experience of a particular people. Christianity is about the fulfillment of the human person and so God's revelation is to be found "not as a separate supracultural message, but in the very complexity of culture itself, in the warp and woof of human relationships, which are constitutive of cultural existence."[30] The danger of this model would be to romanticize culture as invariably good, holy, and valuable, and to close it off to encounter with other cultures (acculturation), something necessary in today's world of increasing global consciousness and interdependence.

The "praxis model" puts the primary focus neither on adapting the message nor on listening to culture but on the dynamic process of social change. Characteristic of the various movements of liberation theology, it assumes that "the highest level of knowing is intelligent and responsible doing."[31] God's presence in history, and so revelation, is discovered in the events of everyday life, in social and economic structures, in situations of oppression. Although this model is valuable in specific situations, its danger would be a kind of reductionism that limits the centrality and importance of culture to conflict situations alone. By way of contrast, the "synthetic model" would develop a "creative dialectic" acceptable to all standpoints. This model might also be called dialectical, conversational, dialogical, or, as David Tracy puts it, an exercise in "the analogical imagination."[32] It assumes that culture is composite, with some elements that are unique and others that are common across cultures. "What is important for the synthetic model is to emphasize both uniqueness and complementarity, since one's identity emerges in a dialogue that includes both. . . . This composite makeup of every culture means that every culture can borrow and learn from every other culture and still remain unique."[33] The danger of this model would be the possibility of one culture becoming dominant and/or of watering down basic convictions and contents in a given culture.

Finally, the "transcendental model" shifts the focus to conversion, that is, to the affective and cognitive operations of the self-transcending subject. "What is important is not so much that a particular theology is produced but that the theologian who is producing it operates as an authentic, converted subject."[34] Bevans cites Lonergan: "Genuine objectivity is the fruit of authentic subjectivity."[35] This model assumes that one starts with one's own experience, one's own historical, geographical, social, cultural, and religious environment or context, so that "theology is conceived as the process of 'bringing to speech' who I am as a person of faith who is, in every possible respect, a product of a historical, geographical, social, and cultural environment."[36] Since for Lonergan the basic cognitive operations are universal, there is a transcultural claim in this approach but certainly no implication that such operations are independent of specific cultures. Genuine contextual theology is open to anyone who is attentive, intelligent, reasonable, and responsible *within* one's own particular context of history, geography, culture, etcetera. The danger of this model would be its tendency toward an idealized, overly intellectualized way of knowing that is not universal and may be too subjective, leading to relativity.

Bevans concludes by asking whether one model is better than another. Each has its advocates today. Surely the dangers inherent in each model must be avoided, but I would venture to say that the extremes inherent in the first two models, i.e., insistence on a supracultural "core" of the gospel message or on a romanticization to the point of denying all criticism of the culture as *a priori* illegitimate, render these models in the terms stated inoperable today. On the other hand theology itself is inoperable today if it does not incorporate the need for praxis, for dialogue, and for authentic subjectivity. Lonergan's notion of "sublation"[37] can help here. Whatever is said about the gospel message and the Church's tradition as transcendent expressions of God's gracious love, they always already exist within particular cultural expressions and should be involved in the process of social change as developments within particular cultures. God's grace introduces something new and distinct in the human condition, puts everything on a new basis, but only insofar as it includes and preserves and brings to fuller realization all that is truly constitutive of human nature, which in turn has "sublated" the physical, chemical, botanical, and zoological dynamics of cosmic nature.

Theological rationality, then, will not seek clear and distinct ideas in the manner of Descartes nor absolute knowledge in the manner of Hegel, but will in the spirit of Lonergan nourish the human capacity to ask the next question in a coherent and systematic way that is open to new knowledge. But are there no boundaries? no definitive norms that are universally valid?

Doctrine as Official Formulations of Christian Faith. What happens when we move from a consensus of a hermeneutical kind to a consensus of a material kind about particular doctrines? Has not the Church in official formulations settled certain questions once and for all? How normative are the Scriptures, the creeds, and the councils? Here it is helpful to return to Robert Schreiter's proposed theory of tradition.[38] The "loci of orthodoxy" (the grammar of faith) have developed and grown in response to performances of Christian communities (= theology understood as a hermeneutical enterprise that involves the gifts of the whole community).

> This is a not uncommon way of reading doctrinal history: doctrinal formulation emerges after the fact, in response to Christian performances proposed. And just as grammar is more successful in determining what is not a well-formed phrase than what is always a well-formed phrase, so too the loci of orthodoxy, even though sometimes positive in formulation, are really negative or delimiting in function. Creedal formulas set boundaries on belief but do not attempt to describe all possible combinations within those boundaries.[39]

Thus priority is given to the creativity of theology (performance) within the community and doctrinal formulations are seen as necessary but secondary to the lived experience of faith. Their primary function is to set certain limits or parameters around what may or may not be legitimately said, but they do not close off new possibilities of creative development. In fact, as with grammar they can undergo change as theology develops new insights and expresses them in creative ways.

How normative are the official texts? "Normativeness unexpressed is lodged in faith; normativeness expressed is lodged in the grammar of orthodoxy, which aids the community in discerning ill- and well-formed performance texts. But for the grammar to maintain its authority, it must be intelligible and credible. It must be adequate to competence and performance."[40] Schreiter goes on to say that Scripture will be read differently as a performance text (via exegetical methods as the expression of a particular community's faith experience, e.g., the Gospel of Mark) and as a normative text (via incorporation into a particular doctrinal statement, e.g., the Nicene Creed). However, I would add that the normativity even of Scripture must cohere with developments in exegesis.[41] Scripture depends on its continuing reception and appropriation within the ongoing lived experience of the community of believers/disciples.[42] This raises the issue of Christian identity. Just as science tests its theories by their capability to make predictions that agree with observation (Hawking), so theological hypotheses and their doctrinal formulations will be judged by their effectiveness or practical consequences, i.e., whether they lead to a true transformation of human consciousness and so of the world in which we live. Schreiter concludes with five criteria for establishing the Christian identity of local communities that all relate to Christian performance and so are practical in orientation.[43] In brief summary, they are: (1) cohesiveness with the community's depth of symbolic experience; (2) affirmation and renewal in a context of worship; (3) credibility through committed action (praxis); (4) unity and catholicity (communion) through openness to the judgment of other churches; (5) outreach to other communities and to the world through missionary and service activity, at times supporting and at times challenging the way things are.

This section has offered a brief summary of the power of imagination and its influence on the various expressions of Christian self-identity that we call faith, theology, and belief. With these basic assumptions or orientations in mind, we can now turn to a consideration of the plan and purpose of this book.

2. Plan and Purpose

From within the Western European cultural tradition, which has its roots in the Jewish and Hellenistic developments of early Christianity, we can recognize today the emergence, at certain critical moments corresponding to "epochal shifts,"[44] of images of Jesus that have become prevalent, indeed normative, for Christian faith. This book will concentrate on four of these moments, although obviously there are other epochal shifts that have led to paradigm change. By way of introduction I will first propose some broad frameworks to locate these key images and then move to an outline of the closer analysis that will be employed.

The four key images and their texts are (1) biblical: the Gospel of Mark; (2) creedal: the Nicene-Constantinopolitan Creed; (3) systematic: the *Summa theologiae* of Thomas Aquinas; (4) social transformation: the "story" of Mexican-Americans. In broad terms these four images and their texts correspond to significant periods in the history of Christianity: (1) the Jewish-Gentile Church; (2) the Hellenistic-Byzantine (imperial) Church; (3) the Latin-Western (papal) Church; (4) the contemporary, post-Vatican II emergence of the worldwide Church that Johann Baptist Metz calls "socially divided and culturally polycentric."[45]

Another way of looking at these four "moments" would be in terms of what David Tracy calls the "publics" being addressed. Following his terms, Mark, the creator of the gospel form as we know it, is one of the foundational "classics" of the Christian faith (though the Creed and Thomas's *Summa* are classics as well). Mark's immediate public would be the local church in which the gospel was formed and brought to expression. On the other hand the Creed's public would be the "Church" now understood after Constantine's edict legalizing and legitimating Christianity in more universal (catholic) terms. In turn while Thomas would surely understand himself as addressing the Church, his public will include the emergent phenomenon of the "academy," that is, those who are being professionally trained (the *Summa* was intended as a handbook for students of theology) or who are already colleagues in the academy. Finally, the public for contemporary movements of social transformation is society, which is the primary concern although the importance of Church and academy are not forgotten. The value of Tracy's distinction of these three "publics" of academy, Church, and society is that it helps us to keep clearly before us how every theological development is affected by the audience that is the target of communication.[46] Every "classic" in theology will address all these publics but normally with greater emphasis on one rather than another.

Finally, employing insights from the sociology of knowledge Robert Schreiter, in another fine section of his book, proposes "a sociology of theology" that "tries to see how particular forms of thought might be related to particular cultural conditions."[47] He is concerned not with a history of ideas (dogma) but with the *forms* ideas can take. Although I read his book after starting this project the "four forms of theological expression" that he treats correspond very closely to the four images proposed in this book.

Thus he first proposes "theology as variations on a sacred text." It is the metaphorical potential of a text, e.g., the Gospel of Mark, that is "basic to the possibility of creating variations." The forms he examines are the commentary, the narrative, and the anthology. While Schreiter's concern is with the cultural conditions, particularly in oral forms of culture, that make such forms of theology possible even to the present day, we will focus on the Gospel of Mark as marking a transition from oral to written text that still reflects the primacy of oral culture and the necessity of narrative. The narrative is structured for an audience that will *hear* the story rather than read it. Thus we will examine the *form* of gospel as a new and creative way to proclaim the significance of Jesus.

Second, Schreiter proposes "theology as wisdom." Characteristic of the patristic period in East and West and of spiritual and mystical traditions, its scope is "cosmic"; its preoccupations center on "the interiority of human experience"; its logic sees human knowledge as a vehicle to "divine knowledge." Analogy (and allegory) become more important than metaphor and a guiding image is that of a "path" or "journey" leading to God. Again noting the cultural conditions that would make such theology possible even today, we will focus on the Nicene-Constantinopolitan Creed as a creedal *form* that seeks to maintain the unity and continuity of the story of Jesus within a context that has changed in dramatic ways, not only culturally but politically and socially as well.

Third, Schreiter proposes "theology as sure knowledge." While having precedents as early as the Greek-speaking apologists (e.g., Justin who died in 165 C.E.), theology as *scientia* that draws on the critical tools of human reason became preeminent by the time of Thomas Aquinas (who died in 1274) and continues to the present. The basic thrust is "to give the most exacting account possible of Christian faith as it relates to reality."[48] Major concerns include relating theology to other forms of knowledge, rigorous analysis, constructing explanatory systems, and preoccupation with method. Cultural conditions such as the development of a more unified Church law and the rise of towns and cities facilitated the birth of the university that in turn provided an environment for academic professionalism in theology. "This was perhaps the greatest revolution in the symbolic forms for reflection and extension of the experience of faith."[49] Such theology functions best in highly developed urban economies and in situations that foster pluralistic worldviews. In this instance we will focus on the *Summa theologiae* of Thomas Aquinas as a *form* of systematic organization that seeks logical and grammatical consistency in telling the story of Jesus.

Fourth and last Schreiter proposes "theology as praxis." Characteristic of the varieties of liberation theologies today that seek to overcome oppression based on class, race, or gender and so to transform society, this theology advocates a constant dialectical interplay between action and reflection. The purpose is to raise consciousness, to reflect continually upon specific committed actions so that they be truly liberative, and to sustain motivation for the ongoing transformation of society. "As a form of reflection, it is geared toward transformation and remains the most powerful approach to social transformation available to theology at this time."[50] This theology functions best in situations of oppression. We will focus on the Mexican-American experience as a *form* of narrative in which the people seek to connect their story with the story of Jesus.

Schreiter's concern throughout is to differentiate ways of doing theology, each of which is legitimate under certain cultural conditions. I agree with this viewpoint. My concern is to examine four key embodiments of these sociologically variant approaches. In sum, Mark represents through the move to written text a certain *distancing* of the story from oral immediacy. The Creed represents an attempt to maintain the *continuity* of the story in a very different cultural setting. Aquinas represents a concern to maintain *consistency* in the telling of the story in the face of challenges from "scientific" ways of knowing. Liberation theology represents a certain *fusing* of the story with the contemporary experience of oppression. All in varying ways are narrative-based, but liberation theology returns to the centrality of narrative that was the genius of Mark.

Moving from these broad frameworks to closer analysis we find that each of these key faith-images of Jesus involves what Alasdair MacIntyre calls a "narrative quest." He maintains that only through the unity of such a quest does one find the unity of human life. This involves at least three elements: (1) some understanding of the good, the goal *(telos)* or desired outcome; (2) a way or journey that involves struggle; (3) a sense of one's identity not only as an individual but more importantly as a social being in community.[51] Adapting this insight, I will summarize the basic structure of the four faith-images as involving: (1) a foundational move that is in response to a particular crisis or struggle; (2) a basic motivation that is the matrix accounting for a new paradigm and taking shape in a concretely lived experience, giving rise to a sense of individual and communal identity; (3) a decisive orientation that expresses the desired outcome or goal *(telos)*. In each case there emerges an image of Jesus that is not the only one but is key for integrating a particular form of the "narrative quest." What follows is an outline of the approach to be used in subsequent chapters.

Chapter Two will examine a biblical image: the Gospel of Mark. The foundational move is from oral to written gospel, most probably occasioned by the crisis of the Jewish–Roman war (66–70 C.E.) that ended in the fall of Jerusalem and the destruction of the Temple. This was a crisis of apocalyptic proportions for all Jews, whether Christian or not. A factor that Mark had to address was the role and influence of early Christian prophets and how they were related to the authority of Jesus.[52] While Mark cannot be classified as salvation history in the sense of Luke's periodization of salvation into epochs (Israel/Jesus/Church), certainly the possibility of developing such a view was rooted in Mark's unrelenting focus on the authority of the earthly Jesus.

The basic motivation is to give testimony through the proclamation of the gospel. The concretely lived experience of this testimony is the counter-cultural act of martyrdom that for Mark means perseverance in the following of Jesus on the way to the cross. Only at the foot of the cross do the disciples know who Jesus truly is and inseparably who they are as disciples. This is the key in Mark for true Christian identity both individually and communally.

The decisive orientation is a journey toward the end of history, identified as apocalyptic judgment that has already taken place in Jesus' authoritative claim to judge those who would presume to judge him, expressed particularly in his self-identification as the Son of Man seated at the right hand of God and coming with great power and authority. Although the title "Son of Man" is crucial to the development of Mark's christology, the key image that integrates all the factors in Mark's narrative quest is "beloved Son."

Chapter Three will examine a creedal image: the Nicene-Constantinopolitan Creed. The foundational move is from a biblical and theological pluralism to confessional unity and continuity occasioned among other factors by the crisis of various positions perceived to be heretical, especially the pervasive influence of Gnosticism among professing Christians, and so by the corresponding need to establish the "rule of faith."

The basic motivation, following Schreiter's analysis, is the drive for wisdom *(sapientia).* The concretely lived experience of this drive is the mystical ascent of the soul to God. This was often associated with monastic life as the new form of Christian witness that replaced martyrdom under the changed circumstance of the legalization and legitimation of Christianity by Constantine. Christian identity, both individually and communally, came to be associated in its purest form with the monks in the desert who renounced the world and lived a coenobitic life.

The decisive orientation is a journey of interiority that has cosmic implications, i.e., that seeks to ascend from this world of illusion and appearance to the realm of true reality that is the divine. The key image of Jesus is "the pre-existent Son" who lives in an eternal relation to the Father and who has descended into this world in order to enable us to ascend with him back to the Father.

Chapter Four will examine a systematic image: the christology of Thomas Aquinas in the *Summa theologiae.* The foundational move is from the patrimony of faith (tradition accepted as authoritative) to the impulse "to give the most exacting account possible of Christian faith as it relates to reality," as Schreiter describes it. The authorities of the past centuries were still central to doing theology, but insofar as the most important and influential authority was Augustine a crisis over Augustinianism arose in the face of the new "science" of the recently rediscovered Aristotle that, in the hands of Aquinas, afforded fresh and creative interpretations of the tradition.

The basic motivation is the drive for sure knowledge *(scientia),* of which the concretely lived experience is the academic professionalism of the university.

Christian identity, both individual and communal, is now intertwined with the capacity of trained professionals to engage the world of scientific discovery and to demonstrate its relationship to the overarching systematization of Christian faith that continues to seek understanding (Anselm).

The decisive orientation is the scientific certitude of explanatory systems, which in the case of theology means demonstrating logical and grammatical consistency, that is, that the claims of faith and the claims of reason can be integrated in the science of theology. The key integrating image of Jesus is "the incarnate Word." The christology of Aquinas appears at the end of the *Summa* not as an appendix but as the articulation of the one reality that can integrate and explain everything in the prior articles. In a word, Aquinas "sublates" the entire preceding discussion of the divine and the human into the image of the incarnate Word.

Chapter Five will examine a social transformation image: the christology of liberation. The foundational move is from the intelligibility of creed and system to the credibility of societal witness. For many authors crisis is practically synonymous with contemporary experience as we move from a modern to a post-modern world. The call is for a post-modern hermeneutic that can overcome ideological bias and provide an adequate account of systemic oppression.

The basic motivation is the liberation of all people from this systemic oppression, especially of race, class, and/or gender. The concretely lived experience is a commitment of solidarity with the poor and oppressed even to the point of martyrdom. Christian identity, both individual and communal, is caught up in a renewed but historically different appropriation of Mark's call to follow Jesus on the way to the cross as committed disciples.

The decisive orientation is service to the reign of God (transformative praxis) understood as an ongoing process of liberation through the power of God's transforming love. The important thing, then, is not so much to understand reality as to change it (Marx). However, the driving force is not Marx but Jesus who came to challenge us to true societal transformation. The key integrating image for many is "Jesus Christ Liberator."[53] However, I will concentrate on the specific experience of Mexican Americans in the United States. I will propose as the key integrating image for *that* particular culture "the rejected prophet."

The analysis of these key faith-images of Jesus, namely beloved Son, pre-existent Son, incarnate Word, and rejected prophet should yield a deepening sense of catholicity. The first purpose of this analysis is to affirm the validity, indeed the necessity, of each "moment" (biblical, creedal, systematic, and transformative) within an unfolding process of catholic openness to all truth and every value.[54] The process can best be imagined as a spiral that is socio-historical, theological, and metaphorical. The process as *sociohistorical* implies two insights. First it is a process of *real change* in which, as with all historical movement, there are times of progress and regress, new insights and lost insights, zigs and zags, lapses, reversals, and new beginnings, continuity and discontinuity.[55] Second it is a process of *contextualization* in which the value and efficacy of each faith-image will vary according to the cultural conditions that have fostered it. Culture can be understood as that web of meanings and values that informs a people's life and is embodied (expressed) in their myths, their symbols, and their affect. If there is to be a contemporary retrieval of any past image, the cultural conditions must be such as to make it possible.

With regard to the *theological process* the spiral image affirms that all of this is going somewhere, that there is a dialectical continuity of identity and difference that will finally yield only identity when Christ "delivers the kingdom to God the Father" so that God may be "all in all" (1 Cor 15:20-28). The power of the "paschal imagination" opens history to the eschatological coming of a nonviolent God[56] whose desire is the transformation, not the destruction, of the whole of creation.

Finally, with respect to the *metaphorical process,* variation within the continuing dynamic is affirmed as both legitimate and necessary. Metaphors matter—indeed they are more fundamental than concepts—but metaphors can and do change as new associations are made in changing cultural contexts. The relationship of metaphor to the centrality of narrative will be the subject of Chapter One. However, it must be noted here that in addition to affirming the validity and necessity of each moment this book has as its second purpose, expressed in this metaphorical approach, the exploration of the interrelationship of these two realities so as to ascertain which is primary and which is secondary in God's self-communication.[57] Symbolic communication, as the analysis will show, clearly gives the primacy to stories that have metaphoric impact. The human drive toward intelligibility (as in creed and system) and credibility (as in transformative praxis) ultimately serves the poetry of creative imagination. When we ask about the validity and necessity of the four key images (biblical, creedal, systematic, transformative), we must ask where they are to be located within the unfolding spiral of metaphoric process.

These four faith-images of Jesus in the history of Christian tradition have had and continue to have profound impact on the consciousness of Western (primarily European-based) Christianity. The ultimate goal of this book is to affirm the legitimacy of each particular cultural development while freeing the normative and authoritative tradition from any form of cultural imperialism. Christology in any age is the culture-specific faith response of the community of believers/disciples (Church) to the mystery of the risen Jesus—a mystery that, identified with the very life, activity, and presence of God, simply transcends any attempt we can make, whether biblical, creedal, systematic, or societal, to bring it to expression. We bear witness to the truth but we do not control it, for the truth of the risen Jesus is for all creatures in God's world.

However, because we are disciples Jesus' freely given obedience on the cross must find its way into our own stories that then, in a very real sense, will be a retelling of Jesus' story.

" The priest calls to the poet "
Karl Rahner

Notes: Introduction

[1] Gerard S. Sloyan, *The Jesus Tradition. Images of Jesus in the West* (Mystic, Conn.: Twenty-Third Publications, 1986) 8. Sloyan offers a brief and readable review of Jesus in the historical framework of the theological and mystical traditions of the West. Another approach that puts more stress on sociocultural history can be found in Jaroslav Pelikan, *Jesus Through the Centuries: His Place in the History of Culture* (New Haven: Yale University Press, 1985). See also Glenn F. Chestnut, *Images of Christ. An Introduction to Christology* (Minneapolis: The Seabury Press, 1984) who offers eight central images in the history of theology that are significant for Christian piety in the modern world. The book is designed primarily for "the ordinary lay person."

[2] William F. Lynch, S.J., *Images of Faith. An Exploration of the Ironic Imagination* (Notre Dame: University of Notre Dame Press, 1973) viii: "Faith is a life of the imagination; it is particularly a life of the ironic imagination, and if there is going to be a continuing collaboration between theology and literature it must be a collaboration between imagination and imagination." Lynch divides his book into two parts. The first attempts to "reimagine faith" and the second to explore how "faith imagines the world."

[3] Jonathan Schell, *The Fate of the Earth* (New York: Knopf, 1982) 5.

[4] Ibid., 177–178.

[5] Stephen W. Hawking, *A Brief History of Time. From the Big Bang to Black Holes* (New York: Bantam Books, 1988) 136. The definitions come from the glossary, which refers to page numbers in the text for fuller explanations.

[6] Ibid., 152: "To summarize, the laws of science do not distinguish between the forward and backward directions of time. However, there are at least three arrows of time that do distinguish the past from the future. They are the thermodynamic arrow, the direction of time in which disorder increases; the psychological arrow, the direction of time in which we remember the past and not the future; and the cosmological arrow, the direction of time in which the universe expands rather than contracts. I have shown that the psychological arrow is essentially the same as the thermodynamic arrow, so that the two would always point in the same direction." There follows the quote in the text.

[7] Schell, *The Fate of the Earth* 117.

[8] Lynch, *Images of Faith* 148. See the whole discussion on "the movement through infinite possibility," 144–156.

[9] Sandra M. Schneiders, *The Revelatory Text. Interpreting the New Testament as Sacred Scripture* (San Francisco: HarperSan Francisco, 1991) 127.

[10] See the whole discussion in Schneiders, *The Revelatory Text* 102–108. Here I offer my own abbreviated summary of her discussion. She sees these characteristics "verified in the proclaimed Jesus-image."

[11] Lynch, *Images of Faith* 83. He sees the Hebraic-Christian faith as "prime imaginer of the world" in four ways: "1. It is a *paradigm* within which we experience or imagine the world. 2. It is not a passive but a *creative* paradigm, one which activates the imagination. 3. It is a *moving* paradigm which will not be understood until it has moved through all the stages of the life of man and, in the same act, all the stages of the life of Christ. 4. It is an *ironic* paradigm. This is so important that I have chosen irony, the ironic imagination, the irony of faith, the irony of Christ, as the real subject of this book" (p. 14). The discussion of these four points follows on pp. 14–33. The emphases in the quotation are mine to highlight the fact that we are talking about a paradigm that is at once creative, moving, and ironic.

[12] Michael L. Cook, S.J., "Jesus From the Other Side of History: Christology in Latin America," *TS* 44 (June 1983) 280. The citation is from Aloysius Pieris, "Contemporary Ecumenism and Asia's Search for Christ," *Teaching All Nations* 13 (1976) 30. This section of my essay analyzes popular religiosity as a possible source for a truly indigenous theology.

[13] Lynch, *Images of Faith* 17.

[14] Avery Dulles, S.J., *The Craft of Theology. From Symbol to System* (New York: Crossroad, 1992) 57–58. Inspired by Lonergan, he treats faith as "radical conversion."

[15] Jürgen Moltmann, "The Interlaced Times of History: Some Necessary Differentiations and Limitations of History as Concept," in Hans Küng and David Tracy (eds.), *Paradigm Change in Theology. A Symposium for the Future* (New York: Crossroad, 1989) 320–339. This is a common theme in Moltmann's writings. It is affirmed by David Tracy in his essay in the same volume: "Some Concluding Reflections on the Conference: Unity Amidst Diversity and Conflict?" 461–471, especially 468–471.

[16] Lynch, *Images of Faith* 175.

[17] For a more complete account of faith, see my article, "Faith," in *The HarperCollins Encyclopedia of Catholicism,* Richard P. McBrien, ed. (New York: HarperSan Francisco, 1995) 510–515. The article elaborates on a description of faith as "a graced but free human acceptance of God's self-communication in Christ as mediated by the Christian community."

[18] Robert J. Schreiter, *Constructing Local Theologies* (Maryknoll: Orbis Books, 1985) 115.

[19] Schubert M. Ogden, "Response to Josef Blank: Biblical Theology and Philosophy in the New Paradigm," in *Paradigm Change in Theology* 287. He refers to Thomas Kuhn, *The Structure of Scientific Revolutions* (2nd ed. Chicago: University of Chicago Press, 1970) 175, 182, 187.

[20] Edward Schillebeeckx, "The Role of History in What is Called the New Paradigm," in *Paradigm Change in Theology* 309, refers to the use of "epochal ruptures" by Karl Rahner and Bernhard Welte but he prefers "conjunctural history." Langdon Gilkey, "The Paradigm Shift in Theology," in ibid. 368, employs "continental shifts" or "epochal shifts."

[21] John E. Thiel, "Theological Responsibility: Beyond the Classical Paradigm," *TS* 47 (December 1986) 573–598.

[22] Stephen P. Bevans, *Models of Contextual Theology* (Maryknoll: Orbis Books, 1992).

[23] In speaking of these paradigm shifts we should note that theologians throughout the ages have been concerned to maintain the tradition, to express the faith in new and

creative ways, and to address the particular cultural context of their times. Herman Schell would be an example of such a theologian at the turn of the century. See George E. Griener, S.J., "Herman Schell and the Reform of the Catholic Church in Germany" *TS* 54 (September 1993) 427–454. What the paradigms seek to describe is "an entire constellation of beliefs, values, techniques" (Kuhn) that have achieved a certain predominance in the community's critical and reflective awareness within a given epoch or period of theological history.

[24] Schreiter, *Constructing Local Theologies* 20–21; 22–38.

[25] Ibid., 39.

[26] Bevans, *Models of Contextual Theology* 7. The reference is to Bernard J. F. Lonergan, S.J., *Method in Theology* (New York: Herder & Herder, 1972) xi. See also Aylward Shorter, *Toward a Theology of Inculturation* (Maryknoll: Orbis Books, 1988).

[27] Ian G. Barbour, *Myths, Models, and Paradigms. A Comparative Study in Science and Religion* (San Francisco: HarperSan Francisco, 1974). Barbour distinguishes among experimental, logical, mathematical, and theoretical models. The last, which is the approach used by Bevans, is described as "an imagined mechanism or process, postulated by *analogy* with familiar mechanisms or processes and used to construct a *theory* to correlate a set of *observations*" (p. 30; emphasis in original. Pp. 30–34 explain the description.).

[28] Bevans, *Models of Contextual Theology,* 25.

[29] Ibid., 111–112.

[30] Ibid., 49.

[31] Ibid., 66.

[32] David Tracy, *The Analogical Imagination. Theology and the Culture of Pluralism* (New York: Crossroad, 1981). He offers a helpful summary of his "revised correlational method" in his essay, "Some Concluding Reflections," in *Paradigm Change in Theology* 466–468. For a clear and helpful review of David Tracy's work to the present see T. Howland Sanks, S.J., "David Tracy's Theological Project: An Overview and Some Implications," *TS* 54 (December 1993) 698–727.

[33] Bevans, *Models of Contextual Theology,* 83.

[34] Ibid., 97.

[35] Ibid., 98; Lonergan, *Method in Theology,* 292.

[36] Bevans, *Models of Contextual Theology,* 98.

[37] Lonergan, *Method in Theology,* 241: "What sublates goes beyond what is sublated, introduces something new and distinct, puts everything on a new basis, yet so far from interfering with the sublated or destroying it, on the contrary needs it, includes it, preserves all its proper features and properties, and carries them forward to a fuller realization within a richer context." This text is cited by Michael Stebbins in an unpublished essay, "Theology and Social Analysis," where he makes a fine use of Lonergan's notion of sublation to argue for the integration of social analysis into theology. See also J. Michael Stebbins, *The Divine Initiative: Grace, World-Order, and Human Freedom in the Early Writings of Bernard Lonergan* (Toronto: University of Toronto Press, 1995) 292 and the review of this book by Bernard J. Tyrrell, S.J. in *TS* 57 (1996) 542-543.

[38] Schreiter, *Constructing Local Theologies* 113–117. This is prefaced by an illuminating discussion of the interaction of local theology and Christian tradition, both problems and contributions.

[39] Ibid., 116.

[40] Ibid., 117.

[41] Karl-Josef Kuschel, *Born Before All Time? The Dispute Over Christ's Origin* (New York: Crossroad, 1992) 489: "It is my conviction that the hiatus between exegesis and dogmatics . . . can be overcome only if dogmatics understands itself as consistent exegesis." He gives priority to the "specific 'perspective' of the New Testament," including its language, and so sees the language of later doctrinal formulations as ancillary and subordinate.

[42] This is the thesis on the "world before the text" in Schneiders, *The Revelatory Text* 157–179.

[43] Schreiter, *Constructing Local Theologies* 117–120.

[44] Hans Küng, "A New Basic Model for Theology: Divergencies and Convergencies," in *Paradigm Change in Theology* 440–443, emphasizes a certain consensus on the use of "epochal shifts" in the symposium that involves the "periodization" of history and the importance of "crises" for paradigm change.

[45] Johann Baptist Metz, "Theology in the New Paradigm: Political Theology," in *Paradigm Change in Theology* 358. Metz also emphasizes the importance of crises for understanding paradigm change. The crisis for theology in a "worldwide church" is "the end of its cultural monocentrism."

[46] David Tracy has used this distinction as programmatic for his own theological project. *Blessed Rage for Order: The New Pluralism in Theology* (New York: Seabury, 1975) is a work in fundamental theology addressed to the academy; *The Analogical Imagination* (cited above) is a work in systematic theology addressed to the Church; a third volume as yet unpublished promises to be a work in practical theology addressed to society.

[47] Schreiter, *Constructing Local Theologies* 80. The whole discussion is on pp. 80–93.

[48] Ibid., 88.

[49] Ibid., 90.

[50] Ibid., 92.

[51] Alasdair MacIntyre, "The Virtues, the Unity of a Human Life, and the Concept of a Tradition" in Stanley Hauerwas and L. Gregory Jones, eds., *Why Narrative? Readings in Narrative Theology* (Grand Rapids: Wm. B. Eerdmanns, 1989) 104–106.

[52] See on this the fine study of M. Eugene Boring, *The Continuing Voice of Jesus. Christian Prophecy and the Gospel Tradition* (Louisville: Westminster/John Knox Press, 1991).

[53] This is the title of Leonardo Boff's popular book, *Jesus Christ Liberator* (Maryknoll: Orbis Books, 1978), but as I pointed out in my article "Jesus From the Other Side of History," 284, the European roots of this term are clearly indicated if one asks indigenous peoples what their favorite image of Jesus is: for example, for the Quechua Indians of the southern Andes (near Puno) the most frequent response is *Cristo humilde,* followed by *justo juez.* Thus it is important to translate this generic image of "liberator"—which may be too dependent on Western abstractions—into the particular circumstances and experiences of diverse cultures.

[54] This is one of the essential characteristics of Catholicism developed by Richard P. McBrien, *Catholicism* (San Francisco: Harper & Row, 1981) 1173–1176.

[55] A *realistic* as opposed to an optimistic or pessimistic view of history recognizes that the one thing that can be said about historical process is that it involves real change. Whether one views such change in a universally progressive (optimistic) or

regressive (pessimistic) way depends on value judgments imported from philosophical and/or theological convictions.

[56] See James W. Douglass, *The Non-Violent Coming of God* (Maryknoll: Orbis Books, 1991).

[57] I first proposed this in my essay, "Revelation as Metaphoric Process," *TS* 47 (September 1986) 388–411. This book attempts to develop further the basic insights of that article.

CHAPTER ONE

The Centrality of Narrative in Christology

Have we lost the art of storytelling in our technological age? At the end of their well-known book Robert Scholes and Robert Kellogg warn that both play (drama) and book (novels) have much to fear from the artistic medium of the motion-picture film, but they see the latter as narrative art nonetheless. "Intellectual prose and journalism will no doubt survive for ages. But the main impetus of narrative art may well pass from the book to the cinema, even as it passed from the oral poet to the book-writer long ago."[1] The comment is a reminder that technological changes have always had a profound influence on the way we tell our stories. A further question is whether such changes eliminate the need for storytelling in any form.

Retrospectively we can recognize certain "epochs" of momentous transition in technology that carry a kind of inevitable necessity for change and development while realizing that the impact of such changes on culture may take generations. On the other hand, once the new technology has been integrated into the culture it is impossible to return to the former state of affairs in a romantic attempt at retrieval. One thinks, for example, of Plato's struggle "to destroy the immemorial habit of self-identification with the oral tradition."[2] In Plato's day oral communication still dominated "all the important relationships and valid transactions of life." But with the invention of the alphabet (ca. 750–700 B.C.E.?) the technology was available for a gradual literate revolution. "It is only too likely that Plato is describing a situation [in the *Republic*] which was on the way to being changed as he wrote."[3]

The gradual shift in Greece from non-literacy to craft literacy to semi-literacy to full literacy, according to Eric Havelock, is a shift from the "Homeric" or "poetic" or "oral" state of mind (which dominated the educational system) to the increasing sophistication of scientific discourse as abstract, speculative, and intelligible *in se*.[4] "It is fair then to speak of Platonism as posing an insistent demand that we think of isolated mental entities or abstractions and that

NB

29

we use abstract language in describing or explaining experience."[5] This was a momentous and revolutionary change, nothing less than "a conversion from the image-world of the epic to the abstract world of scientific description. . . ."[6] Once this step into new technology has been taken there is no possibility of returning to the earlier oral state of mind because, however gradual, the cultural conditions will shift imperceptibly but irrevocably so that a new consciousness will be presumed as the way things have always been.[7]

One can think of other shifts in the technology of communication that have had profound cultural repercussions.[8] After the shift from predominantly oral to written forms of communication a sea-change occurred with the invention of the printing press in the fifteenth century. Among other things, such as the availability of storage and retrieval systems, for the literate there was now the possibility of increased access to books for private reading and correspondingly private interpretation. This surely helped to create the conditions favorable to the Protestant Reformation. Modern electronic media could be said to have begun with the invention of Morse Code (1844) and the possibility of instant communication that came with it. "Beginning with Samuel Morse's invention of a telegraphic code in 1844 a new era dawned in human history. Until that year, information travelled no faster than physical bodies, a few miles per hour at best. Electrical signals, travelling at the speed of light, created the possibility for communicating almost instantaneously across enormous distances. By so doing, they revolutionized the ancient human activities of storytelling and reporting the news."[9]

John M. Staudenmaier sees the development of the telegraph, radio, and television as the most powerful embodiments of a shift in cultural values "that deepens the fragmentation of discourse by teaching the habit of inner passivity and even of contempt for the act of storytelling in every form."[10] The passivity required to watch television creates a deep ambivalence about the worth and value of our own discourse, especially of our personal stories. For Staudenmaier, the art of storytelling is what constitutes our communal and personal identities. In a Christian context this must include the capacity to interweave our stories with the story of Jesus. Staudenmaier's essay is a call to recover the lost art of storytelling. "The vitality and depth of our public and personal lives requires men and women with a mature capacity for telling and listening to the stories that constitute the narrative core of life."[11] Such a renewal of the intimacy of our inner lives will affect the quality of our public discourse. Thus "narrative is essential for human discourse, in our public and communal lives as well as our private and personal identities."[12]

On another level of analysis, that of fictional narrative, Paul Ricoeur likewise asks at the end of a chapter on "the metamorphoses of the plot" whether the contemporary refusal of coherent discourse signals the death of narrative. Or, as he says, perhaps we are on the verge of new narrative forms that we do not yet know how to name. He is convinced of the importance and centrality of narrative in human life. "For we have no idea of what a culture would be where no one any longer knew what it meant to narrate things."[13] Indeed, as he concludes, narratives, whether historical or fictional, are both "preceded by the use of narrative in daily life."[14] In this he connects with Staudenmaier's insight into the importance of our personal stories.

The question of this chapter about the centrality of narrative in christology can only be addressed by responding to the foundational question of the centrality of narrative in human life and experience. It is not only a question of recovering the lost art of storytelling as it has been challenged by technological changes but also of responding to a corresponding phalanx of opposition to or demeaning of narrative by philosophy, science, history, and even literature! It is in the final analysis a question of the necessary and indispensable place of narrative in human consciousness and identity. For the purposes of christology a narrative-centered approach must explore the interrelationship of symbol, metaphor, and story.[15] To put it in summary form, our access to Jesus is mediated by the evocative power of symbols (faith-images) derived from stories that have metaphoric impact. For example "Son of God," as the analysis of the Gospel of Mark will show, is a powerful symbol that evokes a profound Christian response but that is handed on to us through the telling of the story that explores the metaphoric identification: "Jesus is the Son of God." The story is indispensable to the meaning of the metaphor. Stories like Mark that have metaphoric impact hold in tensive unity the radical particularity of Jesus (the man Jesus who proclaimed the reign of God and died on the cross) and a metaphorical potential unlimited in imaginative possibilities and still to be realized in the unfolding of human-divine creativity. Thus a narrative-centered christology would seek to maintain the validity and the necessity of particular, concrete experience within a given sociohistorical and cultural context (first-century Palestine) precisely in order to sustain the truly catholic (in the sense of inclusive of all cultural experience in its diversity) and universal (in the sense of transcultural unity) character of the mystery that is Jesus. True universality and intense particularity are inseparably connected in stories that have metaphoric impact.

To offer a foundation for this as a proposal in christology the rest of this chapter will explore some current positions on symbol, metaphor, and story. Subsequent chapters will develop the proposal's practical applicability to the images of Jesus found in Mark, the Creed, Aquinas's *Summa,* and the Mexican-American experience. The centrality of narrative will involve a discussion of the following: (1) the metaphoric act and its relation to symbolic experience; (2) the centrality of narrative in human experience; (3) narrative as a linguistic category (with special attention to religious stories in the form of myth, parable, and action); (4) text and interpretation as categories of theological thinking. Paul Ricoeur's treatment of "narrated time" as involving a threefold *mimesis* of "prefigured time" (the pre-understood order of action = the world *behind* the text), "configured time" (the ordering of the text into a meaningful whole that is "followable" = the world *of* the text), and "refigured time" (the reading or reception of the text = the world *before* the text) forms a schematic background to the treatment offered here.[16]

1. The Metaphoric Act and its Relation to Symbolic Experience

To understand what is meant by stories that have metaphoric impact we must first examine the centrality and importance of metaphor in human experience and understanding. Metaphors, in turn, can only be understood in relation to the power of symbol arising from symbolic experience on the one hand, and to the unavoidable and necessary employment of language on a literal level on the other hand. Underlying all of this is the foundational and inextricable link between metaphor and analogy. The schematic sequence of symbol → metaphor → story, as in my earlier essay, masks two disputed and unresolved difficulties in our understanding of the linguistic character of human experience, namely the originating ground or foundation for human experience as specifically linguistic and the access to reality in a referential sense that such experience provides.

A fundamental assumption here is that human experience is always already interpreted or, as Bernard Lonergan puts it, mediated through meaning. We may be born into the world naked but we are not born without a world, a body, a self. However we may choose to describe the dialectical breakthrough to human consciousness and self-awareness at the origins of the human race, it cannot be radically and totally other than or different from our experience today as symbol-making animals. Unlike the other animals that can attain a certain "rhythmic movement between instinctual drives and outward gestures (signs, signals),"[17] humans consciously construct symbol systems of language, gesture, artifact, etcetera that communicate meaning. We are, in a word, capable of making connections, of using the creative imagination to associate one thing with another in a new and previously unforeseen way, of seeing analogies between the familiar and the unfamiliar.

This human capacity to construct symbol systems assumes precisely those three realities, however variously they may already be interpreted, of a world, a body, and a self. The coinherence of these three realities constitutes the originating ground or foundation for human experience as symbolic experience, especially in the form of language. The world, which of course includes the whole cosmos and all the wonders of nature, is experienced primarily as social. Symbols *"are intimately related to social cohesion and to social transformation."*[18] F. W. Dillistone refers to two distinct types of human experience and social organization, namely nomadic and settled communities, that give rise to two distinct types of symbolic forms, the struggle for life and the ordered life-cycle. "Symbols have gained their form *either* in complicated strategies of communication and competition *or* in developing processes of production and organization which have characterized the two major types of society in human history."[19] Even universal symbols such as air or water, the body or food, etcetera are expressed in subtly different ways according to the particular social, historical, and cultural conditions in which they are experienced. In any event an indispensable and inseparable condition for the possibility of symbolic experience is the world into which we are born, constructed already for us by interpreted experiences that have come to symbolic expression.

But if we are born into a world it is because we "have" a body or, perhaps better, are embodied persons. "We exist symbolically because the spiritual dimension of our being 'speaks' itself—though never with complete satisfaction—in our bodiliness. . . . Body is the most basic symbol and the root of all other processes of symbolising."[20] This is true as long as we do not forget that we humans experience bodiliness differently from other physical realities in the world such as rocks, plants, and animals. It is the spiritual dimension of our being that "speaks," but always and inseparably as embodied. Specifically human experience includes as always already given and inseparable "the primordial, pervasive experience of the self as a self: active, in process, feeling, embodied, intrinsically social, radically related to all reality."[21] This is the position of "critical realism" advocated especially by Catholic thinkers, including Bernard Lonergan. It has its theological foundation in the central symbolic experience of Christian faith: resurrection. As opposed to the Platonic idea of immortality (understood as the separation of soul and body), resurrection affirms the insoluble and never-ending interconnectedness of world, body, and self. Resurrection is identified with one unique person, Jesus of Nazareth, who is for Christians the final and definitive expression of Dillistone's conclusion: "The most powerful of all symbols is a living person."[22]

Thus we can agree with Paul Ricoeur's thesis that symbolic experience is rooted in the deepest mysteries of life *(bios)*, including our relationships to God, to self, to others in society, to bodiliness, to nature in all its diversity. At the basis of all symbolic experience is the simple, wondrous, at times ineffable experience that Bernard Cooke calls the aesthetic experience of "to be": "This participation in existence roots genuine metaphor; the true poet's mastery of metaphor is inseparable from the insight that what is, *is*. . . ."[23] This symbolic rootedness in life *(bios)* comes to expression as metaphor *(logos)*.[24] While we have been examining the experiential basis of symbols, i.e., the constitution of the human person as an embodied-self-in-a-world, it is important as we turn to the relation of the metaphoric act to symbolic experience to note that symbols are at the same time the result of metaphoric articulation. If a metaphor says A = B, then a symbol is the B term with the A term left unstated. For example, "God is Father" is a metaphor in which

"Father" has become a symbol that evokes a certain kind of human response to the divine mystery.[25] It is also important to note that we sometimes imagine the subject (God) as if it were the symbol (Father), thus making a too-literal identification of God as Father instead of recognizing that symbols evoke a human experience of a mystery that in this case absolutely transcends our human capacities of expression.

We will now offer a definition of metaphor and relate it to analogy on the one hand and to literal use on the other. The metaphoric act, sometimes identified with but certainly inseparable from symbolic experience, will then be related to narrative as equally necessary and intrinsic to the constitution of human experience. An excellent guide to the complexity and variety of metaphor is Peter Macky, who defines metaphor as "that figurative way of speaking (and meaning) in which one reality, the Subject, is depicted in terms that are more commonly associated with a different reality, the Symbol, which is related to it by Analogy."[26] He describes symbol in very similar terms as "a reality (an object, quality, process, state of affairs or image) that stands for and gives insight into some other reality because of the analogy between the two." As with Ricoeur, symbol as rooted in non-linguistic reality comes to expression as metaphor, which makes explicit what symbol implies by applying it to a particular subject. Thus the symbolic reality of "Father" when identified metaphorically with "God" gives the symbolic experience a new depth and specificity. It evokes and explores the implications of a symbolic experience in reference to a particular subject.

What underlies and makes possible such identifications is the simple human capacity to make connections, to see similarities in things that appear to be dissimilar, to combine the familiar and the unfamiliar; in a word, to employ the analogical imagination in a simple act of judgment: A = B. When we talk about metaphor we usually put the stress on the creative imagination that discovers new and previously unseen relationships between two realities thought to be radically dissimilar. The metaphoric act is a moment of discovery, a moment in which we both constitute a world and explore its limits. Such a discovery is always a surprise at first, a shock to the imagination, a goad to the mind to explore its possibilities.

Following I. A. Richards, Max Black describes metaphor as the making of a connection between two "thoughts" that are "active together" or "interact" to produce a new or extended meaning that results from the interaction. While he recognizes that metaphors can be instances of substitution (as a remedy for the temporary imperfection of literal language or as an ornament to give pleasure to the listener/reader) and comparison (as a condensed or elliptical simile, i.e., one that focuses on similarities between two equally known realities), as well as of interaction, he remarks: "Only the last kind are of importance in philosophy." The first two can be replaced by literal translation with no loss of cognitive content, but interactive metaphors "are not expendable."[27] The fundamental human experience of learning anything involves such use of a "subsidiary subject" to further insight into a "principal subject" (one of his examples: "Man is a wolf"). Thus to reduce the tensive and interactive character of metaphor to a literal statement would be a loss of cognitive content, i.e., a failure to produce the same insight.

Similarly, Brian Wicker emphasizes the cognitive role of metaphor that is often misunderstood because of a weakening of analogical language. A shift from Aristotole's and Aquinas's views of metaphor will come when we recognize that language *forms,* and not merely expresses the contents of the mind. Metaphor is a way of *experiencing,* not just describing, things. Metaphor is a lamp, not just a mirror, held up to nature. "To make and to understand a metaphor are alike acts of the creative imagination."[28] That imagination is analogical.[29]

When we talk of analogy in contrast to metaphor we usually put the stress on the similarities and continuities between two realities rather than on the surprising and unexpected connection between the two, but in fact, as all the authors mentioned agree, what grounds the metaphoric act is analogy. Yet the relationship between the two is complex and raises the famous conundrum of which comes first, the chicken or the egg. Of course, as with poultry, either-or questions rarely admit of resolution unless one is dealing with contradictory realities. The fact is that metaphor and analogy are wedded so that one cannot live without the other. Wicker speaks of the "dangerous pull of metaphor" that must be counterbalanced by the recognition that it is only one aspect of language in our experience of reality. Whereas metaphors allow us to see similarities in the apparently dissimilar, analogies affirm underlying causal relationships. Commenting on the fact that many of our metaphors "rest upon the common recognition of some basic analogies," whether A. O. Lovejoy's "great chain of being" for medieval and renaissance times or "natural symbols" in sacramental theology, he avers: "the analogies themselves may have changed, and the repertoire of metaphors with them, but the analogical principle itself, and its capacity for generating metaphors, has not. For underlying the medieval 'Great Chain of Being' was a causal conception—that of creation—which was simply another application of the relationship we have already encountered, between language and speech, between competence and performance, code and message, system and syntagm in the structure of human communication itself."[30] Employing the example of the poem "God's Grandeur," by Gerard Manley Hopkins, he summarizes his position on the relation between metaphor and analogy: "what the poem is saying *is* simply that metaphorical language is itself incomplete without an analogical underpinning. Metaphor (the octave) raises questions that only analogy (the sestet) can answer, while conversely analogy can only answer questions that are raised by metaphorical form."[31]

But does analogy then move us toward a more literal understanding that would make metaphor expendable? What is the relation of metaphor and analogy to the literal use of language? Again Peter Macky offers a balanced overview that can help to address the concerns of Hans Frei. The latter, in an essay on the literal reading of biblical narrative, states his essential position, a plea for "the primacy of the literal sense in Christian interpretation." He wants to resist the tendency he finds in hermeneutical theory (Ricoeur) and deconstructionist interpretation (Derrida) alike "toward global and foundational claims on behalf of inclusive theories."[32] Rather than try to justify general possibilities he calls for a description of "how and in what specific kind of context a certain kind of reading functions."[33] In a word, the "New Criticism" has taken the original, that is, the doctrine of the incarnation of the Word of God in the person and destiny of Jesus of Nazareth (this is the *literal* reality) and turned it into a general class, i.e., "realistic narrative" (or, in hermeneutics, a general context, "human experience"). For Frei, on the other hand, what is primary is the *sensus literalis* as a "case-specific reading" in the context of a sociolinguistic religious community. "Established or 'plain' readings are warranted by their agreement with a religious community's rules for reading its sacred text."[34] These rules include literal ascription to Jesus plus the unity and congruence of the Old Testament and the New Testament. Other readings of a historical or literary kind are permissible only if they recognize the foundational priority of the Christian community's literal reading of its religious tradition.

How does such a literal reading square with the centrality of metaphors to biblical thought? Peter Macky distinguishes literal use as communicable independent use (which is more than empirical or established/conventional use because these can also be figurative) from figurative use as dependent use, especially dependence on literal use—for example, irony that has its effect precisely as the opposite of literal meaning. Metaphors can run the spectrum from new and unusual through familiar and standard (both of which are still recognized as metaphorical) to hidden (established uses, but forgotten as metaphors) to retired or dead, that is, reduced to literal speech (for example, the "fork" in the road). Hidden metaphors often cause difficulty. "Indeed, most theological disputes in the history of the church probably were due to speakers relying on hidden metaphors which they erroneously supposed to be literal speech."[35]

Clearly metaphors can and do come to be understood in a literal sense. We also use literal speech independently of metaphor. Macky offers four criteria for independent literal use: (1) standard, established usage (not novel or unusual); (2) direct participant knowledge of the reality; (3) behavioral concomitants that enable one to share the experience adequately with others; (4) no hint of a figurative meaning in context. To understand the relationship of metaphor to literal speech Macky first excludes the two extremes of "absolute literalism," which insists that everything can and must be re-expressed in literal speech, and "radicalism," which insists upon the unavoidable necessity of metaphorical thinking. Between these extremes there are three options: (1) "sophisticated literalism" that accepts the non-presentative purposes and effects of metaphor but insists that all presentative (cognitive) language can be expressed literally and without distortion; that is, metaphor is never necessary for the communication of insight, information, or understanding of any reality; (2) "modified radicalism" that distinguishes observable realities from non-observable, supersensible realities, which latter can only be expressed or thought metaphorically, e.g., guilt (Macky comments that "guilty" is a literal concept for most adults because the above criteria apply); (3) "critical metaphoricalism," which is Macky's position and is aligned to the "critical realism" of Ian G. Barbour and Janet M. Soskice.[36] Macky agrees with sophisticated literalism that we *can* re-express many metaphorical assertions (especially ornamental ones) in literal speech, but the standard type of metaphor has a more mysterious subject (reference): "We understand such metaphors (when we do) because we have learned to think metaphorically, to 'see' the subject through the window (or picture) which the symbol is, to imagine the subject as if it were the symbol." On the other hand, Macky agrees with modified radicalism that when we speak about and try to describe supersensible realities "we normally are forced to speak metaphorically. The overstatement here is in claiming that this is always the case."[37]

Thus a balanced view affirms the importance and necessity of *both* metaphorical and literal speech. Rather than play one off against the other in either-or fashion, we must analyze the propriety and necessity of each in given speech situations. As a test case Macky asks: did the biblical writers speak literally of God? He affirms at least two instances in which the above criteria for literal independent use apply. First, God is *real* (not imaginary). Paul (1 Thess 1:9) contrasts idols (non-existing) and the "living and true God" (existing). Paul along with prophets like Jeremiah and Deutero-Isaiah evokes an established usage, claims direct participant knowledge of the reality (even if "super-real"), manifests behavioral concomitants such as the willingness to sacrifice his own life for this God—which communicates a corresponding commitment to his audience—and gives no hint that he is talking figuratively in this context. Second, God is *active*. Jeremiah (10:5, 10) contrasts idols unable to do anything (v. 5) and the true and living God (v. 10) who is active, i.e., able to effect things. Here the same criteria for literal use apply. As Macky notes, these uses, if analogical, are independent (i.e., literal) analogical uses for insiders (Paul and Jeremiah). Only for outsiders who claim no direct experience would the usage be a dependent analogy, that is, metaphorical speech.[38]

Finally, Macky asks, where does one draw the line between literal and metaphorical speech about God? Contrast assertions (to idols or to human life) and assertions about the inner lives of human beings are usually meant literally. When we set up contrast pairs and apply both to God, for example, seen/unseen or repents/does not repent, the first is metaphorical and the second literal. Likewise, assertions about personal salvation are intended to be taken literally (whether correctly or not is another issue), but when one asks "how?" one is driven to metaphorical speech. The important point here is that virtually all other cases in which we speak about God are metaphorical. Language about God's "creativity" or God's "forgiveness" or "heart" or "love" or God's "goodness," "justice," and so on are analogies dependent on human making, forgiving, loving, etcetera, and so metaphorical. Up to this point Macky has focused on "presentative speech" (to communicate information or argue for a conclusion). In the rest of his book he shows how the Bible does things metaphorically, going beyond presentative speech to expressive, evaluative, performative, exploratory, dynamic (affective, pedagogical, transforming), and relational metaphors. The great value of his analysis is the demonstration of the variety, complexity, and subtlety of biblical language that is primarily metaphorical.

While we thus can and do use literal speech about God, such language in my view is derivative from and secondary to the metaphoric act and its relation to symbolic experience.[39] If there is a dangerous pull to metaphor that must be balanced by our capacity for literal speech, there has been especially in modern science and philosophy an even more dangerous pull to literalism that reduces all truth to empirical verification. While it is important to affirm the literal intention of assertions about God's reality and activity, it is fundamental to recognize that such assertions derive from embodied-selves-in-a-world who continually probe the richness and potential of human experience in metaphorical language. Assertions about God's being and activity remain rather sterile abstractions if we do not express in a rich variety of metaphors how God loves us, forgives us, nurtures us.

It must also be affirmed that metaphors, even more than literal speech which by definition is limited to literalness, speak about reality, about the way things *are*. In an insightful critique of Ricoeur's approach to metaphor, especially his view of the reference metaphors intended as a potential way of being in the world that ensures a particular view of human freedom, Stephen Happel offers an alternative view "based on Bernard Lonergan's understanding of cognitional judgment and art. For him, metaphors tell us the way the world is and the way it can be *if certain conditions are fulfilled.*"[40] Metaphors, as we have said, are grounded in the analogical imagination's capacity to make the judgment A = B. But the is/is not character of metaphor is not sufficiently understood as a mere confrontational paradox (Ricoeur) that projects purely open possibilities excluding every form of finality. Religious language at least wants to affirm actualization (Jesus *is* the Son of God) so that the tension resides in the affirmation of actualization ("is") and of a future whose conditions have yet to be fulfilled ("is not *yet*"). As Happel puts it, "Metaphors describe a real world which both is and will be under specific conditions." This means that

metaphors, like models, are of value if they establish predictable consequences. Metaphors open up a world of new possibilities but they are not so
open-ended as to move in any direction whatsoever. This would be the romantic, subjectivist ideal of unrestricted imagination. Rather, metaphors are
judgments about the way things are that contain within themselves a hidden
potential for future development if certain conditions are fulfilled. The
metaphoric assertion that Jesus is the Son of God tells us the way he *is* and the
way he *can be* if we allow ourselves as disciples to be drawn into and participate in his vision of the world. According to Happel, a consequence of this is
that "the metaphoric process has an intrinsic temporal asymmetry." The reference of metaphor, in this view, inevitably focuses upon narrative.

2. The Centrality of Narrative in Human Experience

At the outset we must ask which is more important and central to the enterprise of christology: models or narratives? Ian Barbour advocates moving beyond metaphors and symbols, parables and myths, to models that "result from
reflection on the living myths which communities transmit." As he affirms in
summary form:

> Models, like metaphors, symbols and parables, are analogical and open-
> ended. Metaphors, however, are used only momentarily, and symbols and
> parables have only a limited scope, whereas models are systematically de-
> veloped and pervade a religious tradition. A model represents the enduring
> structural components which myths dramatize in narrative form. . . .
> [Models] are neither literal pictures of reality nor useful fictions. They lead
> to conceptually formulated, systematic, coherent, religious beliefs which can
> be critically analyzed and evaluated.[41]

His book is a brilliant analysis of the central cognitive role of theoretical models
and paradigms in both science and religion. The undeniable necessity and
importance of models and paradigms for sustained and systematic reflection
need not lead, however, to the priority of system over story. We are proposing,
on the contrary, that all our human attempts at systematic conceptualization
and formulation have their originating ground in stories that have metaphoric
impact and must constantly return to these stories as the only adequate context
for meaning.

Is narrative, then, so central to human experience that we are indeed not
only symbol-making animals but story-making animals? Can we make sense
of ourselves and our world, of God and the cosmos, without story? Indeed, is
God not the one who in the final analysis is the "teller of the tale"? Is not the
story God's own story? We humans are perhaps most like God in the creativity
of the stories we tell in turn. Do we thereby impose a certain order or sequence
of events upon reality or do we discover and unveil the hidden dynamism of

all life and of the whole cosmos? Are we all part of a larger story? Moreover, can we broaden our account of narrative to include all levels of rational inquiry or should we differentiate and interrelate different levels of human discourse? These and many other similar questions arise from the contemporary turn toward narrative. Narrative has been "rediscovered" in its significance for philosophy, for science, for ethics, for theology, and for the social construction of human emotions. As the introduction to a recent collection of essays that touches on all of these dimensions summarizes: "We are concerned with suggesting that narrative is neither just an account of genre criticism nor a faddish appeal to the importance of telling stories; rather it is a crucial conceptual category for such matters as understanding issues of epistemology and methods of argument, depicting personal identity, and displaying the content of Christian convictions."[42]

In a fine book that provides a clear and nuanced analysis of the complexities involved in narrative Wesley Kort proposes the "unavoidability" of both narrativity and textuality, narrative because of its position between ordinary discourse and mystery, textuality because we always live within a "scripture," that "tacit text" of our beliefs and assumptions. We will return to the question of text and interpretation at the end of this chapter. For now we will follow the outline of Kort's first chapter on "Narrative: A Reassessment," where he treats in succession the status, nature, and function of narrative.

In reference to the *status* of narratives Kort says that they are (1) ubiquitous, i.e., present in all languages and cultures, (2) primary, i.e., not derivative but the foundation that allows us to distinguish facts and ideas, and so (3) necessary, that is, science (facts) and philosophy (ideas) proceed from a common narrative base. "I propose, in contrast to prevailing assumptions, that narrative, rather than a product of originally separated, non-narrative ingredients, is itself originating of those aspects of our world that we abstract from a narrative base and isolate from one another as facts and ideas."[43] This is surely valid in opposition to the contemporary extremes of either empiricism or idealism. But these are concerns of our western culture. Is it true of human experience as such that it is inherently durational and so requires narrative as its most appropriate and central expression? This is the position of Stephen Crites who, in his seminal essay "The Narrative Quality of Experience," offers a "homemade" phenomenological grounding to Kort's view. "Both mind and body are reifications of particular functions that have been wrenched from the concrete temporality of the conscious self. The self is not a composite of mind and body. The self in its concreteness is indivisible, temporal, and whole, as it is revealed to be in the narrative quality of its experience. Neither disembodied minds nor mindless bodies can appear in stories. There the self is given whole, as an activity in time."[44]

Two questions need to be addressed: first, what does Crites's thesis that "the formal quality of experience through time is inherently narrative" mean, and second, how do the "strategy of contraction" and the "strategy of abstraction," both expressive of our apparent need to escape temporality, individually relate to the centrality of narrative in human life?

When we listen to a musical score or engage in athletic competition or simply walk across a room we experience a unity of action through temporal sequence. "An action is altogether temporal. Yet it has a unity of form through time, a form revealed only in the action as a whole. That temporal form is what we mean by style."[45] Crites suggests an analogy between the musical style of action and the narrative quality of experience. Both are cultural forms that express in profound and subtle ways "coherence through time." To be sure we can break up this concretely experienced sequential flow and analyze its various components, as in Zeno's analysis of time into spatial units or Augustine's enigma regarding the extension of a thing (time) that has no extension. But such moves create what Paul Ricoeur calls "the aporias of temporality." Indeed, Ricoeur's entire three volume work on *Time and Narrative* is intended to demonstrate the thesis that only the "poetics of narrativity" can respond and correspond to the aporias of time. "A constant thesis of this book will be that speculation on time is an inconclusive rumination to which narrative activity alone can respond."[46] The major presupposition of his treatment at this point is stated at the outset: "time becomes human time to the extent that it is organized after the manner of a narrative; narrative, in turn, is meaningful to the extent that it portrays the features of temporal experience."[47] Thus time and narrative are inseparable in human experience, even if we can at a second-order level of reflection abstract the one from the other.

The central thesis of Crites's essay is that the experience of consciousness, which "is moulded by the sacred story to which it awakens" and in turn "finds expression in the mundane stories that articulate its sense of reality," has "at root a narrative form."[48] He appeals to Augustine's analysis in the *Confessions* (Books X and XI) as at least establishing the temporality of the subject. Augustine (*Conf.* XI, 20) locates a tensive dialectic within the mind or soul (*anima*) of the present of things past that is memory, the present of things present that is attention, and the present of things future that is anticipation or expectation. Crites suggests that "the inner form of any possible experience" is determined by the union of these three "presents" and requires narrative for its expression and meaning. "Narrative alone can contain the full temporality of experience in a unity of form. But this incipient story, implicit in the very possibility of experience, must be such that it can absorb both the chronicle of memory and the scenario of anticipation, absorb them within a richer narrative form without effacing the difference between the determinacy of the one and the indeterminacy of the other."[49] This all comes to focus in the present of the present as a conscious self-embodied-in-a-world as we analyzed human experience above. "The conscious present is that of a body impacted in a world and moving, in process, in that world."[50] It is, as we have already stated, the full bodily reality of human experience that grounds symbolic consciousness and necessitates its expression in narrative. Exactly how that will come to expression and what the corresponding interpretation of time may be will vary from culture to culture. The only claim being made here is that every culture (and we are all born into a particular culture with its myths and symbol systems) must offer some interpretation of "the inherent temporality of all possible experience."

"So the narrative quality of experience has three dimensions, the sacred story, the mundane stories, and the temporal form of expression itself: three narrative tracks, each constantly reflecting and affecting the course of the others."[51] Symbols such as the cross take on meaning from the stories in which they appear and so it is the narrative form that is more primitive in human experience. Yet stories are not innocent. They must be interpreted in changing historical contexts and sometimes changed or challenged by new stories that signal a radical shift or transformation in consciousness (a conversion or a social revolution). Michael Root makes the important point that the soteriological task within Christian theology cannot be carried out without the construction of augmented forms of the story of Jesus, that is, the creation of new versions of the story that include the ongoing experience of the community so that our stories are included in the story of Jesus (the "sacred story" according to Crites).[52] Similarly, Terrence Tilley sees one of "the tasks of narrative theology" to be the transformation of the narratives of a tradition to bring them into the context of our stories (myths). "Propositional theologians presume that they need merely to update their propositions. Narrative theologians see the need for *new ways to tell the story* of creation."[53]

In this connection narrative theologians would endorse Crites's comments about the two opposite and antagonistic strategies of abstraction and contraction, each of which feeds our very human desire to escape or overcome "the relentless temporality of experience." The strategy of contraction seeks to fragment narrative temporality "by the constriction of attention to dissociated immediacies: to the particular image isolated from the image stream, to isolated sensation, feeling, the flash of the overpowering moment in which the temporal context of that moment is eclipsed and past and future are deliberately blocked out of consciousness. It is commonly assumed that this dissociated immediacy is what is concrete and irreducible in experience."[54] He terms this a "reification" of the body in isolation from the ongoing, concrete temporality of the conscious self. While he applies it to the modern turn toward the immediacy of feeling and sensation, I would like to use his insight in reference to the "contraction" of story to the immediacy of metaphor.

John Hoffman makes the important point that there is a qualitative difference between metaphor and story, so that we should not view story as a mere quantitative extension of metaphor. "While nothing of metaphor is lost when we move to story, significant narrative elements are hidden when we view story merely as extended metaphor."[55] This is said in criticism of Sallie McFague's *Metaphorical Theology,* a criticism that is valid insofar as priority must be given to story as the context of meaning for metaphor. Citing the article by Crites, he affirms: "metaphors, the more elemental units proposed by McFague, find their meaning within a narrative context," and further: "we more accurately speak of metaphor as the limiting case of story—narrative with its temporal life stilled."[56] Thus the "contraction" of the story to the immediacy of metaphor must be recognized as such. It is, or should be, simply a shorthand way of evoking the story, as when we say Jesus is the Son of God. Yet with Michael Goldberg we must still ask *which* story:[57] the Jesus who went about doing good (Acts 10:37-38)? the eternal generation of the Son from the Father (Nicene Creed)? the eternal Word's "use" of humanness as an *"instrumentum conjunctum"* (Aquinas)? the one who worked to free the poor from their oppression (Gustavo Gutiérrez and others)?

The neglect of story can lead to a "strategy of contraction" that isolates particular images from the temporal process. It can also lead to a "strategy of abstraction, in which images and qualities are detached from experience to become data for the formation of generalized principles and techniques. Such abstraction enables us to give experience a new non-narrative and atemporal coherence."[58] As with the immediacy of metaphor the move to secondary, conceptual language must always recognize its source and ground in the primary language of narrative. Thus the function of abstract conceptualization should *N B* not be to replace stories that have metaphoric impact with clear and distinct ideas, but to appropriate their meaning in a critical way that is responsive to the questions human beings ask within the ongoing process of seeking to know. Our definitions and descriptions are indispensable (valid and necessary), but subordinate to the primary and foundational level of human experience: stories whose symbolic power is expressed through the analogical imagination's capacity to think metaphorically. Crites concludes: "So long as the story retains its primary hold on the imagination, the play of immediacy and the illuminating power of abstraction remain in productive tension. But when immediacy and abstract generality are wrenched out of the story altogether, drained of all musicality, the result is something I can only call, with strict theological precision, demonic."[59]

If the status of narrative is thus that it is so central to human experience and expression as to be the sheer wonder of life set to the rhythms of story, we must now explore with Wesley Kort something of the *nature* of narrative. He offers a descriptive definition: "Narrative draws attention to four kinds of force or meaning in discourse: subjects *(character)* involved in processes *(plot)* under certain limits and conditions *(atmosphere)* and in relation to a teller *(tone).*"[60] Narratives combine consistency with variation, as any one of these four kinds of force or meaning can predominate in a particular narrative. Character contributes images of human life. Plot gives rise to the image of

time as coherent movement.[61] Atmosphere establishes the boundaries enclos-
ing the narrative's world, i.e., expectations based on what is possible or impossible, conditions such as setting of time and place. Finally, tone raises
complex questions about the teller of the tale, be that the real author, the
author created by the real author in the story, or the author implied by analysis
of the text itself. Tone has to do with material selection (the author relates
something), voice (the particular style employed), point of view and judgment
(attitude toward the material). Kort offers an analysis of four biblical narratives in which one of these meanings predominates although the others are
important in each narrative: plot in Exodus, character in Judges, atmosphere
in Jonah, and tone in Mark.

We will return to the last of these, and especially the question of the "omniscient" narrator, in Chapter Two. More to the point here is Kort's trenchant
critique of critical methods in regard to biblical narratives. He sees the causes
of critical pluralism to be twofold: orientation to some pre- or post-narrative
interest, and focus on the primacy of one of the four meanings to the exclusion or neglect of the others. His point is that such methods must be subject
to the integrity of narrative and serve it. Thus, briefly, "myth criticism" (for
example, the work of Northrup Frye and Mircea Eliade) attempts to relate
literary works to such human sciences as psychology and anthropology. The
dominant element in such criticism is plot understood as recurring patterns of
order and significance (as found in Exodus). Second, "structural analysis"
(such as that of A. J. Greimas) attempts to infer from human discourse systems of language as synchronic wholes (deep structures below or behind the
surface). The dominant element here is character understood as a system of
units or binary opposites (subject-object; sender-receiver; helper-opponent)
that is fixed (as found in Judges, which juxtaposes a constant paradigm to a
variety of stories).

Third, "critical hermeneutics" (for example, the work of Hans-Georg
Gadamer and Paul Ricoeur) attempts to interpret texts by stressing meaning
as the product of interaction between diverse interests, places temporality at
the very center of human identity (an ongoing process), and invokes three
stages: awareness of another or different point of view, recognition of the
limitations of one's own point of view, and affirmation of a broader horizon
of potential meaning. The dominant element in this form of criticism is atmosphere (although Ricoeur focuses on plot in *Time and Narrative*) understood as
"the spatial quality of the future," a "horizon" (Gadamer) or "world"
(Ricoeur) that opens out to a larger, more encompassing whole not yet realized, that is, breaks the boundaries or conditions of life in the direction of an
inexhaustible future (as found in Jonah, which both establishes and subverts a
world). "Atmosphere is that element principally responsible for granting a
narrative a 'world,' of establishing, that is, the horizon of conditions or possibilities under or within which life in the narrative is carried on."[62]

Fourth, "composition criticism" assumes that literary criticism is interested in the concerns and craft of the author and so attempts a "discourse-oriented analysis." In its application to biblical narratives it overcomes the tendency of redaction criticism to see the author or editor as standing outside the narrative units. The dominant element here is tone, understood as relating the "cultural teller" (known through comparative studies of collective authors, as in the work of Erich Auerbach, Thorleif Boman, or Hans Jonas) to the "individual teller" who is "omniscient" and participates in an "ontologically superior world" (as found in Mark, who presents what appears to be a "realistic" account of Jesus). While recognizing the legitimacy of each of these approaches Kort cautions against an overly zealous enthusiasm for one approach to the exclusion of others. "The mistake of imputing permanent dominance to one of the elements of narrative is almost universally made."[63] Thus the nature of narrative involves *four* kinds of force or meaning in discourse that will always be present even when one or the other predominates in a particular narrative.

Also, as we make the transition to the *function* of narrative, it should be emphasized strongly that narrative has its own unique integrity, coherence, and exigencies, and should not be confused with the specialized language of metaphysics, science, or historical facticity. These languages do derive from the narrative quality of human experience and can also take narrative form, but the important point is to recognize the distinctive mode of communication that is narrative so as not to jump too quickly to another style of language in interpretation. To make the gospel, for example, meet an independent criterion of truth (metaphysical, scientific, historical) "does violence to the form in which the Gospel itself expresses its meaning."[64] The methods employed in biblical criticism must, as Kort says, be subject to and serve narrative. In my view we must recognize the unique mode of expression that is narrative and so not jump too quickly to other modes in the process of interpretation. The narrative quality of human experience implies that narrative is primary and foundational to all other modes of discourse. On the other hand we must also recognize the legitimacy of other modes of discourse that, while derivative and secondary and so subordinate to the primary discourse of narrative, are as necessary as the human capacity to ask questions. In agreement with Brian Wicker we affirm that both metaphor and analogy are necessary as the two poles of adequate discourse and both seek to explore the way things *are* (which is their metaphysical foundation).

How, then, does narrative function? Kort calls it "an articulated belief structure" that responds to anthropological questions about human life *(character),* teleological questions about time *(plot),* ontological questions about boundaries *(atmosphere),* and axiological questions about value *(tone).* These questions, as crucial to human life yet beyond human understanding and control, involve us in mystery yet are "presupposed by and indispensable to an ongoing human life." Thus "narrative plays a liminal or mediating position between ordinary discourse and mystery."[65] Kort's thesis is that the appearance of God in narrative, textual form is indispensable to all narratives, just as corresponding narrativity and textuality are indispensable to all religion. "All narratives contend with mystery. The appearance of God in biblical narratives neither distorts the form nor creates a separate kind of narrative; divine appearance reveals what all narrative is like, what role it plays, and what status it has in and for human life as the vestibule between language and mystery."[66] Narratives, then, are intended to draw us into the deepest mysteries of life and so open us to an experience of the transcendent in a self-involving, participatory way. Stories have metaphoric impact precisely to the degree that they reveal to us new ways of seeing and hearing and so challenge our most deeply held beliefs and assumptions. Such stories address our relations to God, to the cosmos, to the society and culture of which we are a part, and so to ourselves in our personal and communal identities. A common theme among the authors reviewed here is that narratives are indispensable to personal and communal identity and continuity.[67] To ask the question "who?" is to seek the story that constitutes one's life.

The move toward a greater emphasis on character seems to be a modern and perhaps principally western one with deep biblical roots. "The concept of the developing character who changes inwardly is quite a late arrival in narrative."[68] Scholes and Kellogg see this as "primarily a Christian element in our narrative literature" that has its roots in Jesus' revision of the commandments (cf. Matt 5:21-48) so as to emphasize the importance of what takes place inwardly in the heart. The Christian way leads through Augustine and develops in the West beginning with Wolfram's *Parzival* (twelfth century).[69] Herbert Schneidau suggests that this concern for inwardness is rooted even farther back in the Hebrew prophets and in Plato: "Might it not be that the powerful kind of self-criticism which is our individual and collective legacy from the Hebrew prophets [and from Plato] has something to do with an individualistic internalizing of narrative, self-questioning and self-answering, and that this has become our dominant mode of thought? . . . It took Plato and the Bible to make general the kind of 'soul', always anxiously examining its own moral status, that has prevailed in our tradition and that fits so well a concept of internalized narrating."[70] Homer's heroes, Odysseus and Achilles, are types who portray a public concept of heroic excellence whereas the characters in the Bible powerfully suggest inwardness. The freedom of YHWH and the openness to change and history contrast with "a logocentric cosmos in which even the gods themselves function with great regularity."[71]

We must be careful not to allow our modern romantic ideas about the inward development of personality to influence too much our reading of the biblical characterization of YHWH; but the important point, it seems to me, is something we frequently have overlooked or ignored, namely that YHWH is a character, indeed the chief character or protagonist, in a story, i.e., the biblical story that runs from creation to eschaton. Brian Wicker makes this point well: "The very human and changeable characteristics of Yahweh function as metaphors for the activity of the 'Most High', the creator of heaven and earth. For it is Yahweh's significance that he is a character in a story. . . . As such he acts as a metaphor by which the creator can manifest himself in an intelligible form."[72] Indeed, how else could God communicate to us the unimaginable, that is, the intimate relation that the divine desires to have with the human, except in the concrete and personal images of story? Moreover it is important to read the whole story, for as Wicker notes the character undergoes progressive development of a "moral sense." In reference to Gen 12:10-20; 20:1-18; 26:7-11 he comments: "Yahweh is recognizably the same character in each version, but he has been refined and matured during the process of the development of the story."[73]

The basic problem, in Wicker's terms, is how to reconcile YHWH as "a quasi-human character in a story" with "YHWH, God Most High *[El-Elyōn], maker of heaven and earth*" (Gen 14:22)? The basic or root metaphor of Israel's entire history is given here as Abram's (later Abraham at 17:5) identification of YHWH with *El-Elyōn*. This metaphor is a cognitive statement about the personal reality of this character. Abram's identification of this individual personality (YHWH) with *El-Elyōn* is the fundamental act of Israel's faith, yet it is an act of faith that affirms that the reality of God is experienced as storied. "The complex relation thus involved implies that the structure of the story in which this character appears is projected on to the real world to give *it* a structure which otherwise it would not have."[74] This is an act of the creative imagination that makes a connection not perceived before. Metaphors take on meaning when they are given shape (context) by story. But, following Wicker, one cannot tell a story without a cause-effect sequence that leads to an ending.[75] Thus stories with metaphoric impact assume a causal or analogical understanding, while such understanding finds its primordial or foundational experience in the creativity of metaphor. Metaphor and analogy are inseparable. Failure to appreciate the true nature of that relationship is, according to Wicker, the root cause of the divorce between the God of the philosophers and the God of Abraham (Pascal). If there is a duality, it is not in God (Whitehead) but in the language we use to speak about God. Such a duality, it seems to me, is the result of displacing the primacy of story with second-order, abstract, conceptual language.

Finally, in the Jewish and Christian scriptures, who really is the "teller of the tale"? Can the stories truly reveal God if God is not the one who imbues narrative art with ultimate irony? This moves us to the final and most difficult question about the function of narrative, that of tone, which has to do not only with selection of material and style, but above all with point of view.

> The problem of point of view is narrative art's own problem, one that it does not share with lyric or dramatic literature. By definition narrative art requires a story and a story-teller. In the relationship between the teller and the tale, and that other relationship between the teller and the audience, lies the essence of narrative art. The narrative situation is thus ineluctably ironical. . . . Irony is always the result of a disparity of understanding. In any situation in which one person knows or perceives more—or less—than another, irony must be either actually or potentially present.[76]

There are multiple points of view as the interaction variously involves the characters in the story, the audience, the narrator, and at times the author as distinct from the narrator. The possible disparities these various points of view present create the sense of the ironic.

One of the reasons why stories play such a central and important role in human life is, as Scholes and Kellogg suggest, that "they offer a simulacrum of life which enables an audience to participate in events without being involved in the consequences which events in the actual world inevitably carry with them."[77] There is a certain superiority that the audience (readers) enjoy over the characters, a disparity of viewpoint that is ironic. But whose point of view controls the irony in the narrative? Whose authority is primary? The author and/or narrator of the story? The text that includes the implied author, i.e., the very structuring or configuration of the text that creates a role for the reader? The reader who in the act of reading completes the dynamism of configuration by actualizing the role of the reader prestructured in the text and so transforms or refigures it in effective action?[78] Obviously the answer will lie in some form of interaction among author, text, and reader, but at this point perhaps the more fundamental question is the authority of certain kinds of narrative. Historically we have moved from traditional or mythic narrative to creative or romantic narrative. Have we also moved from the "authoritarian monism of the fully omniscient mode of narrative" to the "multifarious relativism of that same mode"? As Scholes and Kellogg put it: "The whole movement of mind in Western culture from the Renaissance to the present—the very movement which spawned the novel and elevated it to the position of the dominant literary form—has been a movement away from dogma, certainty, fixity, and all absolutes in metaphysics, in ethics, and in epistemology. The new philosophical realism, so closely connected with the rise of the novel (as Ian Watt has shown), has led inevitably to a cultural climate we may call relativism."[79]

How and in what sense, then, do narratives (and so texts) have authority in our lives? Are we as readers mere spectators uninvolved in the consequences that the text may imply for the real world? To answer this we must move from the question of the centrality of narrative in human experience to narrative as a linguistic category, that is, to the kinds of narrative that have made authoritative claims. For our purposes we will consider religious stories in the form of myth, parable, and action. Then in the final section we will look at the importance of textuality for the understanding and interpretation of all narratives.

3. Narrative as a Linguistic Category

According to Wesley Kort religious stories are no different from all narratives that are concerned with mediating ordinary discourse and the sense of mystery or transcendence. Stories have little interest if they do not in one way or another (even by way of denial or absurdity) address ultimate questions. We all have such questions even if we are unsure about answers. However, we are concerned here about those stories that have specifically religious interests. And we will focus on the three generic types that Terrence Tilley singles out: "*Myths* are stories that set up worlds. Their polar opposites are *parables*, stories that upset worlds. Between these are *actions*, realistic stories set within worlds."[80]

Modern approaches to myth have been varied and complex. For example, Scholes and Kellogg differentiate Northrop Frye's definition (in *The Anatomy of Criticism*) that "emphasizes the supernatural qualities of myth" from their own that "emphasizes its traditional qualities." For them, following Aristotle's use of *mythos,* myth is "a traditional story" (or plot) that can be further distinguished into folktale ("designed to amuse an audience"), legend ("a quasi-historical tale of ordinary or fantastic events, regarded as true history by the audience"), and sacred myth ("an expression of and justification for primitive theology, manners, and morality"). The emphasis is on the primitive character of myth that has been superseded as narrative emerges into the two antithetical types of empirical narrative "with allegiance to reality" on the one side, and fictional narrative "with allegiance to the ideal" on the other side.[81]

However, myth is not simply a matter of "primitive" experience. Terrence Tilley criticizes the Enlightenment's blindness to its own myth and insists that we always live in a world structured by myth. I would agree. Myths, which are usually enacted in some form of ritual, celebrate a certain stability in human life. They give us a sense of who we are and where we stand, particularly in relation to cosmic powers that are perceived to be saving or threatening. They reconcile contradictions, or at least convince us that such mediation is permanently possible.[82] Joseph Campbell has analyzed myth into a fourfold function: as religious it structures our relation to transcendent mystery; as cosmological it shows where the world came from and where it is going; as moral-social it undergirds the social order; and as psychological it provides individuals with a sense of their own space or role in society.[83] Thus we need myths that give us a comprehensive sense of continuity, order, and participation. We need a story that structures our world in this fourfold relationship, whether it be the Jesus myth of Christian conviction or the emancipation myth of Enlightenment rationality or the work-ethic myth of American capitalism. One can make a religion, a sacred myth, of Reason and Profit as well as of Mystery. Obviously, then, not all myths have the same cognitive and ethical value, nor do they all function equally well. Myths must be challenged by the experience of discontinuity, tension, and iconoclasm. If we need to tell stories that structure our world, we also need stories that warn us against turning such constructions into idols and/or killing them through literalization. These are parables.

Parables subvert the world created by myth. They challenge the assumptions of our myths and call us to envision new possibilities for change. They have metaphoric impact. "You have built a lovely home, myth assures us; but, whispers parable, you are right above an earthquake fault."[84] Parables are only possible in relation to myths. One can live in myth without parable, but parables live only in the tension created by subverting myth. Parable is not another myth, an anti-myth. Parables show the limits of our myths, their relativity. They can shatter worlds. They can also generate new possibilities for those who have eyes to see and ears to hear. As stories that have metaphoric impact, parables are truly revelatory. The stories that constitute Jewish and Christian revelation, the Exodus experience of Moses, the kingdom experience of Jesus, the resurrection experience of Simon Peter are all parabolic. "So we must begin to rethink all our definitions of deity and convert all our worship and our prayers. Revelation is not the development and not the elimination of our natural religion; it is the revolution of the religious life."[85]

The parables of Jesus are the primary exemplification of what I mean by stories that have metaphoric impact. As such they must be understood in the context of Jesus' ministry, for in the hands of the gospel writers they tend to become either allegories that teach or example stories that exhort. Following the pattern proposed in the Introduction, which will be developed in subsequent chapters, the structure of Jesus' ministry might be characterized as follows:

(1) The foundational move is from the silent solidarity of the "hidden" years at Nazareth to the active proclamation of the arrival of God's realm in the power of the Spirit. This was occasioned by the preaching of John the Baptist and Jesus' own baptism in the Jordan. The fundamental crisis that Jesus had to address was Israel's oppression under the political collusion of the Roman imperial power and the Jewish Temple aristocracy.[86]

(2) The basic motivation is to realize the fulfillment of the "time" (*kairos*) and the "drawing near" of God's reign (Mark 1:14-15) that would bring about the liberation of God's people, Israel. The concretely lived experience of this mission is an obedient faithfulness to the will of the God

Jesus called "Abba" even in the face of increasing opposition and rejection. This was a fidelity to God's intention for all humans from the beginning of creation, namely to love one another, even and especially one's enemies, which love is the only possible way to true transformation from personal and societal alienation.

(3) The decisive orientation is the renewal and transformation of relations (social, political, and economic, as well as religious) within the village communities of Israel in order, finally, to bring all Israel to realize its true vocation as a light to the Gentiles. This demanded a radical change of mind and heart *(metanoia)* and a radical trust in God's fidelity *(pistis)* on both the personal and communal level. "Historically speaking, Jesus sought to transform his social world by creating an alternative community structured around compassion."[87] The dominant image he employed was, of course, the reign of God and his favorite way of expressing what he meant by that image was to tell the stories we call parables.

It is not necessary here to go into a detailed analysis of Jesus' parables as a literary genre.[88] What gave his parables their power or authority in the originating context of his historical ministry was their compassionate and perceptive "redescription"[89] of the reality of first-century Palestine. As one who had walked in solidarity with his people for some thirty years, Jesus spoke out of his own experience. He named the realities, particularly the ordinary, lived experiences of human relationships—parent and child, brother and sister, patron and client, master and servant—on all the interlocking levels of social life (familial, religious, political, economic) but in a surprising and new way that effectively called for a revolution in social consciousness. The "transcendent symbol" of the reign of God is identified metaphorically with the ordinary, everyday experiences of peasant village life. The God of Jesus is alive, active, present at the very center of human life in all its relationships, but this God can only be discovered by those who have eyes to see and ears to hear—that is, who can imagine new possibilities in their everyday reality. Jesus did not tell people what to do. Rather he invited them to enter into the parabolic world created by his poetic imagination and so enter the realm of God. As John Donahue puts it so well:

> The parable is a question waiting for an answer, an invitation waiting for a response. It does not really "exist" or function until it is freely appropriated. Theologically this means that the parable is a form of discourse that appeals not only to the fascination of the human imagination with metaphor, or to the joyous perception of a surprise or paradox, but to the most basic of human qualities: freedom. Jesus chose a form of discourse that appealed to human freedom and risked himself with human freedom.[90]

As I put it in the concluding summary to my analysis of five of Jesus' parables (Luke 15:11-32; 16:1-8; Matt 20:1-15; Mark 12:1-8; Luke 10:30-35):

The arrival of the kingdom of God signals a radical transformation of mind and heart (Mark 1:15), a new way of seeing and hearing that is inclusive of wayward sons, unjust managers, poverty-stricken day laborers, desperate tenants who even resort to murder, hated and excluded Samaritans, despised prostitutes, greedy tax-collectors—in a word, "sinners," whatever their class, race, or sex. The "politics of compassion" does not and cannot ignore the suffering of the "other," the one who is not like us or does not belong to us. Thus these parables are at the same time a profound call and challenge to patriarchal fathers, rich businessmen, employers who possess the earth's resources, absentee landlords who demand rents—indeed, to anyone, Jew, Samaritan, Gentile, who excludes others on the basis of race, class, sex, or anything else. Jesus in his parables directs the attention of mind and heart to the concrete realities of everyday life, especially to the inequities created by human divisiveness and hard-heartedness. He did not tell people what to do; if they truly entered into the parabolic world created by Jesus' poetic imagination, however, they would know what to do, for compassion moves the heart not just to sentiments of pity but to transformative action.[91]

Jesus' approach to the social conditions of his day, articulated primarily through the power of stories that have metaphoric impact, finds a close correspondence in contemporary approaches of liberation theology, what we will call in Chapter Five a social transformation image. There, however, it will be Jesus himself, transformed through the resurrection experience, who embodies in a new but still parabolic way the divine intention for human transformation.

Finally a brief word must be said about action stories that, as Tilley puts it, tell us how things go in a world. Between myths that set up worlds and parables that upset worlds, actions allow us to explore worlds. Most of our stories are of this type. We often categorize them into those that tend to be more factual or empirical (e.g., history, biography, autobiography) and those that tend to be more fictional or idealistic (novels, short stories, fables). Paul Ricoeur's detailed and insightful analysis of history and fiction in dialogue with the phenomenology of Husserl and Heidegger is most helpful here. He perceives an "interweaving" of history and fiction, by which he means "the fundamental structure, ontological as well as epistemological, by virtue of which history and fiction each concretize their respective intentionalities only by borrowing from the intentionality of the other."[92] Thus history is "quasi-fictive" insofar as it borrows the role of the imaginary from fiction, while fiction is "quasi-historical" insofar as it borrows the role of verisimilitude from history. The constraints of each type of narrative are operative and the claims of truth, although distinct, are related. Foundationally, however, both are preceded by the use of narrative in daily life, have the same standard of configuring operations (emplotment), and are derived from "narrative understanding," which can include both history and story.[93] By narrative understanding Ricoeur means "the temporal synthesis of the heterogeneous." Or to put it more simply as he does in his conclusions to the three volumes, the lived experience of time in its immediacy, as manifest in the direct discourse of phenomenology, only results in "the multiplication of aporias." Only the "poetics of narrative" can untie these knotty aporias. "In its schematic form, our working hypothesis thus amounts to taking narrative as a guardian of time, insofar as there can be no thought about time without narrated time."[94] Thus his conclusions affirm the central and indispensable place of narrative, whether history or fiction, in any human attempt to articulate the significance of temporal experience.

In the same conclusions Ricoeur explores both the possibilities and the limits of this position under the rubric of three aporias of temporality. The first is "narrative identity." In sum, "Narrated time is like a bridge set over the breach speculation constantly opens between phenomenological time and cosmological time."[95] Hence he proposes a "third time" that has its own dialectic, i.e., the interweaving of history and fiction that in turn produces an offshoot: "The fragile offshoot issuing from the union of history and fiction is the assignment to an individual or a community of a specific identity that we can call their narrative identity." We can only answer the question "who?" by telling the story of a life. (Examples include the case histories of psychoanalysis for individuals and the story of Israel for communities.) The self of self-knowledge is not, therefore, an egotistical and narcissistic ego but "the fruit of an examined life" (Socrates), that is, "one purged, one clarified by the cathartic effects of the narratives, be they historical or fictional, conveyed by our culture." There are limits, of course. Such narrative identity is not stable and seamless nor does it exhaust the question of self-constancy. Much depends on how we respond to the challenge that narratives pose for us.

The second aporia of temporality is "totality and totalization" which corresponds to the Hegelian temptation to find a unitary historical consciousness in the eternal present of speculative thought. In place of the speculative solution of "totality" proposed by Hegel, Ricoeur proposes the practical solution of "totalization" that is "the fruit of an imperfect mediation between a horizon of expectation, the retrieval of past heritages, and the occurrence of the untimely present."[96] The unitary ideal of one time, one history, one humanity can only be realized in a practical and dialogical way. Thus the future and the past must contribute to the present as initiative. In my terms this means to evoke what is deepest and best in the heritage of the past and bring it into present awareness in such a striking way that it is creative of the future. In a word, the future comes through the past into the present. This, I believe, is what Jesus as eschatological prophet sought to evoke among his people Israel. His primary and most fundamental way of doing this was by telling stories that referenced the reign of God. In this, as Ricoeur says, narrative does not resolve the aporias of time but puts them to work. Jesus' parables have validity if they initiate concrete action but they are by their very nature limited.

Thus the third aporia is "the inscrutability of time and the limits of narrative." Time ultimately is a mystery that remains inscrutable and unrepresentable. Its limits are seen, for example, in the appeal to mythic origins on the one hand, or to the triumph of eternity over time on the other. Here narrative meets its final limit. But this limit drives us back to the continuing search for narrative identity: "the reaffirmation of the historical consciousness within the limits of its validity requires in turn the search, by individuals and by the communities to which they belong, for their respective narrative identities. Here is the core of our whole investigation, for it is only within this search that the aporetics of time and the poetics of narrative correspond to each other in a sufficient way."[97]

Stories have a way of ending and yet continuing. The search for human self-knowledge and identity cannot do without them. In distinguishing different kinds of stories within narrative as a linguistic category we wish to affirm not only the centrality of narrative to human experience but also our need for the rich diversity and pluriformity that different types of stories provide. As Terrence Tilley puts it: "A narrative theology of myth without parable would be stifling; of parable without myth would be baffling; of action alone would be boring."[98]

4. Text and Interpretation as Categories of Theological Thinking

What do we, as readers or listeners, expect of a story? Surely we expect a certain degree of followability based on an intelligible sequence of events and some kind of closure or ending that gives the story a sense of completeness and integrity. Frank Kermode, in two distinct works, challenges our assumptions about both. In the earlier work, *The Sense of an Ending,* he proposes a qualitative transformation of the myth of the apocalypse from imminence to immanence, that is, to a myth of crisis with the unsettling effect of being unending.[99] The corresponding crisis for literary paradigms is seen in contemporary works that either have no ending or are open-ended. But as Ricoeur notes, such stories are interesting only to the degree that they deviate from or violate the normal expectation of closure. What is new or unexpected can only be such in reference to what is traditional and expected, as we saw in the relation of parable to myth. We must, says Ricoeur, maintain our basic confidence in the power of language and this means above all in the power of narrative to bring poetic closure, the triumph of concordance over discordance, of consonance or order over dissonance or disorder. In contemporary literature it is often the reader who is expected to bring order out of the disorder of the work. For this to happen there must be some "paradigmatic expectations" operative (Ricoeur). Thus, as Kermode would agree, expectations persist even if they are changed.

In his later work, *The Genesis of Secrecy,* Kermode continues a theme begun in the earlier work, namely that we must separate truth and meaning. Fictions deceive us in order to console us. This responds to the basic need all humans have to make sense, to find order, in the midst of chaos. Thus Kermode subscribes to the notion of a schism or divorce between fiction and reality. The theme of his later work is "the radiant obscurity of narratives."[100] Such obscurity calls for an ongoing work of interpretation but we should be aware of what we are dealing with: "A 'convincing' narrative convinces mainly because it is well-formed and followable, though for other reasons also; for instance, it reassures us by providing what appears to be an impartially accurate rendering of reality."[101] His famous phrase "the benign deceit" refers to the cultural identification of meaning and truth, whereas he maintains: "All modern interpretation that is not merely an attempt at 're-cognition' involves some effort to divorce meaning and truth."[102]

In Paul Ricoeur's view Kermode needs to isolate "the problems of configuration in terms of mimesis$_2$ from the problems of refiguration in terms of mimesis$_3$."[103] This roughly corresponds to the distinction between text and interpretation, but it also implies their unity. We will consider, then, the importance of textuality, what counts for adequate interpretation, and the relationship between the two. "What is involved in an integral, that is, a transformative, interpretation of the biblical text? My answer, in a nutshell, is that integral transformative interpretation is an interaction between a self-aware reader open to the truth claims of the text and the text in its integrity, that is, an interaction that adequately takes into account the complex nature and multiple dimensions of the text and the reader."[104]

At the outset we must recall Sandra Schneiders's thesis about the world behind the text of the New Testament (Ricoeur's mimesis$_1$). What gave rise to the text was the "paschal imagination" of the believing community that "transformed its historical experience into a dynamic image."[105] For Ricoeur, although mimesis$_2$ (configuration) constitutes the pivot of his analysis, i.e., the mediating role of emplotment in the constitution of narrated time, it assumes a preunderstanding of the world of action, a "prefigured time," as its inseparable ground or source. To put it simply, we humans share enough experience of human acting in common—semantics, symbolic resources, temporality—to make textual emplotment possible. "What is at stake, therefore, is the concrete process by which the textual configuration mediates between the prefiguration of the practical field and its refiguration through the reception of the work. It will appear as a corollary, at the end of this analysis, that the reader is that operator par excellence who takes up through doing something—the act of reading—the unity of the traversal from mimesis$_1$ to mimesis$_3$ by way of mimesis$_2$."[106]

Wesley Kort would put greater stress on the unavoidability of textuality even on the level of mimesis$_1$ because we always live within a "scripture," that "tacit text" of our beliefs and assumptions. "The textual is that which we can

assume or to which we can refer; it provides a world we have in common."
And further: "The crux of the matter is that textuality is unavoidable, as unavoidable as is narrativity. A concept of scripture . . . must rest on that
point."[107] This is true, but the narrative/text of our normal human experiences
(Ricoeur calls this a "quasi-text") is still fruitfully distinguished from the configuration of such experiences into a particular text through the imagination of
an author.

The pivot, then, for Ricoeur as for many authors, is "the world of the text,"
mimesis$_2$, understood as a written form of discourse. Although we can speak
of the "text" of oral communication (which indeed was the only possibility in
the period prior to the invention and development of writing), we are heirs to
a written culture that remains such even when modified and transformed
through the invention of the printing press and the development of electronic
media. Unlike the immediacy of speaker, audience, and situation in oral communication, a written text creates in Ricoeur's term a "distanciation" that calls
for the appropriation of the text in the very different world of the reader.
Historical criticism seeks to reconstruct the originating circumstances of the
text (author, audience, situation) and this remains a legitimate quest, but literary criticism focuses on the text itself as a work of art that can be analyzed in
terms of its own semantic autonomy, including both its sense (whether it communicates a coherent meaning) and its reference (what it claims to be talking
about, i.e., reality). As applied to narrative texts by Ricoeur, the text embodies
a "configurating operation" that is a dynamic and creative synthesis of heterogeneous factors (plot, character, etc.). Most importantly it moves beyond
the episodic (the linear representation of time) to the configurational, that is,
a meaningful whole that is followable, has "a sense of an ending" (Kermode),
and enables the reader to reverse the "natural" order of time (the "arrow of
time"; cf. Hawking) by reading the ending in the beginning and the beginning
in the ending. "In short, the act of narrating, reflected in the act of following
a story, makes productive the paradoxes that disquieted Augustine to the point
of reducing him to silence."[108] Thus the narrative text produces a new and
qualitatively different experience of time.

Since a text has a life of its own, as it were, independent of its original
author, audience, and situation, it is open to multiple meanings and so various
possible interpretations. Indeed, if the text is a "classic" as David Tracy uses
that term it has a perennial human relevance because it communicates effectively in a variety of historical and cultural circumstances. A full and adequate
understanding of interpretation must, therefore, include the "world before the
text" (mimesis$_3$), the appropriation of the text by a reader. Werner Jeanrond
makes this point well in reference to theology: "This process, the process of
reception or reading, is foundational for theology: in the first place theology
draws its original dynamic from the disclosure of texts which have been
handed down; in the second place the reception of these biblical textual tradi-

tions has itself left texts behind it which both bear testimony to the reception of the biblical texts at a particular point in time (historical dimension) and also influence the future acts of reception (effective historical dimension)."[109]

"It is important to realize that the 'world the text projects' is not the imaginative, fictional world of the work, for example, the land of Oz or the inn to which the Good Samaritan took the victim of the robbers. The fiction is the vehicle that carries the reader into a possible alternative *reality*. This is precisely the dynamic of the parable."[110] Application (Gadamer) or appropriation (Ricoeur) or transformative understanding (Schneiders) can only take place through a form of participation that allows the listener/reader to be personally affected and transformed by the subject matter (reference) of the text. Significant texts make truth-claims that demand a response that is ethically responsible. Such a response demands that we move from the immediacy of the experience of the text (Ricoeur's first naïveté) to a critical appropriation of the text. This involves both bringing critical questions to the text (historical, literary, etc.) and allowing the text to maintain its own integrity and otherness so that in turn it questions us. The full process of appropriation can only take place, however, when we return to the text with a second, post-critical naïveté and allow the text's evocative power to be truly transformative in our lives. Sandra Schneiders, employing Ricoeur's insights, makes this point well: "The process involves two distinct but non-separable interactive moments: aesthetic surrender and critical existential interpretation."[111]

The first involves experiencing the text as text, entering into the dynamics of the text as it is structured to create the aesthetic experience (the implied reader that is actualized in the actual reader). The second moves beyond the critical phase of exegesis and various "criticisms" to "a radical personal engagement with what Gadamer calls the truth claims of the text." As with Jesus' parables, a new way of existing is affirmed that one can either accept or reject. The critical process continues as an ongoing dialogue with the text about its subject-matter. In reference to Christian texts this "transformative interpretation . . . is not blind submission to the text as answer but an in-depth engagement of the text's subject-matter, of its truth claims, in terms of the developed Christian consciousness of the contemporary believer within the contemporary community of faith."[112]

Thus an adequate understanding of the hermeneutical process sees it as a dynamic interaction of the world behind the text (mimesis$_1$), the world of the text (mimesis$_2$), and the world before the text (mimesis$_3$). Though distinct, these three dimensions are inseparably one. Two final points must be made. The first is that this process is primarily communal in nature. One can speak of the individual act of reading, but reception involves some kind of permanence over a period of time and from a wide range of people. This brings us to the second point which is the necessity of a canon of writings to provide permanence, recognizable limits, and a sense of normativity. As Wesley Kort puts it, we need a "textual center" to counter the contemporary tendency to press too far the decentering, disorienting, and disruptive character of writing. The "interpretive community" constitutes "a kind of textuality" in that it offers a set of assumptions and beliefs that must be critically appropriated. A "scripture" should be understood as "those texts which have authority because of their ability to challenge the assumptions and beliefs with which we address our world at those points when they are affirmed as obviously true. . . ."[113] The authority of scripture is always a call to "greater complexity and catholicity." The biblical texts provide a suggestive model, in Kort's terms, for scripture because the canon, as a veritable library of literary works, is intertextual and polyphonic in its literary strands and forms and in its historical and cultural diversity, not to mention its theological polyphony. The biblical texts both provide a center and decenter, grant certainty and subvert it, offer identity and challenge it. This, says Kort, is what all scripture ought to be like. Or as Werner Jeanrond puts it in summary, the Christian reading community "confesses its belief in a pluralistic norm of scripture and understands itself as on the way to an always new interpretation of life by reference to the divine logos becoming manifest in the texts. In this process it is never a single reading genre which is in question but rather always a new creative synthesis of traditional reading genres and the individual-communitary activity of faith. This process of communal plurality hosts the unitary dynamic of the Christian quest for truth."[114]

In conclusion we may say that theological thinking is a matter of a communal reading of texts in such wise that they are critically appropriated for the sake of contemporary reality. In all of this we must not forget the centrality of narrative and hence the priority of the story we seek to tell. For Christians that is the story of Jesus inseparably intertwined with our own stories. The basic thesis, which we now wish to explore through the analysis of four foundational texts in the experience of Christian self-definition, is that we begin in story and end in story. The move toward conceptual definition and/or experiential description is legitimate and necessary but always subordinate to the primacy of story.[115]

Notes: Chapter One

[1]Robert Scholes and Robert Kellogg, *The Nature of Narrative* (New York: Oxford University Press, 1966) 281. Compare the reflections of Walter J. Ong, especially on television, in his *Interfaces of the Word. Studies in the Evolution of Consciousness and Culture* (Ithaca: Cornell University Press, 1977) 315–323.

[2] Eric A. Havelock, *Preface to Plato* (Cambridge: Harvard University Press, 1963) 201. In the Foreword, Havelock comments: "the crux of the matter lies in the transition from the oral to the written and from the concrete to the abstract, and here the

phenomena to be studied are precise, and are generated by changes in the technology of perceived communication which are also precise" (xi).

[3] Ibid., 38, 41.

[4] "In short, this kind of knowledge which is built up in the tribal memory by the oral poetic process is subject precisely to the three limitations described by Plato as characteristic of 'opinion' *(doxa)*. It is knowledge of 'happenings' *(gignomena)* which are sharply experienced in separate units and so are pluralized *(polla)* rather than being integrated into systems of cause and effect. And these units of experience are visually concrete; they are 'visibles' *(horata).*" Ibid., 180. And further: "It may indeed be suggested that it was increasing alphabetisation which opened the way to experiments in abstraction. Once rid of the need to preserve experience vividly, the composer was freer to reorganise it reflectively." Ibid., 189.

[5] Ibid., 257.

[6] Ibid., 259.

[7] Havelock (91ff.) recognizes the difficulty of modern analogies to peasant oral traditions (such as Albert B. Lord's *The Singer of Tales* [Cambridge: Harvard University Press, 1960]) because such oral traditions are no longer central to our culture. Similarly Scholes & Kellogg, *The Nature of Narrative* 31–32: "Speculation about the process in which the Homeric epic achieved its traditional written form probably ought not to depend entirely upon our knowledge of analogous situations in present-day Yugoslavia or in Northern Europe during the Middle Ages. It is difficult to imagine that a foreign written tradition could have exercised anything like the terrific pressure and potential influence on Greek oral epic that written Christian culture brought to bear on native oral traditions elsewhere in Europe. The Greek transition must have been gradual, evolving from within the dominant literary culture, one form in a sense voluntarily giving over to the other. Elsewhere in Europe, however, oral traditions have either been quickly suppressed by a dominant alien written tradition or have been driven underground, to the sod huts and smoky chimney corners of an ignorant and impotent peasantry. The cultural alternatives available to a Homeric singer of seventh-century Greece on one hand, and to a Bosnian or Karelian singer of the nineteenth century on the other, are hardly comparable. The ancient Greek was singing-master to princes, but the others performed before audiences of cultural illiterates, in the full, terrible, modern sense of that word."

[8] Walter Ong has developed this insight in various writings. See especially *The Presence of the Word* (New Haven and London: Yale University Press, 1967); *Interfaces of the Word* (cited above); and *Orality and Literacy. The Technologizing of the Word* (London and New York: Methuen, 1982).

[9] John M. Staudenmaier, "Restoring the Lost Art. Storytelling, Electronic Media and Fragmented Public Discourse," *The Way* (October 1988) 317.

[10] Ibid.

[11] Ibid., 320.

[12] Ibid., 313.

[13] Paul Ricoeur, *Time and Narrative* 2 (Chicago: University of Chicago Press, 1985) 28.

[14] Ibid., 156.

[15] This was the purpose of my essay, "Revelation as Metaphoric Process," *TS* 47 (September 1986) 388–411, but I hope now to refine and develop the schema of that essay.

[16] Paul Ricoeur, *Time and Narrative* 1 (Chicago: University of Chicago Press, 1984) 52–82. Sandra Schneiders employs the threefold pattern of the world behind the text, the world of the text, and the world before the text as the main outline of her book, *The Revelatory Text. Interpreting the New Testament as Sacred Scripture* (San Francisco: HarperSanFrancisco, 1991).

[17] F.W. Dillistone, *The Power of Symbols in Religion and Culture* (New York: Crossroad, 1986) 14.

[18] Ibid., 15 (emphasis in original).

[19] Ibid., 17 (emphasis in original).

[20] Bernard J. Cooke, *The Distancing of God. The Ambiguity of Symbol in History and Theology* (Minneapolis: Fortress Press, 1990) 296. Cooke sees the alienation or distancing of basic human experience from God to be the result of three factors: the cultic distancing of ritual sacrality (Jewish roots), the philosophic distancing of an abstract ontological participation rather than experienced personal relationship (Platonic roots), and the structured distancing of institutional mediation through an ecclesiastical hierarchy (Roman roots).

[21] David Tracy, "The Particularity and Universality of Christian Revelation" in Edward Schillebeeckx and Bas van Iersel, eds., *Revelation and Experience*. Concilium 113 (New York: Seabury Press, 1979) 109.

[22] Dillistone, *The Power of Symbols* 231.

[23] Cooke, *The Distancing of God* 332 (emphasis in original).

[24] Paul Ricoeur, *Interpretation Theory* (Fort Worth: Texas Christian University Press, 1976) 65: "Everything indicates that symbolic experience calls for a work of meaning from metaphor, a work which it partially provides through its organizational network and its hierarchical levels. Everything indicates that symbol systems constitute a reservoir of meaning whose metaphoric potential is yet to be spoken." See also Sallie McFague, *Metaphorical Theology. Models of God in Religious Language* (Philadelphia: Fortress Press, 1982) 119–122, commenting on Ricoeur's insights.

[25] In my essay, "Revelation as Metaphoric Process," I express it this way: "Symbol has power to evoke mystery because it addresses itself to the whole person—to the imagination, the will, and the emotions, as well as to the intellect—and because it is deeply rooted in human experience and human history. One cannot simply invent true symbols. They emerge from the depths of human consciousness, both individual and collective, and they last as living symbols only as long as they continue to evoke those depths" (392).

[26] Peter W. Macky, *The Centrality of Metaphors to Biblical Thought* (Lewiston/Queenston/Lampeter: The Edwin Mellen Press, 1990) 49–56 for his "working definitions" of metaphor, analogy, symbol, and model. Standard resources for these definitions include Max Black, *Models and Metaphors. Studies in Language and Philosophy* (Ithaca: Cornell University Press, 1962), ch. 3 on "Metaphor," 25–47 and ch. 13 on "Models and Archetypes," 219–243; Ian G. Barbour, *Myths, Models, and Paradigms. A Comparative Study in Science and Religion* (San Francisco: HarperSanFrancisco, 1974).

[27] Black, *Models and Metaphors* 46.

[28] Brian Wicker, *The Story-Shaped World. Fiction and Metaphysics: Some Variations on a Theme* (Notre Dame: University of Notre Dame Press, 1975) 12. He describes the purpose of his book as "a new kind of synthesis based upon a marriage

of the two partners, *metaphor* and *analogy*" (p. 8; emphasis in original) and asks whether the medievals had "a highly developed sense of the *analogical* but a correspondingly under-developed sense of the *metaphorical* use of words."

[29] David Tracy, *The Analogical Imagination. Theology and the Culture of Pluralism* (New York: Crossroad, 1981). Barbour, *Myths, Models, and Paradigms* 18. Similarly George Lakoff and Mark Johnson, *Metaphors We Live By* (Chicago: University of Chicago Press, 1980) speak of metaphor as "imaginative rationality." In opposition to the "objectivist view" of absolute and unconditional truth and the "subjectivist alternative" of truth obtainable through a totally unrestricted imagination, they propose "an experientialist synthesis" that views metaphor as a matter of thought and action as well as of language. The value of their book is that they demonstrate the pervasiveness of metaphor in human life. They show that "conventional metaphors" underlie practically all of our thought processes and that we should not overstress the novelty or creativity of metaphor. "The reason we have focused so much on metaphor is that it unites reason and imagination. Reason, at the very least, involves categorization, entailment, and inference. Imagination, in one of its many aspects, involves seeing one kind of thing in terms of another kind of thing—what we have called metaphorical thought. Metaphor is thus imaginative rationality. Since the categories of our everyday thought are largely metaphorical and our everyday reasoning involves metaphorical entailments and inferences, ordinary rationality is therefore imaginative by its very nature. Given our understanding of poetic metaphor in terms of metaphorical entailments and inferences, we can see that the products of the poetic imagination are, for the same reason, partially rational in nature." Ibid., 192–193 (emphasis in original).

[30] Wicker, *Story-Shaped World* 22. The latter part of the quotation refers to his analysis of Saussure's binary opposites which is on pp. 15ff.

[31] Ibid., 27.

[32] Hans W. Frei, "The 'Literal Reading' of Biblical Narrative in the Christian Tradition: Does It Stretch or Will It Break?" in Frank McConnell, ed., *The Bible and the Narrative Tradition* (New York: Oxford University Press, 1986) 59.

[33] Ibid., 62.

[34] Ibid., 68. Frei's opposition to any theory of "narrativity" as a general class for Christian theology leads him to see narrative as secondary and fortuitous: "The reason why the intratextual universe of this Christian symbol system is a narrative one is that a specific set of texts, *which happen to be narrative,* has become primary, even within scripture, and has been assigned a literal reading as their primary or 'plain' sense." Ibid., 72 (emphasis mine). This does not seem to allow subsequent developments in biblical hermeneutics to qualify or modify the so-called "assigned" literal reading. However, I believe Frei's intent is simply to say that one can never exclude the literal sense, and indeed in certain instances must give it priority, to remain within the tradition of Christian self-understanding.

[35] Macky, *The Centrality of Metaphors* 86.

[36] Barbour, *Myths, Models, and Paradigms* 11, 37–38, 172; cf. Janet M. Soskice, *Metaphor and Religious Language* (Oxford: Clarendon Press, 1985).

[37] Macky, *The Centrality of Metaphors* 182.

[38] Nicholas Lash, in his analysis of Aquinas, would question whether analogical use can be independent of metaphorical use: "By applicability, Aquinas, having begun by sharply distinguishing metaphorical from analogical usage, has ended by acknowledging

that there is an 'irreducibly metaphorical dimension to analogous expressions' . . . only God would be in a position to use analogical terms without any touch of metaphor." Nicholas Lash, "Ideology, Metaphor, and Analogy" in Stanley Hauerwas and L. Gregory Jones, eds., *Why Narrative? Readings in Narrative Theology* (Grand Rapids: Wm. B. Eerdmans, 1989) 131.

[39] F.W. Dillistone, commenting on the essay of Owen Barfield, "The Meaning of the Word Literal" in L.C. Knights and Basil Cottle, eds., *Meaning and Symbol* (Butterworth Scientific Publications, 1960), maintains that language, originally born through human experience in relation with the environment, was first symbolic and only later made literal. Literal definitions (rules, laws, etc.) always give way to new discoveries of structures and energies that must first be expressed in symbols. Thus the sequence is: symbolic → literal → symbolic. Cf. F.W. Dillistone, *The Power of Symbols* 26.

[40] Stephen Happel, "Metaphors and Time Asymmetry: Cosmologies in Physics and Christian Meanings" in Robert John Russell, Nancey Murphy, and C. J. Isham, eds., *Quantum Cosmology and the Laws of Nature: Scientific Perspectives on Divine Action* (Vatican City: Vatican Observatory Publications, 1993) 118 (emphasis mine). The whole discussion of Ricoeur is on 118–120.

[41] Barbour, *Myths, Models, and Paradigms* 27.

[42] Hauerwas and Jones, *Why Narrative?* 5.

[43] Wesley A. Kort, *Story, Text, and Scripture. Literary Interests in Biblical Narrative* (University Park and London: The Pennsylvania State University Press, 1988) 12.

[44] Stephen Crites, "The Narrative Quality of Experience" in Hauerwas and Jones, eds., *Why Narrative?* 85. This article originally appeared in *JAAR* 39 (1971) 291–311 and is analyzed as a foundational essay by Terrence W. Tilley, *Story Theology* (Wilmington: Michael Glazier, 1985) 23–26.

[45] Crites, "The Narrative Quality of Experience," 66.

[46] Ricoeur, *Time and Narrative* 1.6 (cf. 84). He gives a fine analysis of Augustine's treatment of time in Book 11 of the *Confessions* on pp. 5–30.

[47] Ibid., 3.

[48] Crites, "The Narrative Quality of Experience," 72. We will return to the relation between "sacred stories" and "mundane stories" under the rubric of the function of narrative as mediating between ordinary discourse and mystery.

[49] Ibid., 78.

[50] Ibid., 79.

[51] Ibid., 81.

[52] Michael Root, "The Narrative Structure of Soteriology" in *Why Narrative?* 263–278.

[53] Tilley, *Story Theology* 14 (emphasis mine). He is using as an example the doctrinal statement, "God created the heavens and the earth," which never loses its truth but must be reinterpreted in the light of the stories we tell today about the cosmos.

[54] Crites, "The Narrative Quality of Experience" 85.

[55] John C. Hoffman, "Metaphorical or Narrative Theology," *Studies in Religion* 16 (1987) 174.

[56] Ibid., 180, 182.

[57] Michael Goldberg, "God, Action, and Narrative: *Which* Narrative? *Which* Action? *Which* God?" in *Why Narrative?* 348–365. I believe Goldberg is asking the right question in reference to Christian claims for their stories but his essay reveals a serious mis-

reading of the Gospel of Matthew, particularly his views that Matthew excludes the importance of human activity in response to God's saving inititatives and that he excludes the importance of the whole people (359–360). On the contrary, Matthew has a strong sense of the communal identity of the *ekklēsia* and of the importance of *doing* the word that we hear.

[58] Crites, "The Narrative Quality of Experience," 85.

[59] Ibid., 86.

[60] Kort, *Story, Text, and Scripture* 17 (emphasis mine). Cf. Scholes and Kellogg, *The Nature of Narrative* for a fuller account, especially of the historical development of each of these meanings.

[61] Kort recognizes variations in temporal patterns, e.g., rhythmic or cyclical time expressed in natural metaphors, interaction of contemporary forces expressed in social and political metaphors, actualization of human potential expressed in psychological metaphors.

[62] Kort, *Story, Text, and Scripture* 82–83.

[63] Ibid., 96.

[64] Stephen Crites, "A Respectful Reply to the Assertorical Theologian" in *Why Narrative?* 296. He is replying to the question of Julian Hartt, "Theological Investments in Story: Some Comments on Recent Developments and Some Proposals" in ibid., 279–292. "Is aesthetic truthfulness the strongest and most reliable bridge to actuality? If we grant that metaphor is the indispensable specialty of imagination in story, what enables us to discern the 'fit' of a metaphor with actuality?" Ibid., 289. Crites, in turn, recognizes the legitimate role of theology as a hermeneutical discipline, but he makes a plea not to confuse "the exigencies of narrative locution with the generalized language of metaphysical definition. No doubt the story requires critical interpretation, but a hermeneutical theology will not be quick to dogmatize, either with the story or against it, about what God is everywhere and always." Ibid., 297. Similarly Stanley Hauerwas, "Why the Truth Demands Truthfulness: An Imperious Engagement with Hartt" (ibid., 303–310), insists that there is no independent criterion of truth separate from the concrete story of Jesus of Nazareth: "my concern has been to insist . . . that the kind of truth entailed by the Gospels, the kind of demand placed on reality, cannot be separated from the way in which the story of God we claim as revealed in Jesus' life, death, and resurrection forces a repositioning of the self vis-à-vis reality." Ibid., 304. The position of Crites and Hauerwas here contrasts with that of Brian Wicker who maintains that metaphor and analogy are the two poles of "any adequate discourse whether about ordinary things or about God" and that there is a metaphysical basis for the connection between the metaphorical–analogical axes of language. Cf. Wicker, *The Story-Shaped World* 4–8, 23, 76–77. Nicholas Lash, "Ideology, Metaphor, and Analogy" in *Why Narrative?* 117–123 agrees with Wicker's approach.

[65] Kort, *Story, Text, and Scripture* 21. This is where I would locate Crites' discussion of "sacred stories" and "mundane stories" (n. 48 above).

[66] Ibid., 109. He states his thesis in the Introduction: "The appearance of God in narrative, textual form, I shall argue, challenges attempts to talk about religion without also addressing narrativity and textuality. Conversely, I shall argue that the appearance of God in narrative form . . . reveals the nature, function, and status of all narratives." (4)

[67] To add yet another voice, a fine review of the relation of narrative to a sense of self can be found in Anthony Paul Kerby, *Narrative and the Self* (Bloomington and

Indianapolis: Indiana University Press, 1991), especially ch. 2 "On Narrative," 32–64. "It is, I shall maintain, the narrated past that best generates our sense of personal identity, and the emphasis is on the word *personal* because emplotment may indeed create the individual meaning or story of our lives for ourselves. Narration into some form of story gives both a structure and a degree of understanding to the ongoing content of our lives" (p. 33; emphasis in the original).

[68] Scholes and Kellogg, *The Nature of Narrative* 165.

[69] Ibid., 165–170. The authors "distinguish between two kinds of dynamic characterization: the *developmental,* in which the character's personal traits are attenuated so as to clarify his progress along a plot line which has an ethical basis . . . and the *chronological,* in which the character's personal traits are ramified so as to make more significant the gradual shifts worked in the character during a plot which has a temporal basis. This latter kind of plotting and characterization is highly mimetic and is perhaps the principal distinguishing characteristic of such realistic fictions as the novel, which does not emerge as a literary form until Western culture develops a time-consciousness sophisticated enough to make the kind of temporal discrimination which this sort of characterization requires. E. M. Forster summed up this situation neatly when he contrasted ancient and modern narratives as 'life by values' and 'life by time'" (169; emphasis in original). Thus by the eighteenth century time becomes a major structural element.

[70] Herbert N. Schneidau, "Biblical Narrative and Modern Consciousness" in Frank McConnell, ed., *The Bible and the Narrative Tradition* 140–141.

[71] Ibid., 145. Scholes and Kellogg agree with the mythic regularity of Hellenic literature, but view the Hebraic as no different. Citing the story of David and Bathsheba, they comment: "The inward life is assumed but not presented in primitive narrative literature, whether Hebraic or Hellenic." *The Nature of Narrative* 166.

[72] Wicker, *Story-Shaped World* 92. For a fine treatment of YHWH as character based on the Hebrew canon, see Jack Miles, *God. A Biography* (New York: Random House, 1995).

[73] Ibid., 93. Correspondingly, the character of Satan receives a progressive denigration, e.g., compare 2 Sam 24:1 with 1 Chr 21:1. In the former YHWH's anger incites David; in the latter Satan incites David.

[74] Ibid., 96 (emphasis in original).

[75] Ricoeur's emphasis on plot (*mythos* in Aristotle) as the most fundamental aspect of narrative is certainly correct. Scholes and Kellogg define plot simply as "the dynamic, sequential element in narrative literature" (*The Nature of Narrative* 207). They see it as the most essential and least variable of all the aspects of narrative, but more important for the greatest narratives is "quality of mind." "Quality of mind (as expressed in the language of characterization, motivation, description, and commentary) not plot, is the soul of narrative. Plot is only the indispensable skeleton which, fleshed out with character and incident, provides the necessary clay into which life may be breathed." Ibid., 239.

[76] Ibid., 240.

[77] Ibid., 241.

[78] On the relationship of text and reader see Ricoeur, *Time and Narrative* 3 (Chicago: University of Chicago Press, 1988) 157–179. He notes that his treatment of the phenomenology of reading as the necessary mediator of refiguration is the most obvious difference between this work and his earlier *Rule of Metaphor.*

[79] Scholes and Kellogg, *The Nature of Narrative* 276.

[80] Tilley, *Story Theology* 39 (emphasis in original). He cites J. D. Crossan, *The Dark Interval. Towards a Theology of Story* (Niles: Argus, 1975), who also includes *apologues* that defend worlds and *satires* that attack worlds.

[81] Scholes and Kellogg, *The Nature of Narrative* 12ff., 28, 134–136, 218ff.

[82] Crossan, *The Dark Interval* 53.

[83] Joseph Campbell, *The Masks of God: Creative Mythology* (New York: Penguin, 1976), as analyzed by Tilley, *Story Theology* 42–44. Barbour, *Myths, Models, and Paradigms* 19–28 offers a useful summary of the character and functions of myth.

[84] Crossan, *The Dark Interval* 57.

[85] H. Richard Niebuhr, *The Meaning of Revelation* (Toronto: Macmillan, 1941) 138.

[86] According to Marcus J. Borg, *Jesus, A New Vision: Spirit, Culture, and the Life of Discipleship* (San Francisco: Harper & Row, 1987), Jesus connects the experience of Spirit with the social and cultural concerns of his day and so seeks the transformation of his social world. The book is a very readable account of Jesus' historical ministry and includes results from the more recent approaches of sociology and cultural anthropology. Although much in this approach is hypothetical and open to debate, Borg's central contrast between "the politics of holiness" of Jewish renewal movements in first-century Palestine (Essenes, Pharisees, resistance fighters) that sought to maintain Jewish separateness and purity by radicalizing Torah and Jesus' "politics of compassion" that seeks to overcome boundaries and create an alternative community of inclusivity and reconciliation seems to me fundamentally sound and correct. Another helpful resource in this regard is Richard A. Horsley, *Jesus and the Spiral of Violence: Popular Jewish Resistance in Roman Palestine* (San Francisco: Harper & Row, 1987). I employ this approach in my essay, "Jesus' Parables and the Faith That Does Justice," *Studies in the Spirituality of Jesuits* 24/5 (November 1992) 12–15.

[87] Borg, *Jesus, A New Vision* 142.

[88] Such an analysis can be found in my essay, "Jesus' Parables and the Faith That Does Justice" 8–12. The analysis is based on C. H. Dodd's well-known description of parable in *The Parables of the Kingdom* (New York: Scribner's, 1961) 5, but with modifications from Bernard Brandon Scott, *Hear Then the Parable* (Minneapolis: Fortress Press, 1989) where parable is described as follows: "A parable is a *mashal* [= "to be like"] that employs a short narrative fiction to reference a transcendent symbol" (p. 8). Another analysis based on Dodd can be found in John R. Donahue's excellent *The Gospel in Parable. Metaphor, Narrative, and Theology in the Synoptic Gospels* (Philadelphia: Fortress Press, 1988) 1–27.

[89] Paul Ricoeur, *The Rule of Metaphor* (Toronto: University of Toronto Press, 1977) 244ff. calls the parables "fictional redescriptions" of reality.

[90] Donahue, *The Gospel in Parable* 19.

[91] Cook, "Jesus' Parables and the Faith That Does Justice," 33–34.

[92] Ricoeur, *Time and Narrative* 3.181.

[93] See Ricoeur, *Time and Narrative* 2.156–158.

[94] Ricoeur, *Time and Narrative* 3.241.

[95] Ibid., 244. The quotations that follow in the text are on pp. 244–249.

[96] Ibid., 250. See the full discussion on pp. 249–261.

[97] Ibid., 274. See the full discussion on pp. 261–274.

[98] Tilley, *Story Theology* 53.

[99] Frank Kermode, *The Sense of an Ending: Studies in the Theory of Fiction* (New York: Oxford University Press, 1966). I am relying here on Ricoeur's analysis of this work in *Time and Narrative* 2.22–28.

[100] Frank Kermode, *The Genesis of Secrecy. On the Interpretation of Narrative* (Cambridge: Harvard University Press, 1979) 47.

[101] Ibid., 118.

[102] Ibid., 122.

[103] Ricoeur, *Time and Narrative* 2.27.

[104] Schneiders, *The Revelatory Text* 3.

[105] Ibid., 127, cited above. See the whole discussion in ch. 4: "The World Behind the Text: History, Imagination, and the Revelatory Text," 97–131.

[106] Ricoeur, *Time and Narrative* 1.53.

[107] Kort, *Story, Text, and Scripture* 110, 111. He views opposition to textuality to be a product of either idealism or empiricism: "Texts are the consequences, the more or less inadequate substitutes for the real or true things—thoughts or speech, on the one hand, and entities and events, on the other" (113). We desire to be grounded in something nontextual, but for Kort realities as particular and present "become real to us, they become part of a world, by becoming textual" (116). Thus we cannot avoid textuality.

[108] Ricoeur, *Time and Narrative* 1.68. The discussion of mimesis$_2$ is on 64–70.

[109] Werner G. Jeanrond, *Text and Interpretation as Categories of Theological Thinking* (New York: Crossroad, 1988) 5.

[110] Schneiders, *The Revelatory Text* 167 (emphasis in original).

[111] Ibid., 172.

[112] Ibid., 177.

[113] Kort, *Story, Text, and Scripture* 130.

[114] Jeanrond, *Text and Interpretation* 119. In his hermeneutical theory Jeanrond prefers "assessment" to application (Gadamer) or appropriation (Ricoeur) in the inseparable triad: understanding – explanation – assessment, because it brings out more strongly the constant need for critical activity. He states his thesis as follows: "no concept of understanding can lay claim to adequacy unless it includes right from the start a dimension of criticism regarding both the matter *(Sache)* of the text and the situation in which the interpretation takes place" (p. 65). He offers a fine analysis of reading, which is always ethical, i.e., responsible or irresponsible, and reading genres that give rise to a pluralism of readings as they involve both the reading context (extratextual) and the reading style (intratextual).

[115] Robert A. Krieg, *Story-Shaped Christology. The Role of Narratives in Identifying Jesus Christ* (New York: Paulist Press, 1988) offers a helpful analysis of gospel, history, and biography, but seems to conclude that while there is continuity, narrative discourse is subordinate to conceptual discourse: "The retelling of the Synoptic story, or the recounting of an historical narrative, in conjunction with the Gospels and with the study of Christian biography, is not the last word but yields to conceptual discourse" (p. 162). Further: "'Christology shaped by story' means that narratives function within a larger, intellectually-disciplined, investigation" (p. 164). We are saying just the opposite.

NB

CHAPTER 2

A Biblical Image: "The Beloved Son" in the Gospel of Mark

"In the beginning was the story and the story was in relationship to God and the story was God." The Gospel of John (1:1-18) tells the story of the creative and saving power of Wisdom (*Sophia* identified as *Logos*) by telling the story of Jesus (*Logos* identified as incarnate in the human, earthly life of Jesus). It is the story of "the only Son" *(monogenēs)* coming forth from the Father. Mark also begins at the beginning *(archē)* with the subtle and ironic opening line that functions like a title or superscription for the whole gospel: "The beginning of the good news of Jesus Christ, the Son of God" (1:1). Does *archē* here mean (1) the beginning of the story that immediately follows, that is, the story of Jesus' baptism by John; (2) the "beginning of the sufferings" (Mark 13:8), that is, of the end of history as we know it, the apocalyptic finale; or (3) the beginning of the creation of the "new human being" (Son of Man) who already in his baptism is anointed by the Spirit (Christ) and declared to be God's "only" or "beloved" Son (Son of God)?[1] The answer lies within the narrative world that Mark has created.

Why Mark? That is the same as asking "why narrative?" Mark represents a critical transition point, indeed an "epochal shift" in the way early Christians sought to express the significance of Jesus. As such Mark is perhaps the most intriguing and puzzling of all the documents in the Christian canon of scripture. Frank Kermode sees Mark as "a strong witness to the enigmatic and exclusive character of narrative, to its property of banishing interpreters from its secret places."[2] Elizabeth Struthers Malbon, reviewing the multiple readings of one small text (the poor widow at 12:41-44), concludes: "The critical question is how to interrelate the multiple readings of a single text that result from multiple interpreters focusing on multiple contexts."[3] Obviously there is value in each approach of these interpreters insofar as each responds to real questions raised by the text itself (historical, socio-cultural, literary, religious, etc.)

and so there is need to strike a balance that will include the world behind the text, the world of the text, and the world before the text.[4]

Mark is particularly intriguing because this gospel represents the foundational move from oral to written gospel (as narrative). How complex this is can be seen in the question of Walter Ong: "How far is the biblical message the more participatory message of pure orality and how far is it imbued with the analytic, explanatory possibilities implemented by writing and indeed enforced by writing?"[5] He makes the further point, critical to our theme, that irony as a creative work of the imagination is the product of the distancing created by writing and print. Oral cultures permit certain standard ironies, such as riddles, tricksters, etcetera, but "oral performance cannot readily achieve the distance from life which complex irony demands."[6]

But has Mark achieved this distancing or is it a product of *our reading* of Mark under the pervasive influence of our own print culture? Mark was produced in a culture that was primarily oral and yet, as written, conveys a certain distancing of the story from oral immediacy. We will return to this shortly in our analysis of the textuality, structure, and genre of the gospel, but first we must explore more fully the turn to narrative as a new and creative way to proclaim the significance of Jesus (the "good news" of 1:1). Why indeed did Mark embark on this "narrative quest"?

1. Mark's Turn to Narrative

Prior to Mark there were writings. The sayings material common to Matthew and Luke (called "Q") probably existed in a written form by at least 50 C.E. Likewise many scholars believe that an earlier form of the Gospel of Thomas as a collection of "wisdom sayings" of Jesus may have existed around the same time. More significantly, Paul wrote his first letter (1 Thessalonians) around 51 C.E. In his letters he refers at times to "words of the Lord" but it is hard to know whether these were pre-Easter or post-Easter sayings. For Paul it made little difference, for his focus was on the crucified and risen Lord who was central to his faith experience. His letters, which he began to write only after some eighteen years of active ministry (assuming that Paul had his conversion experience around 33 C.E.), were a necessary but inadequate substitute for the power of personal presence and oral immediacy in the proclamation of the gospel. "Q," Thomas, and Paul are all representative of the primacy of oral communication. Why then was it necessary to create a narrative form of the gospel and just how central or indispensable is such a narrative form to Christian proclamation?

The simplest and most basic answer is the fundamental human need to remember a loved one as time passes. Can we imagine what our image of Jesus would be like if we only had the letters of Paul? In a chapter entitled "Jesus in the Memory of the Church," Luke Johnson says that the process of transmission, both oral and written, that culminates in the writing of gospels demands an appreciation of "the art of storytelling." He employs the analogy of "remembering Grandmother."[7] As time passes and memories become faded or confused it helps to have collections of grandmother stories and eventually perhaps even a full narrative so that the "beloved founder" of the family will be remembered in future generations. This is a true and important dimension of all the gospel narratives. Historical memories embedded in narrative form help to give concreteness and particularity to this man Jesus now proclaimed as the Christ and Lord. But narrative does more.

A second and more fundamental answer, then, is that we cannot really understand who Jesus is without telling the *whole* story. For the first Christians the foundational experience upon which everything else was built was the death and resurrection of Jesus. This was the focal point. It evoked what Sandra Schneiders calls "the paschal imagination," "the theological-spiritual imagination of the believing community" that enabled them to transform the historical experiences of both Jesus and the communities themselves into a dynamic image of Jesus as Christ and Lord. As Luke Johnson puts it: "The conviction that Jesus is alive and powerfully active in the believing community is the implicit, and sometimes explicit, presupposition of all the writings of the NT."[8] This was, as he notes earlier, an "experience of power," "the continuing presence of a personal, transcendent, and transforming power within the community."[9] This power was identified as the Spirit of Jesus and as such inseparable from Jesus himself who in turn was inseparable from the God he called *Abba*. The Christian movement was born out of this experience but it could not long remain satisfied with a simple kerygmatic focus on the event of Jesus' death and resurrection. This was already in essence a story, a recounting of an event, but to be understood the communities needed to explore the larger story that could give this event context and meaning. For an adequate account there was need to move back behind the event to the stories that preceded and forward from the event to the stories still to come. The story of Jesus, as God's own story, finally had to embrace all the stories from creation to eschaton.

"Midrash (from the verb *darash,* 'to search') is a method of contemporizing sacred texts."[10] In the light of this new experience of death and resurrection the early communities searched the traditions *(Torah)* and reinterpreted them. They also searched their collective memories for the words and deeds of Jesus and reinterpreted them as well. Inseparably intertwined with memories of Jesus were their own memories of becoming community in the power of the Spirit. All of these are recorded in the gospel writings so that they recount in one and the same story (but in a distinct and particular way in each community) not only the life of Jesus that preceded his death but also the ongoing life of the communities that were born out of the resurrection experience. The story of Jesus has become the story of every Christian disciple and indeed the story of every human person, for it is the story of death and life at the center of all human experience. As such it is nothing less than the story of God because, as Wesley Kort has emphasized, *all* narratives mediate between ordinary discourse and mystery.

The genius of Mark is that he was the first to configure all this into a plot with a coherent and followable storyline. In doing so he addressed what Paul Ricoeur calls "the aporias of time" with "the poetics of narrativity." In the ongoing discussion over Mark's ending it is important to keep in mind that one of the primary functions of narrative is to mediate temporality as memory (the present of the past), attention (the present of the present), and anticipation (the present of the future). There can be no thought about time, as Ricoeur says, without narrated time. Thus the configuration of the world behind the text into a narrative text produces a new and qualitatively different experience of time. As such it inevitably projects a world before the text as the reader/listener engages the truth claims of the text itself and so refigures the text. In this process we meet the limits of narrative in the inscrutability of time. But what narrative does is allow us to discover our personal and communal identities as active participants in an ongoing story, the story of God.

The text of Mark embodies a "configurating operation" that, in Ricoeur's terms, is a dynamic and creative synthesis of heterogeneous factors. These can be subsumed under the four kinds of force or meaning in discourse (Wesley Kort): character, plot, atmosphere, and tone. While all are clearly present in Mark, Kort sees tone as particularly predominant in Mark's narrative. Mark's primary concern is to communicate the significance of Jesus as *God* sees him. The point of view of the narrative is the point of view of God so that anthropological questions about human life (character), teleological questions about time (plot), and ontological questions about boundaries (atmosphere) are all taken up and resolved in the supreme value: *the faith of God* (Mark 11:22) that overcomes boundaries such as the Temple mount, perplexities such as the nearness of the end, and intransigence such as fear and hardness of heart in the face of the divine will. For Mark, God is indeed the one who tells this tale. For those who have eyes to see, ears to hear, and feet to walk,[11] this is a story about the faithfulness of God embodied in Jesus and available to all who listen and obey. God's fidelity can be our fidelity! The key to the gospel is whether we think the thoughts of God (Mark 8:33; in the story world this refers principally to "men" such as Simon Peter but in actuality it refers to anyone, man or woman, who is opposed to God because of hardness of heart).[12]

Mark communicates these truths not in abstract, propositional form but by telling the story of Jesus. In the face of a wide-ranging diversity of opinion with regard to what kind of text (genre/form) Mark is and what this text is trying to say (content),[13] this chapter makes the following assumptions under the threefold rubric proposed by Paul Ricoeur and Sandra Schneiders. First, with regard to the "world behind the text" (mimesis$_1$), social criticism, especially cultural anthropology, is extremely important in order to avoid misunder-standings caused by imposing alien meanings on the text.[14] Thus issues of boundaries, especially "purity maps," cannot be ignored in the interpretation of the text. On the other hand there are two realities behind the text that seem to me more fundamental. The first is the death and resurrection of Jesus as a manifestation of power that has transformed the first Christians. Mark's Jesus communicates a sense of power that cannot be defeated, for the victory has already been won. The word "good news" *(euaggelion)* already signals victory. The second is the crisis of the destruction of the Temple (whether imminent or already a *fait accompli* seems impossible to determine definitively but it is clear that Mark was written in the shadow of that event and the crisis it pro-duced for all Jews, Christian or not). This crisis demanded a radical reinter-pretation of Jewish traditions (especially of Torah in relation to Temple). Mark was written to offer one such interpretation in the light of the crucified and risen Jesus. It should be emphasized, however, whether we search for cultural and social clues or Christian convictions or apocalyptic events that create crises of interpretation, that these realities behind the text are configured into a new synthesis by the text itself and must be understood primarily within the story world that Mark has created.[15]

Second, and most importantly then, is the "world of the text" (mimesis$_2$). Mark was written by a creative theologian who pulled together many oral and written sources, including prophetic sayings, miracle stories, apocalyptic and passion traditions, into a single coherent narrative with a rhetorical or persua-sive rather than a strictly poetic or aesthetic purpose. Thus Mark is a *narra-tive* theologian who communicates not in abstract, propositional form but by telling the story, the story that centers on one person, Jesus of Nazareth. Recall the view of Stephen Crites that "the self is given whole, as an activity in time" only in stories. There is no other way that Jesus can be adequately communi-cated. The key question is: "how does the story mean?"[16] The plot, or story-line, responds to the questions "what" and "why"; that is, the story is the reality structured into a cause and effect sequence. It evinces the fundamental conflict that the narrative must resolve. The settings, or atmosphere, respond to the questions "where" and "when": they provide the background and the boundaries for the dramatic action, both spatial and temporal. The characters respond to the question "who": they raise the question of identity in terms of the characterization of contrasting or conflicting types who embody certain values.[17]

To answer the question "who?" by identifying with the central character is to discover the story that constitutes one's life. If YHWH is the chief character or protagonist in the biblical story that runs from creation to eschaton and so gives the real world a structure it otherwise would not have, in Mark it is Jesus who effects the practical reconciliation with or mediation of "God Most High" *(El-Elyon)* and so structures the world in a new way.

All these dimensions of narrative discourse are found in Mark, but it is tone that predominates. Tone responds to questions of material selection and voice (style), but most acutely to the question of point of view. Who is the teller of the tale? Mark is permeated with a sense of irony. Although we refer to the Gospel according to "Mark," in fact the only author we know is the one who can be reconstructed on the basis of the text or narrative itself. This "implied author" is clearly omniscient and reliable as narrator of the story.

> The salient features of Mark's narrator are these: the narrator does not figure in the events of the story; speaks in the third person; is not bound by time or space in the telling of the story; is an implied invisible presence in every scene, capable of being anywhere to "recount" the action; displays full omniscience by narrating the thoughts, feelings, or sensory experiences of many characters; often turns from the story to give direct "asides" to the reader, explaining a custom or translating a word or commenting on the story; and narrates the story from one overarching ideological point of view.[18]

That point of view is both implicitly and explicitly God's point of view that gradually unfolds as Mark through the use of various rhetorical devices draws the listener/reader into the story world to explore its various levels of meaning. This includes both the "implied reader" (or listener), a hypothetical, imaginary reader/listener "with the ideal responses implied or suggested by the narrative" and the "actual reader" (or listener), a first-century reader/listener who "would have seen the events of the story world in relation to the events of the real world at the time of writing."[19] Irony always involves a certain disparity of understanding created by multiple possible interactions among characters, audience, narrator, and author. This brings us to the third rubric, the "world before the text" ($mimesis_3$).

"When the reader-response critic discusses the implied reader or narratee, she will return constantly to the question of what happens in the temporal flow of language in the act of reading."[20] Reading itself is a temporal experience, as indeed is listening to oral performance. It is "kinetic," "dynamic," involving a sense of "flow." We are not, or should not be, mere passive readers or listeners. In Sandra Schneiders' terms we enter into the experience of the text as text ($mimesis_2$) in an act of "aesthetic surrender" in order to engage the truth claims of the text through "critical existential interpretation" ($mimesis_3$). The world the Gospel of Mark projects is our world, new possibilities for our reality, if we have eyes to see, ears to hear, and feet to walk. In order to enter into that world we must first raise the question of genre: has Mark created a new literary genre? Then we will be in a position to offer a proposed reading of the gospel as a whole. Finally, the key image of Jesus that integrates all the factors in Mark's narrative quest, i.e., the "beloved Son," will be examined by way of a synthetic conclusion.

2. A New Genre?

To understand the genre of Mark two presuppositions must first be addressed: textuality and structure. Hence a first presupposition to the identification of genre in Mark is an understanding of the move from oral to written Gospel.[21] Werner Kelber sees the written gospel as a radical alternative to oral gospel because in Mark the earthly Jesus has replaced and silenced the voice of the living Lord. Mark represents a drastic reconstruction of "oral integrity." This means a loss with regard to the immediacy of live communication but a gain with regard to the distance of textuality that allows for multiple and diverse interpretations across succeeding generations. Yet Mark more accurately represents a tension between oral and written modes of communication because it was probably written to be *read aloud* or, more properly, dramatically enacted in a communal context of liturgical celebration such as a baptism or Eucharist.[22] The author would thus have structured the gospel in such a way as to make it easy to follow and memorable for *listeners* rather than for readers. Such rhetorical devices as "the repetition of words, the two-step progression, the use of questions in dialogue, the framing of one episode by another, the arrangement of episodes in a concentric pattern, and the repetition of similar episodes in a series of three"[23] are all characteristic techniques of oral narration. Such techniques provide both reinforcement through repetition and progressive development. Yet in Mark tension resides in the fact that the basic oral impulse of presence and immediacy confronts the capacity for absence and distance that written fixedness engenders.[24]

A second, closely connected presupposition to the identification of genre in Mark is the way in which the author has structured the story. "The implosion and linearization of oral pluralism, the construction of a comprehensive journey, the valorized spatial world, the narration of the kingdom's story, all that gives sayings, parables, stories, and episodes a semblance of plot, sequentiality, and followability is the achievement of the new technique of writing."[25] Mark's structure has been plausibly described as concentric, thus employing an oral technique in the service of written discourse.[26] A concentric or ring structure (it is worth noting that "Galilee" means "ring" or "circle") is a device for oral remembering and so dependent on oral signals rather than on graphic ones as in a printed text. Mark employs such patterns in subsections of the gospel,[27] but can we say that the gospel as a whole is structured in this way? Admittedly the value of a proposed structure for the entire gospel is that it fits our hermeneutical condition as text-centered. Oriented around a print culture, it is we who need a table of contents, as it were, an outline that allows us to see how the individual parts relate to the whole. Mark certainly did not provide one, so any such proposal is a hypothetical construction from the text itself.

Joanna Dewey offers a very valuable insight into how we should approach Mark. She notes that Mark is not a "single structure made up of discrete sequential units" but "an interwoven tapestry or fugue made up of multiple overlapping structures and sequences, forecasts of what is to come and echoes of what has already been said."[28] Mark's gospel with its forecasts and echoes, its variation within repetition, its development of themes and dramatic climaxes, is designed for a listening audience and can best be compared to the experience of listening to classical music in our own times. This is in line with the analogy suggested by Stephen Crites between the musical style of action and the narrative quality of experience. Thus in opposition to an overemphasis on linearity in Mark we need to pay more attention to "oral hermeneutics" while still recognizing, as Dewey observes, that *we* are readers, conditioned by a print culture, who interpret the gospel according to sophisticated techniques of literary analysis. Keeping in mind the difference between a first-century listener and a twentieth-century reader, we propose the following concentric structure:[29]

> A. The Wilderness (1:2-13)
>   Hinge/Transition (1:14-15)
> B. Galilee (1:16–8:21)
>   Hinge/Transition (8:22-26)
> C. The Way (8:27–10:45)
>   Hinge/Transition (10:46-52)
> B'. Jerusalem (11:1–15:39)
>   Hinge/Transition (15:40-41)
> A'. The Tomb (15:42–16:8)

This proposed structure indicates the most fundamental concerns of the gospel, so it may be helpful to indicate some of these at this juncture. A–A', which function as prologue and epilogue respectively, show a concern to begin and end with God's voice proclaiming the good news through a messenger or herald (John the Baptist dressed in camel's hair as the voice in the desert and the young man dressed in a white robe as the voice in the tomb). In each case there is a "going before" (1:2, 7; 16:7) that echoes the importance of the "way," but whereas John's voice is superseded by God's voice (1:11) Jesus' "going before" at 16:7 calls attention to all that has preceded in the story world and evokes the expectation of a response that now only the listener/reader can give. As Stock remarks with regard to both wilderness and tomb: "The paradox is that in these places of death new life begins."[30]

The hinge or transition passages function in a typically oral fashion as both prospective, anticipating what is to come (foreshadowing), and retrospective, looking back to what has transpired (echoing). The effect is to condition the listener to absorb the movement of the story. For example 1:14 looks forward to Jesus' preaching in Galilee (the "good news of *God*" exegetes the "good news of Jesus Christ, the Son of God" at 1:1) and to John's arrest (narrated as a flashback at 6:17-29), while 1:15 looks back to the fulfillment already announced by John and realized in the revelation of who Jesus is as Christ/Son of God (1:1 as exegeted at 1:10-11) and what he is about as victor (the "stronger" one) over Satan, thus inaugurating the eschatological age of salvation (1:12-13).[31] This first "hinge" is especially important for it encapsulates the whole gospel and thus indicates how it should be heard. The other hinges also function in a prospective/retrospective way. Particularly interesting is 15:40-41, for v. 40 looks forward to the role of the women at the tomb and v. 41 offers a retrospective focus on the whole preceding structure: Galilee – the Way – Jerusalem. And of course the two cures of blind men (8:22-26; 10:46-52) offer poignant contrast to the continuing blindness of the disciples and frame the central and key section of the gospel.

B–B' is a study in contrast. The veritable explosion of oral forms in Galilee eventually gives way to the slowed-down tempo, space concentration, and tightly plotted narrative of the passion in Jerusalem. Immediacy and presence give way to distance and absence, the pulsating activity of life to the crushing passivity of death. Kelber, in his chapter on "Mark's Oral Legacy," shows how the "heroic stories" (the ten healing stories), the "polarization stories" (the three exorcism stories), the "didactic stories" (the six controversy stories that culminate in a memorable saying), and the "parabolic stories" (the six parables and the general use of parabolic discourse) correspond to the oral dynamics of formulaic structure and social contextuality. The latter refers to the interaction of hearer and speaker that determines a specific interpretation (out of multiple possible ones) only in the immediacy of oral interchange. The purpose of these stories as oral media is not so much theological or historical as oral remembering, to make Jesus live in the imagination of the audience in a wholly unambiguous way (especially in the heroic and polarization stories). "In sum, orality's principal concern is not to preserve historical actuality, but to shape and break it into memorable, applicable speech."[32]

In Mark it is Jesus' ministry in Galilee (1:16–8:21) that principally corresponds to this oral legacy, although the linear dynamics of textuality have already introduced ambiguity into the picture of an unambiguous Jesus mighty in word and work (especially at 3:6; 6:1-6a; 8:14-21). As Kelber puts it: "The terrifyingly ambiguous notion that the protagonist must first be crushed himself for evil to be conquered lies outside the mental horizon of this *oral christology* of heroism and polarization."[33] It is the contrasting parallelism of Jerusalem (11:1–15:39) with its triple death, namely that of Jesus, the Temple,

and the disciples (so Kelber) that brings into focus a different kind of christology, one of faithful trust in the face of the overwhelming and massive evil
of death by crucifixion, and so gives a particular dynamic shape to the whole
gospel that transforms the meaning of Jesus' success in Galilee. "What is most
noticeable about Markan christology is its exclusive cast in a pre-resurrec-
tional framework . . . it is the written medium that facilitates this sweeping,
retrospective reach for the earthly Jesus. . . ."[34]

In Mark Jesus is the only one who teaches, and it is C (8:27–10:45), the
center and key of the entire gospel, that articulates the most important and
fundamental content of that teaching. This central section is structured by the
three passion predictions at 8:31-32a; 9:30-31; 10:32-34, each of which is accompanied by the resistance and/or fear and misunderstanding of the disciples
and followed by an extended teaching on the nature of discipleship. Jesus now
speaks the word "plainly" (*parrhēsia* at 8:32) in contrast to parabolically or in
riddles (*en parabolais* at 4:33). The voice from heaven in the transfiguration
scene (9:2-8, which occurs at the physical midpoint of the whole gospel and
at the center of a concentric structure at 8:34–9:13) gives the definitive exhortation: "Listen to him!" *(akouete autou)*. The capacity to *hear* what Jesus
is saying (the thoughts of God at 8:33) is key to the entire gospel. Thus the
image of Jesus as teacher functions as the "hermeneutical bridge" to Mark's
way of doing christology.[35] Jesus in this central teaching section communicates the divine will (*dei* at 8:31) both for himself and for his disciples. For
Mark the question of who Jesus is (8:27-30) is inseparable from the question
of who we are as disciples. Christology is inextricably intertwined with discipleship, and the only adequate answer is not a theoretical one based on an
intellectual understanding, e.g., of the titles of Jesus, but the very practical one
of actually taking up one's cross and following Jesus on the way (8:34-38).
The significance of Peter's response lies not in his "correct" answer ("You are
the Christ!") but in his refusal to take up the cross (8:32b-33). To convey this
Mark tells the story of Jesus' faithfulness and Peter's denial.[36]

For Mark, in sum, it is not the titles such as Christ, Son of God, and Son of
Man that provide the interpretative key for unlocking the mystery of who
Jesus is. Much rather it is the story of Jesus' personal journey to the cross that
provides new understanding of such titles. If Jesus is God's Son, he is such
only as the crucified Nazarene (15:39; 16:6), as the one who died with a loud
cry of abandonment (15:34, 37). This is a story that, like the parables of Jesus,
has metaphoric impact. It does not seek to provide information so much as to
invite participation. Is the genre of Mark's gospel then, as some have proposed, that of parable?[37] The very diversity of proposals, including tragedy,
comedy, aretalogy, biography, apocalyptic myth, apocalyptic history, and parable would seem to indicate that the best category is "host-genre,"[38] which is
to say that Mark has integrated a wide variety of forms and/or genres with
respect to the Jesus tradition (mostly oral but with some written sources) into

a narrative framework that appears to be a realistic, chronological, and/or historical account. The author has created a *text* structured by oral concerns, which raises three questions: (1) Has Mark created a completely *new genre* or is there a contemporary model for this style of writing? (2) Does the gospel as *story* take the shape (form) of myth, parable, action, apologue, or satire? (3) Is the *purpose* rhetorical or aesthetic?

First, is this a new genre in the sense that Mark is trying to communicate something that has never before been communicated? In a sense the answer must be both yes and no. There are precedents in "the biographically oriented biblical histories" of the First Testament.[39] The strong presence of Elijah, Moses, and David as well as the prophetic literature, especially Isaiah and Daniel, indicate that the primary model employed, consciously or unconsciously, would have been the First Testament tradition of recounting God's mighty acts on behalf of Israel. Neither biography as analyzed by Talbert nor apocalyptic as analyzed by Kee[40] exactly corresponds to this even though there is a vaguely generic biographical orientation and a very strong apocalyptic interest in Mark. Yet the gospel is nothing if not "realistic narrative."[41] What is new and unprecedented is that the "good news of God" (1:14), God's eschatological victory over the power of "the strong man" (3:27), is the story of this rejected, crucified "carpenter" and "son of Mary" from Nazareth in Galilee. The apocalyptic drama is set in the real world; it is a popular story in which ordinary, sometimes downtrodden and socially marginated people play significant roles, as is clear for example in the case of Simon the fisherman who was called Peter. "Gospel" is no longer oral proclamation in the Pauline manner but proclamation in narrative form that manifests a profound interest in historical realism.[42]

Second, with regard to the gospel's character as story, the question has been raised whether Mark's primary shape is that of myth or of parable. Elizabeth Struthers Malbon proposes that it is both. "The pattern of Markan spatial oppositions both establishes world and subverts world. The literary world to which the Gospel of Mark is related is myth-parable, or parable-myth."[43] Mark appears to be at one and the same time subverting the established world of Jewish religiosity and establishing a new world of Christian discipleship, but even this new world is structured parabolically by the paschal mystery of Jesus. Mark's "double ending" illustrates the tensive character of this relationship. Chapter 13 is an apocalyptic myth (or history, according to Collins) that focuses on the unmistakable coming of the Son of Man ("they will see," vv. 24-27 is the center of a concentric structure) but at the same time contains a parabolic passion prediction for Mark's community (vv. 9-13).[44] The characteristic "Beware!" (*blepete* at vv. 5, 9, 23, 33) signals an exhortation to persevere until the end (v. 13) in the face of persecution by authorities (v. 9) and hatred among families (v. 12). At the center of this exhortation stands the divine will *(dei)* that the gospel be preached to all the nations (v. 10) and the promise of the eloquence of the Holy Spirit (v. 11). Mark's community can with mythic awareness be confident of Jesus' final victory but that victory is surrounded by an unsettling parabolic challenge to their own perseverance. If the first ending focuses on mythic resolution challenged by parabolic awareness, i.e., that the "new insiders" (women, fishermen, tax-collectors, and others as over against the Jewish religious leaders) have no definitive guarantees of their own fidelity, the second ending (chs. 14–16) is primarily parabolic with its focus on Jesus' death as the abandonment and absence of God (15:34), yet contains the mythic hope of Jesus still "going before" (16:7). Malbon offers a good summary of the paradoxical tension. "As I read Mark's Gospel, to 'see' (16:7) Jesus is not to await a literal parousia in Galilee (as in Kelber's myth), but it is really to 'see' something, not nothing (as in Crossan's parable). . . . To 'see' Jesus is to perceive that being a disciple is following the way he took, the way on which he is still 'going before' (16:7). To 'see' Jesus is, according to the Gospel of Mark, to see that the new world established 'on the way' is a world that challenges establishment itself."[45] Thus just as the genre of "biographically oriented biblical histories" has transformed the story forms of myth and parable into a kind of history, so these story forms have transformed history into a self-involving myth-parable that draws the reader/listener into the mystery of the reign of God.[46]

Finally, Mark's purpose in all of this is not to create an aesthetic object that finds its purpose solely within its own coherence and beauty but to persuade, to function as an instrument within a social process.[47] For example, Mark's use of parable in chapter 4 has "taken what is essential to the parable, the double-meaning effect, and made it the starting point of a theological theme concerning the audience's resistance to hearing the word."[48] Thus the "mystery of the kingdom of God" (4:11) has to do not with secret knowledge but with hardness of heart (cf. 4:12 with 6:52; 7:6-8, 20-23; 8:17-18; 10:5), with the tension between the divine will and human wills. It is essential to hear with an understanding heart (4:9, 12, 13, 14-20, 23, 24, 33; 6:52; 7:14, 18; 8:17, 21) so as to be able to do the will of God (3:35).

3. A Concentric Reading of Mark

Mark has textualized and structured the oral tradition about Jesus so that his words will never pass away (13:31) but will have their fulfillment (13:23). Jesus lives on in the "written fixedness" of a text that preserves his words, his deeds, and his fate and in the promise given in the text that he will return. Past and future come together in the present of the listener's capacity to hear. "Listen to him!" (9:7). The most fundamental question is not about Jesus' own sense of personal identity but about his relationship to God. Does he, or his story, truly embody God's will? If so, then it makes sense to follow him.

2 Beautiful, Powerful Ideas !!

However, the answer is provided not in a prior theoretical understanding but in the concretely lived experience of actually following Jesus on the way. Jesus' story claims to embody the very reality of God and invites us to participate in the same way. The paradox is that there are no answers apart from the risk involved in making the journey. The surprise and indeed shock of the narrative comes in the image of God, caught well in the ingenuous claim of the vineyard owner: "They will respect my son!" (12:6)[49] What indeed was God thinking about (8:33)? And, perhaps more to the point, what do we think of such a God?

Given the above analysis of textuality, structure, and genre, it becomes evident that Mark must be read/heard not simply in a linear fashion that follows the progressive development of the story but at the same time and more profoundly in a concentric or ring fashion that reinforces the memorable dimensions of the story through the kinds of variations and developments of themes that one hears in a musical score (as in a fugue). We must enter into the dynamics of the story and imaginatively participate in its unfolding by identifying with the characters, their interaction, and their fate; that is, we must have a narrative experience of the fundamental conflict and its resolution—or challenge thereto. This means at a more profound level that we must let the story enter into our lives, make the story our story, through its memorable applicability. The concentric structure helps us to remember and understand the gospel as a whole, to read it not only from beginning to end but also from end to beginning, to hear the foreshadowings and echoes, the variations, and the dramatic climaxes that allow the whole story of Jesus to live in our hearts.

The reading that follows employs the proposed concentric structure. It is intended to focus upon and highlight essential features of the gospel's movement without giving a detailed exegesis. Obviously, given its summary nature it cannot be read without a text of Mark at hand. Moreover I would agree with Herman Waetjen on the importance of a close, literal translation (in lieu of reading it in the original Greek) both to hear the thematic variations played on the same words and to sense the social context out of which the text arose. "The words or signifiers that convey the instructions for the production of meaning are encoded in Hellenistic Greek and, more specifically, the Hellenistic Greek of the uneducated lower-class residents of the rural countryside.[50]

A. *The Wilderness* (1:2-13). The prologue begins with the voice of God announcing through the writings of "the prophet Isaiah" the messenger (v. 2, citing Mal 3:1 as referring to Elijah?) who will construct *"your* (sing.) way" (v. 2, citing Exod 23:20 as referring to Israel?). The parallel reference to "the way of the Lord" (v. 3, citing Isa 40:3 as referring to YHWH?) with its shift to the plural ("prepare" and "make straight") indicates that only the story can unravel this mysterious evocation of the prophet Isaiah. However it is already clear, as Jack Dean Kingsbury notes, that the omniscient narrator "aligns both his own evaluative point of view and that of Jesus with the evaluative point of view of God" so that God's point of view is normative for the whole story. Hence "the central question facing the interpreter is not, strictly speaking, how Mark, as narrator, conceives of Jesus or even what Jesus' conception of himself is, but . . . what God's conception of Jesus is."[51] The principal function of John the Baptist as Elijah *redivivus* (v. 6) is not to perform his own ministry of preaching and baptizing (vv. 4-5) but to announce the coming of "the stronger one" (vv. 7-8). The stronger one who is expected to come is God but paradoxically it is Jesus who arrives from the obscure and insignificant Nazareth of Galilee (v. 9, which forms an inclusion with 16:6).[52]

In contrast to the people from Judea and the Jerusalemites who allowed themselves to be baptized by John *in* the Jordan river, Jesus, as Herman Waetjen has noted so well, was baptized *into* the Jordan. He is the only one in whom is fulfilled the promise that "the stronger one" will baptize with the Holy Spirit (v. 8). "Surrendering himself to John's baptism, Jesus alone expresses the repentance that God's forerunner was demanding. In effect, he drowned; he died eschatologically; he embraced the reality of his death before his physical expiration. Nothing less than such a comprehensive experience of nothingness corresponds to the announced purpose of John's baptism. It is a genuine act of repentance."[53] What follows, according to Waetjen, is the eschatological moment of the re-creation of Adam into the new human being (who will identify himself in the story world as "the Son of Man" = "the New Human Being"). "And immediately coming up from the water he saw the heavens torn apart and the Spirit as a dove coming down into him. And a voice from the heavens: 'You are my Son, the beloved, in you I began to take pleasure.'" (vv. 10-11).[54] This sequel to the baptism of Jesus is structured by a two-step progression that corresponds to the initial claim at 1:1 that Jesus is the Christ, the Son of God: v. 10 is a visual revelation of Jesus as Christ (= anointed by the Spirit); v. 11 is an auditory revelation of Jesus as Son of God (citing in turn Ps 2:7; Gen 22:2; Isa 42:1). Therefore it is God who definitively declares who Jesus is. "The passage 1:11, then, is a divine asseveration whereby God solemnly affirms that Jesus, the Anointed One (Messiah-King) from the line of David, is his only, or unique, Son whom he has chosen for eschatological ministry."[55] The composite citation from Scripture evokes some powerful metaphors: because he is God's Son (Ps 2:7) Jesus' story is clearly identified as God's own story; as the servant in whom God "began to take pleasure" (Isa 42:1), Jesus is the one who embodies God's will; but as the "beloved" Son (Gen 22:2, repeated at 9:7 in the context of the necessity of the cross and at 12:6 in the context of the murder of the Son), Jesus is the one whose willing repentance, descending into the water (dying) and ascending from the water (rising) already in the originating event of his ministry (baptism), is the key to the mystery of the reign of God and so to God's very Self.

The prologue concludes (vv. 12-13) with an anticipatory "binding of the strong man" (3:27). The triad of being tempted by Satan for forty days, being with the wild beasts, and being served by angels signals the messianic victory: the eschatological age of salvation has begun. Thus in these few short verses of prologue Mark has already indicated God's view of who Jesus is and what he is about in his mission. The rest of the story will unfold the implications of this tightly-knit opening.

Hinge/Transition (1:14-15). Jesus preaches in Galilee "the good news of God" that as the story unfolds will more and more be seen to be identified with Jesus himself (already stated at 1:1; note the parallel between Jesus and the good news at 8:35 and 10:29, implied also at 13:10 and 14:9), but the fulfillment anticipated in his baptism, with the consequence that the reign of God has drawn near, depends on human responses. What is required for the fullness of the kingdom to come is a change of heart and mind *(metanoeite)* and a capacity to believe, despite all obstacles, in this good news of victory. If hardness of heart and lack of understanding will cast the shadow of failure over the success in Galilee, the need for faith will be the key to the way of the cross. The exhortation to have the faith of God (11:22) promises that it will enable one to move "this mountain" (the Temple) and cast it into the sea, for "all things are possible" to one who believes (9:23), for God (10:27), and above all for Jesus' *Abba* (14:36). Already in this first transitional passage the basic tension between the fulfillment of God's intention and the ambiguous and uncontrollable character of human response is programmatically announced.

B. *Galilee* (1:16–8:21). Following Schweizer and Perrin we can subdivide this section according to the threefold repetition of the call to discipleship: summons (1:16-20), naming (3:13-19a), and missioning (6:6b-13), and the threefold rejection/misunderstanding: leaders (3:6), people of Nazareth (6:1-6a), and disciples (8:14-21). A more concentric reading recognizes the pivotal centrality of Jesus' teaching in parables (4:1-34) which Ched Myers calls "the first sermon on revolutionary patience" so that what precedes (1:16–3:35) focuses on the *newness* of what Jesus brings and what follows (4:35–8:21) on the *disciples'* growing estrangement and incomprehension.

There are three coherent units in what precedes: 1:21-45; 2:1–3:6; and 3:20-35. First, 1:21-45 is a unit that portrays an extraordinary burst of energy and power. Jesus teaches *with authority (exousia)* in contrast to the scribes (1:22). His power to command unclean spirits in the synagogue (1:27) is a challenge to that place as demon-possessed. The scribes will counterattack at 3:22-30. His power is so great that people are coming to him from everywhere (1:45; cf. vv. 28, 32-33, 37).

Second, 2:1–3:6 is a concentric structure that centers on the character of this *newness* as a radical break with the old order. (A) 2:1-12. In a house he defends himself against the charge of blasphemy by the scribes who were "rationalizing in their hearts" (*dialogizomenoi*, repeated three times). Jesus poses a central question: "Why do you rationalize these things in your hearts?" (v. 8). (B) 2:13-17. In a house he defends his disciples against the charge made by "the scribes of the Pharisees" of associating with sinners. Jesus makes a key pronouncement: "I did not come to call the just [the self-righteous?] but sinners." (C) 2:18-22. Against the charge of not observing the old order (fasting as do John's disciples and the Pharisees) Jesus counters that there can be no fasting while the bridegroom (= Jesus) is among them. This culminates in the parallel sayings about the need for a new garment (baptism?) and new wineskins (Eucharist?). (B') 2:23-28. On the Sabbath he defends his disciples against the charge made by the Pharisees of breaking the Sabbath. This culminates in another key pronouncement: "The Sabbath was made for human beings, not human beings for the Sabbath. Therefore the Son of Man is lord even of the Sabbath." (A') 3:1-6. On the Sabbath in a synagogue he again defends himself against the (implicit) charge of blasphemy by the Pharisees who are characterized by their "hardness of heart." Jesus poses another central question: "Is it lawful on the Sabbath to do good or to do evil, to save a life or to destroy?" The unit ends with the notice that the Pharisees and the Herodians are plotting to destroy him (3:6).

Third, after a transitional summary (3:7-12) and the naming of the Twelve (3:13-19), 3:20-35 uses a framing technique to proclaim a *new family* of "insiders" constituted by anyone who does the will of God. Those "near Jesus" consider him to be out of his mind (vv. 20-21). The scribes accuse him of being possessed and of casting out demons by the prince of demons (vv. 22-30). Jesus responds to the second with his saying about binding the strong man (v. 27) and to the first with his severe condemnation of those who blaspheme against the Holy Spirit (vv. 29-30, an implicit reference to his baptism into the Spirit). Then in parallel to those near him (v. 21) Jesus' mother and brothers seek him (vv. 31-32) only to find that he declares those sitting around him in a circle to be his mother and brothers, i.e., those who do the will of God (vv. 34-35).

Correspondingly what follows the parabolic teaching (4:35–8:21) focuses on the growing estrangement and incomprehension of the *disciples*. Key to this section are the crossings of the sea in the boat and the feedings of the crowds in the desert. The first crossing, when Jesus calms the storm on the sea (4:35-41) puts into sharp relief the disciples' fear and lack of faith (v. 40). They raise the christological question for the first time: "Who then is this that both wind and sea obey him?" (v. 41). On the other side of the sea (in Gentile territory) Jesus exercises power over the "legion," i.e., the Roman occupying army, by employing the destructive power of the sea.[56] This exorcism in Gentile territory parallels the earlier one in the synagogue (1:23-28). When Jesus returns in the boat to the other side he heals two "daughters" in Israel, one of a leader of the synagogue (5:22-24, 35-43) and the other a marginated and socially outcast woman (5:25-34, intercalated within the story of Jairus' daughter). In both cases fear is overcome through faith and each is restored to full membership in the true community of Israel (symbolized by the number twelve).

After the notice of his rejection at Nazareth because of their unbelief (6:1-6a), the missioning of the Twelve (6:6b-13), and the flashback on the death of John the Baptist (6:14-16, 17-29, 30-31) intended as a reminder that the disciples as well as Jesus can expect the same fate, the first feeding in the desert (6:32-44) is striking in its challenge to the disciples: "You give them to eat" (v. 37), which they can understand in only the most material of terms. That challenge is compounded when Jesus immediately forces the disciples to get into the boat and go before him *(proagein)* to Bethsaida (6:45), which they fail to do because of their hardness of heart about the loaves (6:52).[57] These two notices frame the second crossing when Jesus walks on the sea as if it were dry land (6:47-51). Once again the exhortation is crucial for true discipleship: "Have courage in your hearts. I am! Do not be afraid" (v. 50).

After another transitional summary (6:53-56) Jesus engages the failure to understand (because their heart is far from God) first of the Pharisees and scribes from Jerusalem (7:1-13), then of the crowds (7:14-15; the exhortation for all to hear and understand is the center of this section), and finally of the disciples (7:17-23) who once again are chided for their lack of understanding (v. 18). Then he abruptly departs for Gentile territory where as a parallel to the healing of two "daughters" in Israel (5:22-43) he now heals two Gentiles, one a Greek woman who will not be denied her fair share in the kingdom (7:24-30) and the other a deaf-mute whose cure occasions a zealous proclamation about those who can now hear and speak (7:31-37). This Gentile ministry comes to its focal conclusion with the second feeding in the desert (8:1-10), which the disciples can understand no better than the Pharisees who demand a sign from heaven (8:11-13).

All the themes or motifs of this section come together in a third and final confrontation of Jesus with the disciples (8:14-21). They are in the boat crossing the sea and the disciples are arguing *(dielogizonto;* cf. the scribes at 2:8) about their lack of bread (cf. 6:52), ignoring Jesus' warning about the leaven of the Pharisees and of Herod (echoing 3:6; 6:14-29; 7:1-13). Jesus' questions put into sharp focus all that has preceded. "Why do you argue *(dialogizesthe)* over the fact that you have no bread? Do you not perceive yet nor understand? Do you have your heart hardened?" (v. 17). The biggest obstacle, however, remains the significance of the loaves (vv. 19-21). What is it the disciples refuse to see, and struggle against, in their crossings of the sea if not Jesus' call for a new social order that is equally inclusive of Jew and Gentile, male and female, rich and poor, insider and outsider? This is the impact of the parallel exorcisms in Jewish and Gentile settings, the parallel healings of two "daughters" in Israel and two Gentiles outside Israel, and above all the parallel breakings of bread in the desert for Jew (twelve baskets) and Gentile (seven baskets). In all of these actions Jesus is breaking the social boundaries of hostility between Jew and Gentile and of "purity maps" within Israel. "People who continually have even passing contact with sinners, lepers, blind, lame, menstruants, corpses and the like are perceived as spurning the *map of persons.* People who show no respect for holy places such as the temple (see Mark 11:15-17) are crossing dangerous lines on the *map of places.* People who 'do what is not lawful on the Sabbath' disregard the *map of times,* and would be judged in some way as rejecting the system. Not only are they themselves polluted, they become a source of pollution to others."[58] Such a challenge to the cultural, economic, and political codes of the times carries with it the threat of rejection and death, and herein lies "the mystery of the kingdom of God" (4:11) for those who have eyes to see and ears to hear (8:18).

Jesus' teaching in parables (4:1-34) is an exhortation to hear (vv. 3, 9, 12, 15, 16, 18, 20, 23, 24, 33) intercalated between Jesus' initial success in Galilee (1:16–3:35) and the growing estrangement and incomprehension of the disciples (4:35–8:21). As such it functions as a commentary on both. The concentric structure given here is dependent on John Donahue's analysis.[59]

(A) vv. 1-2. Introduction. Jesus teaches a large crowd many things in parables while sitting in the boat on the sea.

(B) vv. 3-9. The parable of the sower is addressed to this large crowd. There is strong emphasis on the failure of the seed (vv. 3-7) reversed only at the end (v. 8). "Let the one who has ears to hear, hear!" (v. 9).

(C) vv. 10-12. Private instruction is given to "those around him" (cf. 3:34) with the Twelve. To them has been given the mystery of the reign of God but for those outside everything happens in parables (riddles). The reason is the divine will cited from Isa 6:9-10. This raises in acute form the question of who really are the "insiders" and who the "outsiders."[60]

(D) vv. 13-20. Allegory. This is the center of the concentric structure and thus indicates what is of central importance, namely that the new "insiders" have no guarantee (as might seem to be implied by vv. 10-12) but rather have received a challenge to true discipleship = "whoever hears the word and accepts it and bears fruit" (v. 20). To understand this is to understand all the parables/riddles (v. 13).

(C') vv. 21-25. Enigmatic sayings. As parallel to "the mystery of the kingdom of God," for "insiders" or true disciples three things are necessary: to let the light shine (= Jesus: vv. 21-22), to hear what is being communicated by the light (= the necessity of the cross: v. 23), and to be aware of *what* they hear and with what degree of generosity (v. 24) lest they suffer the fate of the excluded (the warning of v. 25 parallels v. 12).

(B') vv. 26-32. The parables of the seeds are addressed once again to the crowd in public (vv. 34-35). As with the failure of the seeds (vv. 3-8), so here hiddeness (vv. 26-29) and insignificance (vv. 30-32) will not have the final word, as Donahue has noted so well.

(A') vv. 33-34. Conclusion. There is an emphatic contrast between speaking publicly in parables/riddles according to the capacity of the listeners (the large crowd) and explaining everything privately to the disciples. But the paradox as the story continues is that the disciples pose the greatest obstacle by their refusal to hear the message of the cross. The parables on failure, hiddeness, and insignificance are metaphors for the central teaching of Jesus on the necessity of the cross. True disciples are those who hear this word, accept it, and bear fruit by doing the will of God (3:35; cf. 8:31; 14:36). Thus the understanding of the true significance of the cross, while it appears to be predetermined by God's will (4:10-12), is in reality a matter of human intransigence. Throughout his ministry in Galilee, Jesus manifests incontestable power over demons, infirmities, and nature. It is the human heart that he cannot and will not control. He can only invite a response. The message, for those who have eyes to see and ears to hear, is that the true enemy, the leaven of the Pharisees and of Herod, is within, i.e., in what comes from the heart.

Hinge/Transition (8:22-26). Over against the blindness and deafness of the disciples (8:18) stand four healings: of the "deaf and dumb" at 7:31-37 (gradual) and 9:14-29 (with a simple word but dependent on faith), and of the "blind" at 8:22-26 (gradual) and 10:46-52 (faith). These healings function as "a counter-discourse of hope."[61] The present transitional story functions to point ahead toward the possibility and hope of a gradual opening of the eyes of the disciples to true understanding and to remind us of the original intent to go to Bethsaida (6:45) and what has happened since: the disciples' hardening of heart (6:52; 8:14-21) and the gradual healing of deaf and dumb in Gentile territory. Also the command not to enter the village evokes the previous ambiguities surrounding Jesus' fame (1:45; 3:7-10, 20; 5:17-20, 43; 6:1-6a, 33, 54-56; 7:24, 36-37) as well as the need to stand apart from the crowd in order to have faith (2:3-5; 4:35-41; 5:21-43; 6:1-6a; 6:45-52; 7:24-30; 9:14-29; 10:46-52).[62]

C. *The Way* (8:27–10:45). Throughout the ministry in Galilee, as Jack Dean Kingsbury notes, there is an intertwining of demonic knowledge and human ignorance with regard to Jesus' identity. For each demonic cry there is a corresponding human question: 1:24/1:27 (crowd); 1:34/2:7 (scribes); 3:11/4:41 (disciples); 5:7/6:3 (people of Nazareth). Only at 6:14-16 are some tentative answers proposed. Ironically, during the disciples' forced boat journey toward Bethsaida (6:45-52), a scene powerfully evocative of Jesus' resurrection power, Jesus identifies himself with the very name and power of God (*egō eimi*) but the disciples—even though the text emphatically states that they saw him—could not understand because of their fear and hardness of heart. Now at the beginning of the journey from Caesarea Philippi to Jerusalem Jesus himself proposes the question in a two-step progression: "Who do people say that I am?" recalls the previous answers at 6:14-16 and leads to the decisive question around which the whole gospel turns: "But you—who do you say that I am?" Peter's answer is "correct" (1:1, 10) yet receives the same stern rebuke *(epetimēsen)* given to the demons and the storm (1:25; 3:12; 4:39). The Pharisees had just sought from him "a sign from heaven" to test or tempt him *(peirazontes auton* at 8:11; cf. 1:13) and as the text unfolds it is clear that Peter too is on the side of Satan and must be equally "rebuked" (8:32b-33). Only a true disciple, one who thinks as God does, will finally know who Jesus is. Hence Jesus' task is to teach quite openly and plainly the way of the cross as the way of God for Jesus and for anyone who would be his follower.

As noted above, this central teaching section is articulated by three passion predictions accompanied by the disciples' confused and alienated reactions and followed by an instruction on discipleship. It is worth observing at the outset that each kind of seed in the allegory of the seeds (4:13-20) finds an exemplification here: 4:15 (Satan) at 8:33; 4:16-17 (scandal) at 9:42-50; 4:18-19 (riches) at 10:22-25; 4:20 (hundredfold) at 10:29-30.[63] The passion predictions evoke an apocalyptic atmosphere of divine necessity *(dei)*, confrontation with the political and religious powers (elders, chief priests, and scribes, plus the Gentiles at 10:33), and above all the destiny of the Son of Man who, according to Daniel 7, is vindicated by God against the four "beasts" that represent the imperial powers. Jack Dean Kingsbury correctly observes that "Christ" and "Son of God" are confessional titles that have to do with Jesus' identity, already indicated at 1:1, 10-11 and to be affirmed by Jesus himself at 14:61-62, while "Son of Man" is always used in the context of public conflict to express Jesus' mission and destiny.[64] Thus the Son of Man "on earth" has the power to forgive sins and to interpret the Law (2:10, 28); the Son of Man coming "in clouds" has power to judge and to gather the elect (8:38; 13:26-27; 14:62), but the primary emphasis is on the Son of Man who is "handed over," "rejected," tortured, and "killed" (8:31; 9:12, 31; 10:33-34; 14:21, 41), who in the very giving of his life redeems us all (10:45). The question of Jesus' *identity* as Christ and Son of God is inseparable from his actual *destiny* as Son of Man so that it is only in the telling of the story that these titles can be correctly interpreted.

The disciples' reactions of outright rejection (8:32b), lack of understanding (9:32), shock, and fear (10:32) necessitate the teaching on true discipleship. The first instruction, addressed to the crowd along with the disciples (8:34), centers on the paradox of losing one's life to save it. The central scene of recognition (9:7) is surrounded by the cross in a ring structure.

(A) 8:34-38. Cross: to lose your life "for me and for the good news" (v. 35) parallels being ashamed "of me and my words" (v. 38).

(B) 9:1. Expectation: the reign of God will come soon with glory (8:38) and power (9:1) envisioned together at 13:26.

(C) 9:2-8. God's view of Jesus as "the beloved Son" culminates in the central exhortation of the whole gospel: "Listen to him!" What they must hear is the message of the cross.

(B') 9:9-10. Expectation: the resurrection will be the time to proclaim freely what they had seen (the glory and power of Jesus).

(A') 9:11-13. Cross: as "it is written" of Elijah (= John the Baptist), so of the Son of Man (referring to the suffering servant of Isaiah 53). But none of this is possible unless one has faith (9:23). Precisely what the disciples lack is faith (9:19) and prayer (9:29). The healing of the boy with the dumb and deaf spirit (9:14-29) brings into startling focus both the disciples' failure to have faith (and to pray) and Jesus' agony as he is stretched between heaven and earth. Elizabeth Struthers Malbon has pointed out the verbal echoes between this scene and the agony in the garden (14:32-42). Both the boy and Jesus fall upon the earth (9:20; 14:35) "in the felt presence of a greater power"; both stories evoke the power of faith and prayer in the face of overwhelming circumstances; both involve a sense of death (9:26; 14:34). Yet the hope of resurrection surrounds both narratives.[65]

If the first instruction is addressed to the crowd with the disciples, the second is principally concerned with the disciples and the Twelve (9:31, 35). Taken together 9:30–10:31 could be called "a manual of instruction" for the community whose interpretative key is the paradox of eschatological reversal: the first will be last and the last first (10:31). Jesus has already established his "true family": "Whoever does the will of God is my brother and sister and mother" (3:35). As the story unfolds this proves to be anyone in solidarity with Jesus in his suffering for the sake of others. Now he promises a "new family" to those who have left everything to follow him (10:28 echoes 1:16-20). Those who have left all "for me and for the good news" (10:29 echoes 8:35) will receive "a hundredfold now in this time" (10:30 echoes 4:20) with the following distinguishing features.[66] First, this promise is based not on natural kinship or class status, as in the case of the man with large landholdings, but solely on the power of God (10:27). Second, this new family/community is radically opposed to oppressive dominance and control as evidenced not only by the omission of any mention of a father but also by the emphasis on being a "servant" (9:35 foreshadows 10:43) and on renouncing dominating power. This latter is seen in Jesus' identification of himself with a child (9:36-37), in his acceptance of those who "do not follow us" (9:38-41), and in his concern for the "little ones" and the protection of the whole body, the community (9:42-50). It is carried through in his condemnation of the practice of divorce (10:2-12), which was oppressive of women, and of the exclusion of children (the "least of the least"[67]) by the overbearing disciples (10:13-16). Particularly challenging to the disciples is Jesus' call to renounce economic status and privilege and to redistribute one's wealth for the sake of the poor (10:17-27). Third, the promise of the hundredfold in this age will include persecutions (10:28-30), a comment that ties together the cross of Jesus and the social setting of Mark's community. "A Christian community which evokes a saying of Jesus to claim that doing the will of God is more important than loyalty to the natural family and which actually counsels leaving the family to form a new family without the governing power of the father and which rejects those structures of interrelationships which govern normal family life would naturally evoke suspicion and persecution."[68]

Finally, the third instruction centers on the Twelve alone (10:32d, 41-42a) to bring out the true nature of leadership in the community. To become truly great one must be "your servant" (10:43, affirmed of Jesus at 10:45a) and "slave of all" (10:44, affirmed of Jesus at 10:45b). True leadership in the community is not exercised by lording it over others or by the use of brute power (10:42); still less is it recognized by status positions of glory (10:37). True leadership is only found in one who serves and who follows Jesus' way of the cross, that is, in a practice of discipleship that is willing to give one's whole life (12:44). Clearly, such leadership is found in women as well as men.[69] But the most startling aspect of this third and culminating section on discipleship is Jesus' association of his death with baptism (echoing 1:9-11) and the cup (foreshadowing 14:23) which he promises that the disciples will share (10:39). The image that brings everything into focus is the Son of Man identified with the suffering servant (Isaiah 53) who gives "his life as a ransom in place of the many" (10:45) and who gives his blood "poured out for the sake of the many" (14:24). Clearly this is key to Mark's understanding of Jesus. This is something that only Jesus can do, not the disciples, because he is the only or unique Son, constituted the new human being (Son of Man) at his baptism, the meaning of which will be recognized on the cross. He must "go before" and only so will the disciples be empowered to follow. He is the only one who, as the metaphor of ransom suggests, can "buy back" the whole of the human race by giving his very life's blood, that is, by making himself the victim of our violence in place of us and for our sake.[70]

Hinge/Transition (10:46-52). Once again, in contrast to the blindness of the disciples, Mark presents a poor, marginated blind beggar as a model of faith.[71] This transitional story points forward to Jesus' entry into Jerusalem as the Son of David (vv. 46-48, 52d) and reminds us of the beginning of this journey when another blind man was healed gradually (8:22-26). It is only faith that can enable the disciples to see and to follow Jesus "on the way" (10:52).

B'. *Jerusalem* (11:1–15:39). As in the parallel section (1:16–8:21), the dynamics of this part of the gospel can be seen to revolve around what Myers calls "the second sermon on revolutionary patience" at 13:1-37. What precedes, 11:1–12:44, communicates Jesus' image of God in confrontation with the whole phalanx of authorities in Jerusalem: "the chief priests, the scribes, and the elders" as well as the Pharisees, Herodians, and Sadducees. It divides into two parts: Jesus' prophetic challenge to the Temple (11:1-33) and his teaching on the true nature of God's action (12:1-40) over against the authorities' failure to know either the Scriptures or the power of God (12:24). The entry into Jerusalem is described by Myers as "political street theater" since, with its anticlimactic ending (11:11), it functions as an ironic preparation for the true message: not the triumphal seizure of the Temple to reform it but the shocking declaration that it has no continuing validity! Thus Mark frames the casting out of the oppressive profiteers (11:15-19) with the image of the fig tree withered "to its roots" (11:12-14, 20-21). The Temple and the power structure it represents are replaced with the exhortation: "Have the faith of God!" Such faith empowers one with God's point of view. It is this power, God's faith, that will cast "this mountain" (= that on which the Temple stands) into the sea (like the "legion" at 5:13). Who gave Jesus such authority or power *(exousia)* that he could do these things? The answer resides in the mystery of Jesus' baptism (11:27-33 echoes 1:9-11). This leads to a confrontation with the authorities over the activity of God in the present crisis.

Mark 12:1-40 has a concentric structure that centers on the theme of resurrection.[72]

> A. Vv. 1-9 relate the parable of the "patient vineyard owner" who at the climactic moment sends his "beloved Son" (12:6 echoes 1:11 and 9:7) in the ingenuous belief that the tenants will respect him. They kill him and cast him out of the vineyard, which results in their destruction and the giving of the vineyard to others.
>
> B. Vv. 10-12 cite Ps 118:22-23, a widely used apologetic text of early Christianity. God has laid the cornerstone for a new Temple, which as the story of the passion unfolds will be Jesus' body in place of the destroyed Temple (15:29-32, 37-38).
>
> C. Vv. 13-17 contain an antithetical saying that forever separates the way of Caesar and the way of God. There is irony in the double meaning of *apodote,* i.e., "pay allegiance" or "pay back" to get rid of Caesar's claims. Thus one pays according to the allegiance one has established in one's life. Those who carry Caesar's coin (the Pharisees and the Herodians, cf. 8:15) owe allegiance to Caesar. But Caesar, like the Temple, has no continuing validity.
>
> D. Vv. 18-27 propose the central question concerning the resurrection. It calls for an ascending response framed by the charge that the Sadducees are "deceived" *(planasthe* at vv. 24 and 27). First, they know neither the Scriptures nor the power of God (v. 24). Second, they should not view this eschatological reality in materialistic terms (v. 25) for it depends on the power of God (as evidenced by the verbs *anastōsin* and *egeirontai*). Third, they should not forget their scriptural heritage (v. 26) that God is a God of the living, not the dead. "At the center of his theological treatise on God, the Marcan Jesus reaffirms the core of Jewish monotheism, that God is a God of

the living and a living God. . . . Resurrection is not return from the grave, but enduring life hidden in the power of God. God is not met primarily in figures who return from the dead, but in the one who has power over death."[73] Herein lies the full significance of having "the faith of God." All things are possible if we have God's faith (9:23; 10:27; 14:36).

C'. Vv. 28-34 present a synthetic saying in contrast to the antithetical saying at vv. 13-17, combining in inseparable unity two commands, love of God and love of neighbor, that had never been joined together before. Jesus associates them with Israel's central confession of faith (Deut 6:4, cited at v. 29). The scribal repetition, however, (vv. 32-33) emphasizes that these two commandments transcend the "whole burnt offerings and sacrifices" of the Temple.

B'. Vv. 35-37 cite Ps 110:1 which, along with Psalm 118, is another widely used apologetic text. Son of David, while "correct" (10:47-48; 11:9-10) as an interpretation of Christ, is inadequate and will be transcended as the story unfolds (14:62; 15:39).[74]

A'. Vv. 38-40 warn against the scribes and condemn their pride and their oppression of the poor. The "greater condemnation" (v. 40) parallels the destruction of the tenants (v. 9). This section comes to a climax with another "model of faith" (12:41-44 that with 14:3-9 frames the sermon of 13:1-37), this time a poor widow who, though victim of oppression at the hands of the wealthy scribes and others (v. 40), still trusts the God of Israel, the one God who is a "God of the living," and so out of her poverty "threw in everything she had, her whole life" (v. 44).

What follows the second sermon, 14:1–15:39, would seem to negate such trust. It too can be divided into two parts: Jesus' prophetic challenge to the disciples (14:1-42) and his utter abandonment by all, including God, so that he is crushed by the power of evil (14:43–15:39). Framed by notices of conspiracy (14:1-2, 10-11), this section opens with yet another woman of faith, probably wealthy given the great value of the ointment, who while repudiated by some (male disciples?) is defended by Jesus for having performed a prophetic action (v. 8) that forevermore will be inseparable from a true understanding and proclamation of the gospel (v. 9). By her courageous act she has named a reality that the disciples refuse to face. There is great irony in the location (the house of Simon the leper as opposed to the Temple) and in the fact that this woman is the only one who understands what is going on (except perhaps Judas).

With the preparation of the Passover meal and its celebration we have another example of "political" or "messianic" theater in Myers' terms. The earlier polemical imagery surrounding eating (2:15-17, 18-20, 23-28; 7:1-23) and especially bread (6:35-44, 52; 7:27-28; 8:1-9, 14-21) comes into focus with the third breaking and sharing of bread (14:22-25). "In Mk 6–8 . . . leaven pervades mistaken perceptions held by the Pharisees, Herod, and the disciples. In contrast, the Last Supper takes place on the first day of 'unleavened bread'. Evidently for Mk leaven signifies power which inflicts death upon others but refuses to internalize the meaning of suffering and death."[75] Jesus' body anointed beforehand to be buried (14:8) and his blood to be poured out as the covenantal redemption (14:23-24) recalls the proclamation of something radically new (2:21-22) that will necessitate fasting (14:25 echoes 2:18-20).

Sadly, this final attempt to break through the disciples' hardness of heart is surrounded by betrayal and denial. Mark 14:18-21 again evokes both divine necessity ("the Son of Man goes as it is written of him") and human capacity for evil ("woe to that one . . ."), while vv. 26-31 again invoke Scripture face to face with human rejection, although this time injecting a note of hope ("but after I am raised up, I will go before you into Galilee") foreshadowing 16:7. All of this comes to a poignant climax in the disciples' final failure to heed Jesus' warning to stay awake in Gethsemane (14:32-42). The "hour" has come and they are asleep (echoing 13:32, 35-36).[76] But while the disciples close themselves off, Jesus experiences extreme terror and anguish before death (vv. 33-34); still, what he dreads is not so much suffering and death as being abandoned by God.[77] Even so, he affirms the will of his *Abba* for whom "all things are possible" (vv. 35-36, echoing 9:23 and 10:27). Jesus suffers his last and most severe temptation and affirms the will of God who alone has power over death before all else. The "hour" has come and he speaks his last word to the disciples while they sleep (v. 41).

So begins the drama of Jesus' abandonment. Judas betrays him with a kiss (14:43-46) and at his arrest (once again in fulfillment of the Scriptures) all abandon him and flee for their lives (vv. 47-50), including the young man who followed but finally fled naked with shame (vv. 51-52 foreshadow *sindōn* at 15:46 and *neaniskos* at 16:5). With this sudden intrusion of the young man the implied reader/listener is reminded that he or she is also part of the scene. Peter's denial (vv. 54, 66-72) frames Jesus' trial before the Sanhedrin (vv. 55-65). Cursing and swearing, he denies that he ever knew Jesus at the very moment that Jesus is affirming his true identity. The parallelism of the two trials shows that in Mark's story world Jesus was equally condemned by Jews and Romans alike. Confronted with false testimony at the Sanhedrin trial, Jesus remains silent, but when the high priest ironically affirms in question form what God's view (1:11; 9:7; 12:6) and the narrator's view (1:1) has consistently been: "You are the Christ, the Son of the Blessed One?!" Jesus responds with a resounding "I am!" Jesus' identity can now be revealed because it is declared in the context of the cross. It is immediately followed by an affirmation of his destiny as Son of Man, not to be judged but to judge.[78] There is a double irony here. On the one hand hardness of heart prevents the high priest from recognizing the truth. "Mark is concerned to show in his story that Jesus is sentenced to death on no lesser grounds than that the high priest and the Sanhedrin repudiate as blasphemous the very claim Jesus affirms to be true."[79]

On the other hand the irony is that the high priest's condemnation has no validity for it is Jesus as Son of Man vindicated by God who is the true and universal judge. Finally, if the Jews condemn him for blasphemy, the Romans in the parallel trial condemn him for being "the King of the Jews," a designation that Jesus accepts with reserve: "(So) you say." Pilate would understand the title to mean a political rebel, yet the irony continues in Pilate's implicit admission that Jesus was more dangerous to Rome than Barabbas, one of the insurrectionists "who had committed murder during the uprising" (15:7).

Jesus is condemned by the Jews as a blasphemer and mocked for being a false prophet (14:65). He is likewise condemned by the Romans as a rebel and mocked for being the "King of the Jews" (15:16-20a). But as he dies crucified he is mocked for not being able to save himself (15:27-32 echoes 8:35). He is taunted to come down from the cross with words that reverberate throughout the gospel, "that we may see and believe" (v. 32), precisely what he cannot do if they are to have true faith, the kind of faith that accepts God's point of view. The "stronger one" is crushed by the power of darkness. God is the stronger one expected by John the Baptist who will baptize with the Holy Spirit (1:7-8). This God came in the new human being, Jesus, and in the unfolding of his story. It is this same Jesus who now cries out in agony to the God who abandoned him (15:33-34). There is no Elijah coming to take him down but only a final heartsplitting cry that "tears apart" the curtain of the Temple (15:38 echoes 1:10) and evokes with supreme irony the "heavenly voice" (1:11; 9:7) on the lips of one who is serving Satan's oppressive and destructive power. The centurion offers the same kind of recognition as the demons who always knew who Jesus was (1:24, 34; 3:11-12; 5:6-7) but it is the supreme and essential recognition for it comes from one who *saw* face to face the way in which Jesus "breathed his last." This ironic recognition seals the fate of both Jewish Temple and Roman empire. The confession, "Truly this man was the Son of God!" (15:39), marks the coincidence of Jesus' identity and destiny in this climactic moment. Mark has told the story of the fully human life and ministry of Jesus who was the Son of God throughout his public ministry beginning from his baptism but whose identity could only be fully revealed at the final *"kairotic"* moment, the "hour" of his death on the cross. Normally our attention focuses on "Son of God" as the full revelation of Jesus' identity, but the truly extraordinary thing is that the centurion identifies "this man" *(houtos ho anthrōpos)* as the Son of God, this man who throughout has consistently identified himself as the new human being, the Son of Man. It is in this man's whole life culminating in his death by crucifixion that one experiences the true power of God.

If the destruction of the Temple and its replacement with Jesus' body on the cross surrounds our hope with parabolic openness, it must be remembered that Mark has already provided another ending of mythic meaning in Jesus' "second sermon on revolutionary patience" (13:1-37). What should the listener/reader remember? The story of Jesus will continue in the story of his disciples. What Jesus says to Peter, James, John, and Andrew (13:3) he says to all: "Watch!" (13:37). Following the introductory verses in which Jesus predicts the destruction of the Temple (vv. 1-2) and the disciples pose the dual question (vv. 3-4) as to when "these things" (cf. v. 29) will be and what will be the sign when "all these things" (cf. v. 30) are about to be fulfilled, there is a concentric structure that centers on the coming of the Son of Man.

A. Vv. 5-13 warn against being deceived (*blepete* at vv. 5, 9, 23, 33) whether by messianic pretenders (vv. 5-6 and 21-22 frame A–B, thus emphasizing the importance of this) or by seemingly cataclysmic events (vv. 7-8) or, most importantly, by the disciples' own experience of persecution, betrayal, and hatred (vv. 9-13). At the center of this exhortation to persevere "until the end" (v. 13) stands the divine imperative *(dei)* to proclaim the gospel to all the nations, the gospel that in their own experience as in that of Jesus (14:9) is inseparable from the cross.

B. Vv. 14-23 describe in apocalyptic terms (v. 14 = Dan 9:27; 11:31; 12:11; v. 19 = Dan 12:1) the imminent destruction of the Temple. What the reader should understand is that the Roman army is about to occupy and destroy the Temple. This is not a time to join forces with the rebels and defend it, but to flee in the face of God's judgment against the Temple.[80] The disciples should pay attention only to Jesus' word that has foretold all this (v. 23).

C. Vv. 24-27 proclaim that the powers of death and destruction will finally be overcome by the coming of the Son of Man (Dan 7:13-14), the new human being whose enthronement on the cross binds together Jesus' earthly ministry, death and resurrection, and parousia. The image is of one who "will gather the chosen ones" (v. 27), i.e., those who have indeed persevered to the end (vv. 13, 20, 22c-23). "History at last will have arrived at its divinely appointed goal. Human destiny will be fulfilled, and those who have recovered the divine image and likeness in which they were created will participate fully in God's power and glory."[81]

B'. Vv. 28-32 echo 11:12-14, 20-23 with the lesson of the fig tree, once again corresponding to the Temple's imminent destruction (vv. 14-23): "he is near, at the very gates!" The original question of v. 4 is echoed in "these things" (v. 29) and "all these things" (v. 30). Whoever hears or reads this gospel now belongs to "this generation." The one and only bedrock reality on which the disciples can rely is Jesus' words, which will endure to the end (v. 31) but have their completion only in the Father (v. 32). The final word is trust in the Father. The absolute use of "the Son" in the immediate context points back to the Son of Man (v. 26) in his eschatological function, but it also points forward to Jesus' relation to God as *Abba* during his agony (14:35-36). "In each place the image of Jesus as son is one of faithful trust in the Father, even in the face of mystery, the mystery of the end-time [13:32] and of the passion [14:35-36]."[82]

A'. Vv. 33-37 again issue a warning to take heed *(blepete)*, to keep awake *(agrupneite)*, and to watch *(grēgoreite)*. The disciples will fail to watch in Gethsemane but they are still called to do so until "the lord of the house comes" (v. 35).

Thus in this concentric structure the image of the final and definitive victory of the Son of Man is encircled by two warnings to disciples and two evocations of the Temple's destruction. The whole of creation (sun and moon) and the structures of oppression (stars and powers in heaven) will be transcended and transformed in the new community of the "chosen ones."

Hinge/Transition (15:40-41). The climactic convergence of Jesus' identity and destiny (15:39) yields to a dramatic transition that looks forward to the conclusion of the story through the experience of three women whose names are given while it remembers their discipleship *(ēkolouthoun)* and ministry *(diakonoun)* to Jesus in Galilee and their companionship with him on the way to Jerusalem.

A'. *The Tomb* (15:42–16:8). The irony continues. As the centurion, representative of oppressive Roman power, recognizes who Jesus truly was, so Joseph of Arimathea, "a respected member of the council" that condemned Jesus to death but one "who was even himself looking for the kingdom of God," does with Roman permission what Jesus' disciples could not do (cf. 6:29). He wraps Jesus' body in a linen cloth *(sindona* at 15:46 echoes 14:51-52) and places it in a rock tomb. It is the women who will seek to give him a proper burial by anointing him (15:47-16:2) even though this had already been done (14:3-9). And now comes the final parabolic thrust. A "young man sitting on the right" (in Jesus' glory, echoing 10:37?) and with a "white robe" (symbol of baptism and/or martyrdom echoing 10:38?) about his body *(peribeblēmenon* again echoes 14:51) announces the good news of victory. Jesus the Nazarene, the crucified, has been raised; he is not here (16:6)! The tomb has yielded life. The God of Jesus is truly a God of the living, not the dead (12:27). The women are to go and announce this good news to the disciples and especially to Peter. Jesus' word has been fulfilled (16:7 echoes 14:28); a new possibility of seeing in Galilee has been opened up by Jesus' death and resurrection. He is still going before on the way. Yet the narrative ends in parabolic tension as Mark skillfully calls upon every listener/reader to continue the story in his or her own life. The women, shocked (v. 5) and afraid (v. 8) like the disciples earlier (10:32), confronted with a mystery at once terrifying *(tromos)* and fascinating *(ek-stasis)*, say nothing to anyone. . . . The reader/listener must finally confront his or her own fear. Who now will herald the gospel? the young man (16:6)? Peter (16:7)? the women (16:8)? or whoever endures to the end (13:13)?

4. The Beloved Son

Mark invites us to return to Galilee where Jesus is still going before us, to complete the circle and read the whole gospel from the beginning in the light of the end, to remember what we have heard and seen and to affirm what is seriously imaginable for our own lives as readers/listeners. What indeed do we remember that allows the story to enter into our lives? What gives this story a future? Having journeyed with Jesus on the way, participating in the promise of Galilee and the threat of Jerusalem, are we ready to confront the God who has been revealed to us?

Mark's move from oral to written gospel in narrative form has produced a plot in which the fundamental conflict, centered on the way or road from Galilee to Jerusalem, is between the promise of life and the threat of death. It is a conflict between the power of God and the power of Satan. The atmosphere or settings evoke the boundaries of death: wilderness and tomb, the Sea of Galilee and the Temple of Jerusalem. These boundaries are broken through "a reordering of power" that includes stilling storms at sea, feeding multitudes in the wilderness, trampling the waves of the sea as if it were a roadway, moving the Temple mount and emptying the tomb.

The story revolves around three primary characters: Jesus, the disciples, and God. The key image of Jesus that integrates all the factors in Mark's narrative quest is God's view of him as the "beloved Son" who must die on the cross in order to give life to others. Unlike Abraham's sacrifice of his beloved son Isaac, this one can no longer offer a sacrificial substitute. Jesus is the beloved Son because he came to defeat the powers of death on their own ground. Jesus is credible as our redeemer not because he came down from the cross and destroyed his enemies but because he experienced death as we do—not as "holy" or "sacred" but as God-forsaken. Jesus' God is a God of the living, not the dead (12:27). Hence new life comes forth from the tomb as previously it had come forth from the wilderness. It was the culture of death that created the cross. Those who refused to listen, to perceive, and to understand demanded their sacrificial victim. Jesus, in the very act of dying and in the way he died (15:39), did not eliminate the reality of death but he did change its meaning. His faithful obedience to the divine will was at the same time a humanly faithful resistance to the powers of death even unto death itself. Jesus became a victim of the vicious and unending spiral of violence. But as victim he was also conqueror, for he freely gave his life (10:45) that others might have life. Mark's point is that Jesus redeems us by being the man he was, the new human being (Son of Man) who had authority on earth, died on earth, and returns to this earth with the transforming power of resurrection life. Mark's root metaphor is expressed at the climactic moment of Jesus' death: "Truly, *this man* was the Son of God!" (15:39). One cannot tell this story without exploring its implications for us as Jesus' followers and for God as Jesus' *Abba*.

Salvation, true liberation, depends primarily on God's initiative but demands as an indispensable condition our response, our free human decision to follow Jesus on the way or not. Mark tells us that it was this man Jesus from Nazareth in Galilee who by his affirmation of the divine will in the face of death has led the way. The gospel challenges us to follow and to persevere until the end in the face of the dominant cultural obsession with death if we would truly save our lives and liberate our world. To those around him with the Twelve Jesus says: "To you is given the mystery of the kingdom of God" (4:10-11). Werner Kelber summarizes: "The Kingdom is open to 'all the nations', Jews and Gentiles, as well as to both males and females. It is not hierarchical in structure but egalitarian in nature. Its fundamental article of faith, love of God and love of neighbor, overrules all laws and regulations. Most importantly, its central authority is Jesus, who was enthroned not by the power of the resurrection but in the humiliation of the cross."[83]

Mark's Jesus proposes a new community of disciples that is inclusive, egalitarian, and grounded in the sole authority *(exousia)* of Jesus' own free gift of his life for the sake of others. Mark's Jesus challenges the purity codes, Torah interpretations, and Temple hegemony of the dominant power structure. Particularly worthy of note is the remarkable treatment of women. Although women in the end (16:5-8) face the same challenge to discipleship as men there is not one story specifically about women that does not present them as "models of faith"—the *sine qua non* of discipleship. "What is unexpected is the presence in Mark of several *chreiai* involving women. . . ."[84] Mark uses *chreiai* (pronouncement stories) about women at 5:25-34; 7:24-30; 12:41-44; 14:3-9, to talk about faith and discipleship. The gospel begins and ends with the image of women performing the communal role of *diakonia* (1:30-31; 15:41; 16:1) that Jesus insists is to be the characteristic of true discipleship (9:35; 10:42-45). There is no indication in Mark that any other ecclesial structure or authority has enduring validity. The Twelve, Peter, or any other disciple will continue as followers of Jesus only to the degree that they along with the women at the tomb are able to overcome their shock and fear (16:8 echoes 10:32) and to proclaim the gospel to the whole world (13:10; 14:9). That gospel, of course, is about Jesus the Nazarene, the crucified (16:6). This teacher from Galilee says that his true followers must lose their lives to save them (8:35) and he leads the way, giving his life as "a ransom in place of the many" (10:45).

In an ultimate sense the most important character in Mark's story world is God. Mark's Jesus proclaims the "good news of God" (1:14) which is parallel to the reign of God (1:15; 4:11) and is identified with Jesus himself. In Mark, as John Donahue points out, there is a strong emphasis on the transcendence of God and an avoidance of anthropomorphisms. Jesus' view of God, inseparable from God's view of Jesus, is expressed throughout the gospel. There is strong emphasis on the divine will, especially in reference to the passion (e.g., 3:35; 8:31 *[dei]*; 8:33 [to think the thoughts of God]; 14:36). This is frequently connected with citations from Scripture: "as it is written" (e.g., 9:12; 14:21, 27, 41, 49). God is the only one who is good (10:18), the one with whom all things are possible (10:27), the one who has prepared the final glory (10:40), the one who alone knows when the end will come (13:32). This God is not God of the dead but of the living (12:27) and should be loved with all our heart, soul, understanding, and strength (12:30). This God is the one who sent Jesus and who can be found in Jesus' embrace of a small child (9:37). This is a God jealous of what belongs to the divine (12:17) but ready to hear our prayers (11:24 echoes 9:29) and to forgive (11:25 echoes 2:7). All that is required is "the faith of God" (11:22).

Surprisingly, in contrast to the other gospels Jesus refers to God as Father only four times. At 8:38 confidence in the final victory is expressed in the image of the new human being (Son of Man) coming "in the glory of his Father." At 11:25 "your Father in heaven" stands ready to forgive as we forgive one another. These two references appear to be traditional formulations, but the last two touch the very core of Jesus' relationship to God and so bring the transcendent God to earth in the human experience of Jesus. At 13:32 Jesus affirms that "only the Father knows" that day or hour. The saying is an affirmation of trust that God will finally reconcile the seemingly irreconcilable opposition of good and evil. At 14:36, the only prayer of Jesus recorded in Mark, it is noteworthy that Mark alone of all the evangelists employs the Aramaic word *Abba* (found elsewhere only at Gal 4:6; Rom 8:15). In the midst of his agony, confronted with the massive and overwhelming evil of his opponents' desire for a victim, Jesus is presented as one who fears that God will abandon him but who unwaveringly places absolute and unconditional trust in God imaged as *Abba*. Whether or not Jesus ever prayed to God with this word on other occasions, its primary impact is surely here when he prays *Abba* in the face of everything that would contradict such trust.

Jesus goes on to affirm that without question he is the Son of this God (14:61-62), yet he dies with a loud cry of abandonment (15:34, 37), tortured to death by the powers of darkness. And this, finally, is the point: however much Jesus' experience of death seems to connote failure, hiddenness, and insignificance (4:3-8, 26-29, 30-32), human evil will not have the last word (13:31).

The circle of death is surrounded by the embrace of the God of the living who has power over death. But such power is effective only for those who, following the way of Jesus, do not deny death because of fear, thus allowing it to be victorious, but willingly lose their lives before death for the sake of others, thus changing its meaning. Only one who has faced death already in this life and defeated it on its own ground is truly free. Only such a one can bring true freedom to others. "Let the one who has ears to hear, hear!" (4:9).

In conclusion we return to the predominance of tone in Mark's narrative. What has his "narrative quest" accomplished? Mark responded to the crisis of the destruction of the Temple in Jerusalem by telling the story of a radically new dispensation from God. This is the God of the living *who has power over death.* That power is made manifest in God's "beloved Son" who as the new human being *transforms the meaning of death.* This has called forth a new community of disciples who, in contrast to Peter's denial of the cross, *must be willing to face death,* to do the will of God by proclaiming this good news and persevering through persecution and martyrdom until "the lord of the house comes" (13:35).

The decisive orientation is a journey toward the end of history. The disciples must continue to follow Jesus on the way but they can be confident that the definitive judgment has already taken place in the new human being (Son of Man) "sitting at the right hand of the power and coming with the clouds of heaven" (14:62).

The gospel of Mark is a story that has metaphoric impact. As such it is open to many possible interpretations. This chapter has offered one possible interpretation but the mythic and parabolic nature of its double ending, that Jesus conquers death (myth) by submitting to death (parable), guarantees that this story will continue to be, as a foundational classic, the primary way for all generations to explore and express the profound depths of the person known to history as Jesus from Nazareth of Galilee (1:9), the one who was crucified (16:6).

Notes: Chapter 2

[1] Herman C. Waetjen, *A Reordering of Power. A Socio-Political Reading of Mark's Gospel* (Minneapolis: Fortress Press, 1989) 68–71, sees Jesus' baptism *into* the Jordan as a death to all indebtedness, so that the conjunction of Jesus' "going up out of the water," the heavens "being torn apart," and the Spirit "going down like a dove *into* him" represents the eschatological moment of re-creation. "God creates a new human being before a new order of reality, the kingdom of God, is established. The New Human Being precedes the inauguration of God's rule. With this surprise reversal a fundamental myth of Jewish millennialism is shattered" (p. 71). Jesus inaugurates "a reordering of power." He is completely free of all debts and obligations and has power over the entirety of God's creation.

[2] Frank Kermode, *The Genesis of Secrecy. On the Interpretation of Narrative* (Cambridge: Harvard University Press, 1979) 33–34. On pp. 134ff. he views Mark 13 as a major intercalation between chs. 1–12 and 14–16 and suggests that the whole book may represent "a greater intervention," i.e., a major intercalation that does not yet have an ending and needs more story to make sense.

[3] Elizabeth Struthers Malbon, "The Poor Widow in Mark and Her Poor Rich Readers," *CBQ* 53/4 (October 1991) 602.

[4] A good review of new approaches can be found in Janice Capel Anderson and Stephen D. Moore, eds., *Mark and Method. New Approaches in Biblical Studies* (Minneapolis: Fortress Press, 1992). The chapters treat narrative criticism, reader-response criticism, deconstructive criticism, feminist criticism, and social criticism by various authors. The earlier approaches of form criticism, redaction criticism, and historical criticism, however, still remain valid.

[5] Walter J. Ong, S.J., *Interfaces of the Word. Studies in the Evolution of Consciousness and Culture* (Ithaca: Cornell University Press, 1977) 270. The complex relationship between written composition and oral speech is seen as one moves from the patristic period ("largely oral, for writing was not deeply interiorized") to medieval times ("highly literate but with very active residual orality") to the Renaissance and beyond ("typographic") (p. 271).

[6] Ibid., 289. He also notes: "The Romantic Movement marked the beginning of the end of rhetoric as a major academic and cultural force in the West. The Romantic Age took form with the maturing of knowledge storage and retrieval processes made possible by print" (pp. 296–297). "Rhetoric" or "discourse" is, of course, essential to understanding Mark.

[7] Luke T. Johnson, *The Writings of the New Testament. An Interpretation* (Philadelphia: Fortress Press, 1986) 131–134.

[8] Ibid., 109.

[9] Ibid., 87, 106.

[10] Ibid., 54.

[11] Bruce Malina describes a "three-zone model" of the human person within the cultural world of the NT: (1) a "zone of emotion-fused thought" expressed in references to the eyes and heart; (2) a "zone of self-expressive speech" expressed in the ears and mouth; (3) a "zone of purposeful action" expressed in the feet and hands. Bruce J. Malina, *The New Testament World. Insights from Cultural Anthropology* (Atlanta: John Knox Press, 1981) 60ff. It is instructive to see how these and related words are employed in the gospel of Mark.

[12] "Mark is full of reversals of insiders and outsiders, rich and poor, the first and the last, male and female. The key Markan distinction is between doing or violating the will of God, being on the side of God or of man (8:33)." Janice Capel Anderson, "Feminist Criticism: The Dancing Daughter" in Anderson and Moore (eds.), *Mark and Method* 132. In the same volume Elizabeth Struthers Malbon, treating characterization in her essay "Narrative Criticism: How Does the Story Mean?" comments: "Norman Petersen has argued that the two evaluative points of view among Markan characters are 'thinking the things of God' and 'thinking the things of men'" (p. 30). She refers to Norman R. Petersen, "'Point of View' in Mark's Narrative," *Semeia* 12 (1978) 97–121.

[13] For a useful overview see Frank J. Matera, *What Are They Saying About Mark?* (New York: Paulist Press, 1987); also the collection of articles with a wide range of views in William Telford, ed., *The Interpretation of Mark* (Philadelphia: Fortress Press, 1985).

[14] "The question is, How can we understand the New Testament as a collection of writings from the eastern Mediterranean world of the first-century rather than impose the meanings we bring to the text from our time and place? The social study of the New Testament addresses this question." David Rhoads, "Social Criticism: Crossing

Boundaries" in Anderson and Moore, eds., *Mark and Method* 136. This essay is a good review of the importance of social criticism. He makes extensive use of Bruce Malina's work (n. 11 above).

[15] Elizabeth Struthers Malbon makes the important point that the gospel of Mark is not an allegory that requires a key outside the text, e.g., the disciples as Mark's supposed opponents (T.J. Weeden). While moves toward first-century or twentieth-century situations outside the text are legitimate, the text as narrative must first be understood in terms of its own internal dynamic. "Without doubt the Gospel of Mark is not simply a literal narrative; it moves and means by metaphors, but it is not an allegory." E. S. Malbon, "Fallible Followers: Women and Men in the Gospel of Mark," *Semeia* 28 (1983) 47.

[16] E. S. Malbon, "Narrative Criticism: How Does the Story Mean?" (n. 12 above).

[17] Recall the remarks above (ch. 1, pp. 46–47 and n. 69) that the inward, psychological development of character, while rooted in biblical stories, is a gradual development that requires "temporal discrimination" and culminates in the modern novel. Earlier characterization, both Hellenic and Hebraic, tends to embody values in typical heroes although the characters in the Bible powerfully suggest inwardness.

[18] David Rhoads and Donald Michie, *Mark As Story. An Introduction to the Narrative of a Gospel* (Philadelphia: Fortress Press, 1982) 36; these points are explained on pp. 36–43.

[19] For a discussion of "implied reader" and "actual reader," see ibid., 137–142.

[20] Robert M. Fowler, "Reader-Response Criticism: Figuring Mark's Reader" in Anderson and Moore, eds., *Mark and Method* 55.

[21] Werner Kelber, employing many of the insights of Walter J. Ong, articulates the importance of "medium transition" and the necessity of recognizing the difference between orality and textuality. "The failure to treat orality as a medium in its own right and apart from textuality has been identified as the root cause for the imposition of linearity upon oral life and the trivialization of the genesis of Mark." Werner Kelber, *The Oral and the Written Gospel* (Philadelphia: Fortress Press, 1983) 32.

[22] Thomas E. Boomershine, "Peter's Denial as Polemic or Confession: The Implications of Media Criticism for Biblical Hermeneutics" in Lou H. Silberman, ed., *Orality, Aurality and Biblical Narrative. Semeia* 39 (1987) 47–68, proposes the phenomena of sound and memory as bridges between the oral and the written gospel. "The phenomenology of sound in the first century is one of those bridges. The gospel continued to be read aloud. The transition from the oral to the written gospel in Mark's context was not a transition from sound to silence but from sounds recomposed by a storyteller to sounds read from a manuscript. . . . A second bridge is memory. . . . Indeed, the phenomenon of the memorization of manuscripts in the ancient world as a transitional stage between orality and literacy may have major implications for the Synoptic problem" (p. 61). Hence a chasm separates the media world of historical criticism from that of the Bible. We should approach the Bible "as hearers and storytellers rather than as silent readers and critics" (p. 64). He refers to silent reading as "media eisegesis." Werner Kelber in "Biblical Hermeneutics and the Ancient Art of Communication: A Response" in the same volume (pp. 97–105) recognizes the tension between the oral and the written in Mark: "The gospel, as I perceive it, is at once more thoroughly entrenched in oral strategies and verbalization than our modern literary aesthetics will let us know and more informed by literary rationality than the thesis of

oral composition would allow" (p. 101). But he also notes that the gospels as sound-conscious discourse will not return us to a primal state of storytelling because *our* hermeneutical condition is that of *text* with its values of stability and permanence, relative semantic autonomy, and potential for decontextualization and recontextualization in succeeding generations of interpretation. We are, for better or worse, conditioned by the hyper-visualism of "print literacy." On this latter see Thomas J. Farrell, "Kelber's Breakthrough" in ibid., 27–45.

[23] Rhoads and Michie, *Mark As Story* 45–55 explain these narrative patterns.

[24] Kelber, *The Oral and the Written Gospel* 198: "If one is to face at all the death of the Messiah, the absence it spelled, the silence it entailed, and the grief it brought, distance is an absolute prerequisite." For this one needs "artistic distanciation by written words that empty events of their immediacy." Yet one wonders how Paul and other early Christians managed to proclaim the death and resurrection of Jesus so forcefully. Adela Yarbro Collins, *The Beginning of the Gospel. Probings of Mark in Context* (Minneapolis: Fortress Press, 1992) 102, considers Kelber's explanation "to be the weakest. As Green has pointed out, much early Christian preaching focused on the death of Jesus."

[25] Kelber, *The Oral and the Written Gospel* 115. He further remarks: "It is difficult to overstate the success of gospel textuality, its 'benign deceit' [Kermode] in seducing readers into taking fact-likeness for factuality. . . . The result of Markan textuality is thus not a copy of the Jesus of history but rather an artistic recreation" (p. 116). The degree to which Mark wanted to write history will be included in my conclusion regarding the genre of the gospel.

[26] I am following here the proposal of Augustine Stock, "Hinge Transitions in Mark's Gospel," *BTB* 14 (1984) 27–31, which it seems to me can incorporate the best aspects of the structure first proposed by Eduard Schweizer, "Mark's Theological Achievement" in Telford, ed., *The Interpretation of Mark* 42–63 and in his essay "The Portrayal of the Life of Faith in the Gospel of Mark," *Interpretation* 32 (1978) 387–399, and later adapted by Norman Perrin, *A Modern Pilgrimage in New Testament Christology* (Philadelphia: Fortress Press, 1974).

[27] Concentric structures have been proposed for 2:1–3:6 (by Joanna Dewey); 4:1-34 (by John Donahue); 12:1-40 (by David Rhoads and Donald Michie). In addition I will propose such a structure at 5:1-20; 8:34–9:13; 13:1-37. For another proposal of the chiastic structure of the whole gospel that places 9:7 at both the physical and theological mid-point or center, see M. Philip Scott, "Chiastic Structure: A Key to the Interpretation of Mark's Gospel," *BTB* 15 (1985) 17–26.

[28] Joanna Dewey, "Mark as Interwoven Tapestry: Forecasts and Echoes for a Listening Audience," *CBQ* 53/2 (April 1991) 224. After an analysis of some commonly posited 'breaks' in Mark, she comments: "In conclusion, none of the commonly posited breaks in Mark's outline are straightforward dividing points or simple transitions between adjacent sections. Rather, they, like other pericopes in Mark, participate in a number of sequences. There is no single linear outline for scholars to identify. . . . Mark is indeed an interwoven tapestry. Yet a fugue is, perhaps, the better metaphor, for Mark certainly contains development and dramatic climax as well" (p. 234).

[29] Elizabeth Struthers Malbon, *Narrative Space and Mythic Meaning in Mark* (San Francisco: Harper & Row, 1986), basing her work on Lévi-Strauss's understanding of

mythical thought as an awareness of oppositions that require progressive mediation, offers a very insightful analysis of Markan space as "geopolitical," "topographical," and "architectural." Her conclusion could offer some support for our proposed outline: "At the level of the opposition GALILEE vs. JUDEA, movement toward the mediation of ORDER and CHAOS is implied in the Markan exchange of connotations between the two regions. When Galilee (supposedly chaotic) connotes a new order, and Judea (supposedly orderly) represents chaos, the fundamental opposition is weakened" (p. 159). And further: "The final mediator of the spatial order of the Gospel of Mark, the WAY (or road), signals not so much another place, as a way between places, a dynamic process of movement. . . . The specific Markan references to the way (*hodos* and *proagein*) sharpen this image of the mediation of CHAOS and ORDER" (165). Also, while the shift from Galilee to Judea at 10:1 might seem to be a major 'break', it is still characterized as a journey 'on the way' (10:32, 52) until the arrival in Jerusalem at 11:1.

[30] Stock, "Hinge Transitions" 27.

[31] On the analysis of 1:1-13 see Jack Dean Kingsbury, *The Christology of Mark's Gospel* (Philadelphia: Fortress Press, 1983) 55–71, and Waetjen, *A Reordering of Power* 63–77.

[32] Kelber, *The Oral and the Written Gospel* 71. He goes on to distinguish speech *about* Jesus (heroic and polarization stories) from stories spoken *by* Jesus (parables and sayings). "The difference suggested is between language imposed upon Jesus and that grasped by himself, or between a Jesus who is brought into conformity with the oral imperative and a Jesus who has entrusted himself to it" (p. 72).

[33] Ibid., 55 (emphasis mine). Kelber sees Mark's move to textuality as a renunciation of direct loyalty to multiple oral interest groups (disciples, prophets, family) as manifest for example in the disciples' oral christology. "What epitomizes the disciples' frame of mind is a preference for ideological simplicity and heroic actuality. It is a mentality that runs afoul of the kind of theological complexities that, according to Mark, characterize the fullness of Jesus" (p. 97). A similar view is held by James Robinson: "Mark, who of necessity worked from oral traditions, nonetheless superimposed the ethos of textuality on the tradition. It is perhaps part of this effort that one can sense a decided repudiation in Mark of the bearers of oral tradition, both the disciples and the family. . . ." James M. Robinson, "The Gospels as Narrative" in Frank McConnell, ed., *The Bible and the Narrative Tradition* (New York: Oxford University Press, 1986) 110. Similarly M. Eugene Boring sees Mark as developing an alternative form to prophetic sayings of the risen Jesus, namely the new literary form of gospel, *"to mediate the continuing voice of Jesus to the church"* in his *The Continuing Voice of Jesus. Christian Prophecy and the Gospel Tradition* (Louisville: Westminster/John Knox Press, 1991) 245 (emphasis in original). E. S. Malbon's caution on not making Mark an allegory (n. 15 above) must be kept in mind in this discussion.

[34] Kelber, *The Oral and the Written Gospel* 209.

[35] M. Eugene Boring, "The Christology of Mark: Hermeneutical Issues for Systematic Theology," *Semeia* 30 (1984) 125–153, in contrast to Paul J. Achtemeier, "'He Taught Them Many Things': Reflections on Marcan Christology," *CBQ* 42 (1980) 465–481, who sees Jesus as teacher to be a corrective to a magician image of Jesus as miracle-worker.

[36] The importance of Peter not just as a foil for a "corrective" christology (see the articles by Weeden and Perrin in Telford, ed., *The Interpretation of Mark,* 64–77, 95–108) but as the poignant embodiment of both the successes and failures of discipleship should be emphasized. For a more balanced view see R. C. Tannehill, "The Disciples in Mark: The Function of a Narrative Role" in ibid., 134–157 and E. S. Malbon, "Fallible Followers" (n. 15 above).

[37] John R. Donahue, "Jesus as the Parable of God in the Gospel of Mark," *Interpretation* 32 (1978) 369–386.

[38] Adela Yarbro Collins, "Narrative, History, and Gospel" in Mary Gerhart and James G. Williams, eds., *Genre, Narrativity, and Theology. Semeia* 43 (1988) 145–153, referring to a phrase employed by David Aune.

[39] David P. Moessner, "And Once Again, What Sort of 'Essence'?: A Response to Charles Talbert" in ibid., 76–84. Talbert in the preceding article, "Once Again: Gospel Genre," 53–73, offers an excellent analysis of the genre of ancient biographies. He locates their "essence" in "what sort of person such biographies reveal." Moessner, using Luke as an example, shows in response that the concern of the gospel is not primarily with "what sort of person" but with God's mighty acts on behalf of Israel. In a similar vein Adela Yarbro Collins, in her article (n. 38 above), writes: "The primary intention of the author of Mark *was to write history. . . .* Mark focuses on Jesus and his identity, not in the interest of establishing his character or essence, but in order to write a particular kind of history, which may be called a narration of the course of the eschatological events, which are yet to be completed (thus the open-endedness of the ending)" (pp. 147–148, emphasis in original). She develops this idea more fully in chapter one: "Is Mark's Gospel a Life of Jesus? The Question of Genre" in *The Beginning of the Gospel* 1–38.

[40] Howard Clark Kee, *Community of the New Age. Studies in Mark's Gospel* (Philadelphia: Westminster, 1977) 105: "In his portrait of Jesus, Mark speaks to and from a community which is influenced both by the Jewish-Hasidic-Essene-apocalyptic tradition, with its belief in cosmic conflict about to be resolved by divine intervention and the vindication of the faithful elect, and the Cynic-Stoic style of gaining adherents by itinerant preaching, healing, and exorcisms from village to village, existing on the hospitality that the local tradition offered." A similar approach is taken by Vernon K. Robbins, *Jesus the Teacher. A Socio-Rhetorical Interpretation of Mark* (Philadelphia: Fortress Press, 1984) who proposes that Mark contains literary parallels not only in Jewish but also in Greco-Roman literature so that both should be employed for comparative analysis. He concludes that Mark's Jesus is a disciple-gathering teacher who, like Socrates, manifests an "internal decision to accept death as a benefit for others" (p. 212).

[41] Ched Myers, *Binding the Strong Man. A Political Reading of Mark's Story of Jesus* (Maryknoll: Orbis Books, 1988) 104–106.

[42] Georg Strecker, "The Theory of the Messianic Secret in Mark's Gospel" in Christopher Tuckett, ed., *The Messianic Secret* (Philadelphia: Fortress Press, 1983) 49–64, calls Mark kerygmatic in its historicizing tendency: "preaching as story" (p. 63). Similarly Martin Hengel, *Studies in the Gospel of Mark* (Philadelphia: Fortress Press, 1985) 41, refers to "the model of Old Testament historiography" as a "unity of narration and proclamation" and so says of Mark that we need not choose between preaching and historical narration. Rather, "he preaches by narrating; he writes history and so proclaims."

[43] Elizabeth Struthers Malbon, "Mark: Myth and Parable," *BTB* 16 (1986) 11.

[44] Helen R. Graham, "A Passion Prediction for Mark's Community: Mark 13:9-13," *BTB* 16 (1986) 18–22.

[45] Malbon, "Mark: Myth and Parable" 11.

[46] In her essay Malbon describes a suggestion of James G. Williams with regard to the relationship between biography and parable. However, the formulation used is my own.

[47] Madeleine Boucher, *The Mysterious Parable. A Literary Study* (Washington: CBAA, 1977) 16: "It is the rhetorical character of the biblical writings which some NT scholars have discerned and described so well in pointing out to us that the gospels are not primarily biography or history, but *kerygma,* or that the parables are 'language-events'" (emphasis in original).

[48] Ibid., 83.

[49] John R. Donahue, S.J., *The Gospel in Parable. Metaphor, Narrative, and Theology in the Synoptic Gospels* (Philadelphia: Fortress Press, 1988) 52–57, interprets the parable at 12:1-9 within the horizon of First Testament prophecy in which a long-suffering God is pursuing humanity, reaching out for a human response, and so calls it the parable of "the patient vineyard owner." In context Mark has turned the parable into a christological allegory in which Jesus, rejected by the Jewish leaders, ironically becomes the cornerstone of a new Temple.

[50] Waetjen, *A Reordering of Power* 3. He cites Etienne Trocmé, *The Formation of the Gospel According to Mark* (Philadelphia: Westminster, 1975) 68–72: "The main feature of Mark's style is its rusticity" (p. 17). Waetjen translates Mark (pp. 27–61). If one reads his translation, especially noting the changes in verb tenses, the feel in English is rustic indeed! Another good translation that stays close to the original Greek can be found in Rhoads and Michie, *Mark As Story* (pp. 7–34).

[51] Kingsbury, *The Christology of Mark's Gospel* 47–51.

[52] According to Waetjen, *A Reordering of Power* 67, John the Baptist, dressed as Elijah, would be the apocalyptic sign of *God's* imminent coming. This is why "the whole country of Judea and all the Jerusalemites" (v. 5) went out to him. By way of contrast, in "the story world of the Gospel" Jesus "is the only Jew from Galilee to present himself for baptism at the Jordan River. Perhaps the narrator is intimating that he is the outsider, for, in contrast to the other Jews, he originates from the insignificant town of Nazareth in the rural province of Galilee."

[53] Ibid., 68. The connection between baptism and death is repeated at 10:38-39.

[54] The translation is my own except for "I began to take pleasure," which follows Waetjen: "The divine sanction that is pronounced on him at the beginning of his new career, 'In you I began to take pleasure,' is based on his radical response to John's call to repentance. There is no indication that it reaches back to any earlier act or event in his life prior to his baptism. The Greek verb *eudokēsa* is in the past, or aorist, tense and is best identified as an ingressive aorist, an entry into an action in the recent past" (ibid., 73). Thus the voice from heaven is recognizing Jesus' full immersion into the baptism of John as freely given obedience.

[55] Kingsbury, *The Christology of Mark's Gospel* 66.

[56] Elizabeth Struthers Malbon, *Narrative Space and Mythic Meaning in Mark* 78-79: "In addition to the manifestations of Jesus' power over the sea by calming it or walking on it, Mark portrays Jesus as utilizing the generally destructive power of the

sea for his own purposes. Jesus grants the request of the legion of unclean spirits to enter the swine rather than be sent out of the country of the Gerasenes, but the possessed swine then rush down the bank into the sea (5:13a) and are drowned in the sea (5:13b). Elsewhere Jesus suggests, in hyperbole, that the destructive power of the sea may be used by those who have faith (11:23) and against those who hinder faith (9:42). This destructive, chaotic power of the sea is the very power Jesus confronts and overcomes in ordering the sea by stilling the storm and walking on the water. The power Jesus manifests on the sea is akin to the power he manifests by the sea, the power of teaching and healing." Mark 5:1-20 is a concentric structure that focuses upon the destruction of the swine (who symbolize the Roman legions):

> (A) vv. 1-5. Description of the man, who is a "strong man" whom no one could bind.
> (B) vv. 6-10. Encounter with Jesus with the recognition of who he is and the plea to remain in the country.
> (C) vv. 11-14. Destruction of the swine in the sea which manifests the power of Jesus over "legion" and over the whole region of the Gentiles (the herdsmen flee and announce it in the city and in the country).
> (B') vv. 15-17. Encounter with Jesus with the notice of fear and the plea for him to leave the country.
> (A') vv. 18-20. Description of the man, who is now a new man who desires to be with Jesus but is sent to his own to preach by way of anticipation the good news of what the Lord has done for him.

[57] When the disciples "go before" *(proagein),* they fail (cf. 11:9). When Jesus "goes before" (10:32; 14:28; 16:7) success is possible even though the way to success must pass through the cross.

[58] Jerome H. Neyrey, "The Idea of Purity in Mark's Gospel," *Semeia* 35 (1986) 105 (emphasis in original).

[59] Donahue, *The Gospel in Parable* 29–52.

[60] Malbon, "Mark: Myth and Parable," sees "two parabolic turns" in Mark, the first of which establishes new "insiders" (women, fishermen, tax-collectors, etc.) over against the Jewish religious leaders as "outsiders" and the second of which recognizes that the new "insiders" have no guarantees that they will remain such.

[61] Myers, *Binding the Strong Man* 238–240.

[62] Robert G. Hamerton-Kelly, *The Gospel and the Sacred. Poetics of Violence in Mark* (Minneapolis: Fortress Press, 1994) 90ff., makes this point well. He sees Mark's gospel as unveiling the violence of the sacred, its "generative mimetic scapegoating mechanism," which often takes the form of mob violence—hence the need to step out of the crowd that Jesus recognizes as faith.

[63] Myers, *Binding the Strong Man* 284.

[64] Kingsbury, *The Christology of Mark's Gospel* 91–102.

[65] Elizabeth Struthers Malbon, *Narrative Space and Mythic Meaning in Mark* 79–81.

[66] This exegesis is based on the first-rate analysis of John R. Donahue, *The Theology and Setting of Discipleship in the Gospel of Mark* (Milwaukee: Marquette University Press, 1983).

[67] Myers, *Binding the Strong Man* 266–271, offers some very insightful reflections on Jesus' solidarity with the child as "least of the least" and on our own need to identify with the child in order to deal with and overcome the roots of violence. I would add that 10:13-16 could be paraphrased to parallel the beatitude for the poor (Luke 6:20): "Blessed are you children, for yours is the kingdom of God."

[68] Donahue, *The Theology and Setting of Discipleship* 45–46.

[69] Donahue in his conclusion notes that Mark's "radical egalitarianism" based on the *sole* authority of Jesus stands in tension with the concern manifest later in the Second Testament for issues of institutionalized authority and ministry. Myers goes further: "How else can a portrait that paints men as power hungry and women as servants function, except to legitimate women as leaders?" *Binding the Strong Man* 281.

[70] Hamerton-Kelly, *The Gospel and the Sacred* 71: "The literal pole of the metaphor of ransom is the buying back of hostages. In this particular application, a person rather than money is given in exchange for the hostages—Jesus goes into captivity instead of us. A sacrificial interpretation would have Jesus giving his life instead of ours to appease the wrath of a vengeful God, which does not fit the metaphor, because captivity does not entail the wrath of the captor and ransom is not the same as appeasement. A careful decoding of the metaphor has one person going into captivity instead of the many, and that makes good sense in terms of our theory." And further: "If we had joined him in a covenant not to inflict violence on the other and to bear the violence inflicted on us without retaliation, the wheel of sacrifice would have ceased to turn and he would not have had to give his life as ransom for many. The wrath that fell on him was human, not divine" (p. 72).

[71] Kingsbury's arguments that Bartimaeus represents not a model of discipleship as such but a model of faith seem convincing (*The Christology of Mark's Gospel* 104–105, n. 159), yet such faith is precisely what the disciples need and lack. Note that Jesus asks the same question at 10:36 and 10:51: "What do you want me to do for you?"

[72] Rhoads and Michie, *Mark As Story* 54. John R. Donahue, "A Neglected Factor in the Theology of Mark," *JBL* 101 (1982) 563–594, concentrates (following Joanna Dewey) on the "ring structure" of 12:13-34, which he sees as a Jerusalem *didachē* for Gentile mission at the precise moment when the vineyard will be given to others (12:9).

[73] Donahue, "A Neglected Factor" 577–578. The idea of the ascending response is taken from his analysis.

[74] John R. Donahue, "Temple, Trial, and Royal Christology (Mark 14:53-65)" in Werner H. Kelber (ed.), *The Passion in Mark: Studies in Mark 14–16* (Philadelphia: Fortress Press, 1976) 61–79, shows how Mark has employed the story of David and Davidic expectations throughout the gospel but has modified such traditions to create the author's own royal christology.

[75] Vernon K. Robbins, "Last Meal: Preparation, Betrayal, and Absence (Mark 14:12-25)" in Kelber (ed.), *The Passion in Mark* 28. In the biblical world leaven is a symbol of corruption.

[76] Werner H. Kelber, "The Hour of the Son of Man and the Temptation of the Disciples" in ibid., 53: "While Jesus' three visits to the disciples (14:37-42) function internally to emphasize their inexcusable blindness, they link up externally (in relation to the total Gospel context) with the three passion predictions, Peter's three denials,

and the three 'hours' on the cross. . . . The correlation of these four threefold scenes, which variously emphasize the divine necessity and human rejection of passion, underscores the tragically irreconcilable conflict between passion Christology and discipleship failure."

[77] Waetjen, *A Reordering of Power* 214: "What he dreads is not the terror of death. That continues to be a fundamental misunderstanding of the cup. Jesus already embraced his mortality at his baptism. Nor is he overwhelmed by the anticipation of the pain of crucifixion. He will refuse to accept the anesthetic of wine mixed with myrrh. . . .What he fears is the horror of being abandoned by God. For, as he announced in his quotation of Zech. 13:7 to his disciples after their arrival at the Mount of Olives, God will take an active part in this eschatological event of Jesus' sacrifice: 'I shall smite the shepherd'. This is the judgment that he must suffer in his self-sacrifice as the New Human Being who has twice been validated as God's beloved son and who came to 'give his life a ransom for many.'"

[78] In opposition to the "corrective view" that sees Christ and Son of God as misunderstood titles that are corrected by Jesus' use of Son of Man, Kingsbury quite shrewdly maintains the distinction between Christ and Son of God as correctly referring to Jesus' identity and Son of Man to Jesus' destiny. "Jesus is condemned to death by the Sanhedrin for being exactly who he is . . ." (*The Christology of Mark's Gospel* 120). Son of Man at 14:62 ascribes to Jesus "the eschatological role that will attend his 'public' vindication, that of exercising judgment over his opponents at the end of time" (p. 124).

[79] Ibid., 122.

[80] Myers, *Binding the Strong Man* 324–353, proposes that the correct sociohistorical context for Mark is the revolt of 66–70 C.E., particularly the crucial year 69 when the rebels were seeking recruits to resist the increasingly ominous movement of the Roman army. The vividness of Mark 13 is best explained by the resistance of the community both to Roman collaboration (as exemplified by Josephus) and to Jewish zealotry (probably reflected in 13:5-6, 21-22). Collins, *The Beginning of the Gospel* 81–91, agrees with Myers. Since the question of the precise time when Mark composed the gospel cannot be decided definitively, it is important to recognize that the reader/listener must reinterpret these images according to subsequent experiences. See Waetjen, *A Reordering of Power* 198–200. Since most of Mark's intended (implied) audience would be illiterate, his aside may be intended for a literate scribe who in reading the gospel to the community would need to interpret it to subsequent generations, especially on this point of apocalyptic expectation.

[81] Waetjen, *A Reordering of Power* 201.

[82] Donahue, "A Neglected Factor" 592.

[83] Werner H. Kelber, *Mark's Story of Jesus* (Philadelphia: Fortress Press, 1979) 94.

[84] Mary Ann Beavis, "Women as Models of Faith in Mark," *BTB* 18 (1988) 5; see also Joseph A. Grassi, "The Secret Heroine of Mark's Drama," ibid., 10–15, who views Mark as presenting the "ideal disciple" in a "gradually expanding dramatic crescendo through key women. . . ." But compare Janice Capel Anderson, "Feminist Criticism: The Dancing Daughter" in Anderson and Moore, eds., *Mark and Method* 131: "Perhaps the strongest aspect of patriarchy is that, aside from Herodias, no women have positions of official authority and power, even those Mark implicitly praises. No women preach or heal. The only powerful woman in Mark is also, after Judas, one of

its most reviled villains." However, the story at 6:14-29 is not primarily about Herodias but about the fate of John the Baptist (and so also of Jesus and the disciples) at the hands of imperial power embodied in Herod. Malbon strikes a good balance in her notion of "fallible followers" that includes "bold and faithful women," "self-denying serving women," and "women as followers from beginning to end." She concludes that the Markan portrait of fallible followers is complex and includes disciples, crowds, women, excluded individuals. There is a twofold message: "anyone can be a follower, no one finds it easy." Malbon, "Fallible Followers" 46.

CHAPTER 3

A Creedal Image: "The Pre-Existent Son"
in the Nicene-Constantinopolitan Creed

What would our image of Jesus be like if we only had the writings of Paul with his almost exclusive emphasis on the cross and resurrection? or again if we only had Paul and the synoptics with the latter's additional emphasis on Jesus as the "new human being" (Mark) whose way to the cross gradually, through a process of historical becoming, unfolds the revelatory and salvific power of God? Indeed, what would our image of Jesus be like without the Gospel of John with its emphasis on Jesus' eternal relation to the Father? *"Only with the Fourth Gospel can we speak of a full blown conception of Christ's personal preexistence and a clear doctrine of incarnation."*[1] There is no question that the Gospel of John set the terms for the postbiblical christological debates of the early Church. Nonetheless, John's gospel as much as Mark's represents a "narrative quest" and so, indeed, do the creeds that were so heavily dependent on the Johannine image of Jesus, especially the one that has become the most widely accepted ecumenical summary of Christian faith, the "Nicene Creed" formulated at the Council of Constantinople in 381.

To explore this creedal image and its relationship to the primacy of story we will employ our threefold rubric of the world behind the text, the world of the text, and the world before the text. The first engages the dynamics of "narrative quest": (1) the foundational move occasioned by the crisis of heterodox views *(hairesis);* (2) the basic motivation of the desire for wisdom *(sapientia)* to be realized in the mystical ascent of the soul to God; and (3) the decisive orientation as a journey of interiority toward the *real* world, that of the divine. This will lead us secondly to a reading of the two texts that reflect this journey, the products of Nicea in 325 and Constantinople I in 381. This will be a multivalent reading according to the diverse functions of the creeds but with an emphasis on the foundational priority of narrative. Finally we will focus on the image of the pre-existent Son and its importance for subsequent Christian faith (the world before the text).

1. From Biblical Pluralism to Confessional Unity

The world behind the text of our creeds is a complex and varied one. The Scriptures themselves evidence a healthy pluralism and the recognition of which writings would eventually be accepted as canonical and which not was part of the search for a "rule of faith" or "canon of truth" (Irenaeus) that would result in confessional unity. The Gospel of John in particular was both problematic and finally decisive in this search. The historical development of the postbiblical quest for Christian identity is often written primarily from the point of view of the intellectual elites, the Church "Fathers" whose views prevailed. This makes sense insofar as they give us the bulk of written documentation that has come down to us. The writings of their opponents were frequently destroyed and only in recent years have we had greater access to Gnostic writings such as those discovered at Nag Hammadi in Egypt in 1945[2] that allow us to see more clearly the pluralism that existed prior to Nicea.

The emergence of authors with great intellectual acumen who could respond to the challenges and objections raised both outside of and within Christianity is only part of the story that explains the formation of the creeds. "It seems that the creeds took the form they did in response to the situation in which they arose, that the selection of details related to the challenges presented to the Christian account of things . . . and the common 'catch-phrases' are deeply traditional in oral confessional material pre-dating the formation of the creeds."[3] The situation was the communal experiences of catechesis and baptism. The challenges relate to the development of the wisdom theology of the Fathers. The "catch-phrases" were primarily, but not exclusively, drawn from Scripture.

We will treat in chronological order the biblical foundations of the creeds, the emergence of creeds from baptismal experience, and the development of creeds as expressions of wisdom theology (as well as "tests of orthodoxy"). The goal is to recognize the complex nature and function of the creeds and to see their fundamental character not primarily as systems of doctrine but as *story:* "they are summaries of the gospel, digests of the scriptures." Or again they are "'confessions' summarizing the Christian story, or affirmations of the three 'characters' in the story."[4]

The biblical foundations of the creeds. J. N. D. Kelly concludes his discussion of "credal elements in the New Testament" (ch. 1) as follows: "Our conclusion must be that one-membered, two-membered and three-membered confessions flourished side by side in the apostolic Church as parallel and mutually independent formulations of the one kerygma; and this is a datum of prime importance."[5] According to the Pauline witness the oral proclamation *(kerygma)* of the good news *(euaggelion)* centered on the "God who raised Jesus from the dead," already a bipartite formula. This basic proclamation was expressed not only in a bipartite structure (e.g., 1 Cor 8:6) but also in a tripartite structure (as in the baptismal formula at Matt 28:19) and in a single-member christological focus including both simple formulas (for example, "Jesus is Lord" at 1 Cor 12:3) and more detailed confessions (for example, in hymns such as Phil 2:6-11). While one cannot "postulate fixed credal forms for the apostolic age, the documents themselves testify to the existence of a corpus of distinctively Christian teaching. In this sense at any rate it is legitimate to speak of the creed of the primitive Church."[6] The diversity of "style, substance, and structure" is best explained by the diverse "life-situations" that occasioned the formulas. Kelly lists baptism, catechesis, preaching, polemic within (heretics) and without (pagans), liturgical worship (including the rite of exorcism), and letters. This biblical pluralism is rooted in the one gospel (Gal 1:6-9) and in the tradition of handing it on (1 Cor 15:3). Eventually the Church will move toward greater fixity of formulation in what we usually understand as the creeds.

The hymns to Christ, which probably developed out of some form of liturgical experience, are particularly interesting as creedal statements. They arise from and celebrate Christ's victory as risen Lord over "the cosmic powers" (Eph 6:12). The imagery employed is the contrast imagery of apocalyptic. The focus is eschatological, that is, it is centered on the final and decisive "event" of Jesus' death on the cross and his resurrection from the dead. Questions of origins (protology) arise from and are interpreted by the central story of Christian faith: Jesus' way to the cross and his victory over the power of death in the resurrection (eschatology). Thus what is being celebrated is not the personal pre-existence of Jesus but the revelatory and salvific significance of his personal relation to God in the light of the resurrection.

Paul, when he seeks to describe what kind of body is involved in resurrection (1 Cor 15:35-57), resorts first to analogies from nature in order to make the point that resurrection depends primarily on God's creativity. "But God gives it [a bare seed] a body as he has chosen and to each kind of seed its own body" (v. 38). When he applies this to resurrection he employs the contrast imagery of apocalyptic: perishable/imperishable; dishonor/glory; weakness/power; physical body/spiritual body (vv. 42-44). The latter gives rise to the christological contrast between the first Adam (he cites Gen 2:7) and the last Adam who "became a life-giving spirit." Paul is not interested in speculation about a pre-existent heavenly man. In fact he denies that possibility in vv. 45-49. His concern is to focus on the eschatological nature of this "last Adam" as the one who has conquered the power of sin, law, and death (vv. 54-57; cf. Rom 5:12-21; 8:1-11).

One of the most famous early hymns is incorporated into Paul's letter to the Phillippians. Although this hymn has often been interpreted as proclaiming the pre-existence of Christ I would agree with those who interpret it as an expression of Paul's normal emphasis on the contrast between Adam and Christ.[7] The hymn (Phil 2:6-11) divides into two strophes: 1 (vv. 6-8): humiliation; 2 (vv. 9-11): exaltation. As Dunn interprets it the hymn communicates the story of Christ as one who, being in the image and likeness *(morphē)* of God as was Adam, did not count equality with God something to be grasped at *(harpagmon)* as did Adam, but freely chose to empty himself and take on the *morphē* of a slave (what Adam became), that is, one subject to the powers of evil (sin, law, death). This means that Christ entered fully and freely into human existence, growing in the likeness of (sinful) human beings (v. 7; cf. Rom 8:3; 2 Cor 5:21). But being found in outward form *(schēma)* like Adam *(anthrōpos),* unlike Adam he freely chose to humble himself and become obedient unto death. Thus the first strophe articulates the same contrast between the disobedience of Adam and the obedience of Christ found at Rom 5:12-21. The hymn is not concerned with pinpointing any particular "moment" of this freely given choice but simply communicating an understanding of Jesus' whole life as expressing his obedience unto death, even (as Paul adds) death on the cross.

The second strophe sees Jesus' exaltation as a consequence of this obedience (v. 9: "Therefore God *[ho theos]* has highly exalted him") that includes a full affirmation of his divinity ("and graced him with the name above every name so that at the name of Jesus every knee should bend . . ."). The whole of creation should now offer adoration *at the name of Jesus,* which appears to be a new reality in the divine life as a consequence of his death on the cross. The hymn concludes (v. 11) with a ringing confession of faith using a bipartite creedal formula: "And every tongue should confess that Jesus Christ is Lord to the glory of God the Father." Thus the hymn affirms what Fuller has called a "two-stage christology" (rather than his view of it as representing a "three-stage christology"). It focuses on the contrasting parallel between the earthly life and the exalted life of Jesus. Because of the Adam imagery the contrast is sharply drawn between humiliation and exaltation.

The letters of Paul universally accepted as authentic (1 Thessalonians, Galatians, 1–2 Corinthians, Romans, Philippians, and Philemon) do not manifest an interest in Christ's personal pre-existence, including the hymn just analyzed.[8] Neither do the other hymns that Fuller analyzes, though they move back toward the origin of all things in the creative and revelatory power of God. The hymn in the letter to the Colossians (Col 1:15-20) expresses a cosmic view that is close to 1 Cor 8:6. It too divides into two strophes: 1 (vv. 15-18a): protology; 2 (vv. 18b-20): eschatology. The key to the hymn lies in the qualification attached to v. 18b: "who is the beginning, the firstborn from the dead, *in order that he may become in all things preeminent"* *(prōteuōn).*

It is his resurrection from the dead that allows us to speak of his preeminence or primacy over all creation (vv. 15-18a). Thus the two strophes interpret each other. The resurrection makes possible the affirmation of Christ's primacy in all creation but at the same time such an affirmation interprets the true significance of the resurrection as an eschatological event that embraces the whole of creation from beginning to end. Hence once again there is no question of a temporal sequence or pre-existence; rather there is a theological affirmation in the light of the resurrection. Likewise the hymnic fragment at Heb 1:2b-3c is set in the context of "these last days" (v. 2a) and the death and exaltation of the Son (vv. 3d-4). Both of these hymns are intended to identify Jesus with the Wisdom of God, that is, the fullness of God's creative power. Dunn summarizes:

> Again, we repeat, the thought is not of Jesus himself as there in the beginning, despite what to us seems the "obvious" meaning of the language used in I Cor. 8.6, Col. 1.16 and Heb. 1.2, but of Jesus as the man Wisdom became— not merely inspired, but became. He who espouses a Wisdom christology does not assert that Christ was a pre-existent being, but neither does he assert that Christ was simply a man used by God, even in a climactic way. He asserts rather that *Christ fully embodies the creative and saving activity of God, that God in all his fullness was in him, that he represents and manifests all that God is in his outreach to men.* . . . Herein we see the origin of the doctrine of the incarnation.[9]

The hymn reconstructed from 1 Pet 3:18-19, 22 is once again a two-stage christology based in the death and resurrection (v. 18: "put to death in the flesh, made alive in the spirit"). The verse at 1:20 that Bultmann saw as part of the hymn does not speak of personal pre-existence and incarnation but of the intention in the mind of God *(proegnōsmenou)* revealed *(phanerōthentos)* in the last days (cf. Acts 2:23; 1 Cor 2:7; Eph 1:3-14), that is, of an ideal pre-existence, not a real or personal one. This notion of the mystery *(mysterion)*[10] also introduces the hymn at 1 Tim 3:16 that again is clearly a two-stage christology based on Jesus' death and resurrection. It is worth noting, however, that with this hymn we have a higher valuation of the earthly life as epiphanic ("manifested . . . proclaimed . . . believed") that is similar to the Gospel of John.

Thus far we have been arguing that the creedal confessions of the early Church, especially in their hymnic forms, are basically liturgical celebrations of the significance of Jesus in the light of the death and resurrection. As such they do affirm a doctrine of incarnation understood as the eschatological embodiment of God's creative, revelatory, and salvific power in the person of Jesus. Such confessions do not, nor need they, affirm the personal pre-existence of Jesus. The question that is crucial for subsequent creedal development is whether the Gospel of John represents a new moment, indeed a departure, with its affirmation of the personal pre-existence of Jesus. There are two questions that must be kept distinct. First, does the hymn in the Prologue affirm the pre-existence of Jesus and if so, in what sense? Second, how does the Prologue relate to the rest of the gospel that does clearly affirm the personal pre-existence of Jesus?

The hymn as we have it now has been interpolated into what was probably the earlier beginning of the gospel at 1:6-9 with explanatory expansions at vv. 12c, 13, 15, 17-18.[11] It divides into four strophes: 1 (vv. 1-2): the Word *(logos)* in relation to God *(ho theos);* 2 (vv. 3-5): the Word in relation to creation/revelation; 3 (vv. 10-12b): the Word in relation to the world (rejection/acceptance); 4 (vv. 14, 16): the Word in relation to the community as witness. This hymn, like the ones in Colossians and Hebrews, draws its imagery from the Wisdom traditions of the Jewish Scriptures but employs one of the alternative ways of speaking of God's creative, revelatory, and salvific activity (the divine immanence), i.e., the Word.[12] It is clear that although "in the beginning" would evoke Gen 1:1 the intent is to affirm the existence of the Word prior to creation (which is first mentioned in the next strophe). This contrasts with Prov 8:22; Sir 24:9. Three times in the first strophe the Word is said to exist *(ēn):* prior to creation *(en archē),* in relation to God *(pros ton theon),* and as divine *(theos).* The beginning of the second strophe (v. 3) probably refers to all of God's activity *ad extra* that is then made explicit: creation (v. 10), revelation (vv. 4-5, 14, as well as the explanatory expansions at vv. 9, 18), and salvation (vv. 12, 16, as well as the explanatory expansion at v. 13).[13]

What is said of the creative, revelatory, and salvific activity of the Word in the second and third strophes would be at home in the Wisdom speculations of the late Jewish Scriptures. What is absolutely new and unique, indeed startling, is the affirmation of the fourth strophe (v. 14): "And the Word became flesh" *(kai ho logos sarx egeneto).* As Dunn puts it: ". . . the revolutionary significance of v. 14 may well be that it marks *not only the transition in the thought of the poem from pre-existence to incarnation, but also the transition from impersonal personification to actual person."*[14] However, as an originally independent hymn (though probably composed within Johannine circles, given the characteristic vocabulary), this affirmation is not far removed from the image of Jesus embodying divine Wisdom in the hymns of Colossians and Hebrews. The pre-existence of the *logos* (= Wisdom) is an ideal pre-existence in the sense that such imagery (Wisdom, Word, Spirit, etc.), controlled by a strong monotheistic faith, was always intended to affirm the divine immanence (God's creative, revelatory, and salvific activity) while preserving the divine transcendence. John 1:14 affirms, as did 1 Cor 8:6; Col 1:16; Heb 1:2 that Jesus is the person that Wisdom became. It is the same affirmation of incarnation but in a much more explicit and inescapable way.

What makes it new in this way, and so supremely important for subsequent christological development, is how the evangelist relates this hymn to the rest of the gospel. With regard to our theme the simple fact is that he does so by telling the story of Jesus in gospel form and in this his work is very similar to the Gospel of Mark. As T. E. Pollard points out, John employs the *logos* to establish contact with contemporary readers/listeners who may have had interest in the many forms of *logos* speculation but the fact that he never uses it again after 1:14 indicates that it was inadequate to express fully what he wanted to say and also that it was to be interpreted in the light of the rest of the gospel and not the other way around.

> While the Prologue can stand by itself it is evident that St. John is far more interested in Jesus Christ, the Son of God, than he is in the Logos, and that he intended the Prologue to be interpreted in the light of the rest of the Gospel. Or, to put it more specifically, he intended the Logos of the Prologue to be interpreted in the light of Jesus the Christ, the Son of God, whose earthly life is the theme of the Gospel. The subject of the Gospel is Jesus Christ, not the Logos.[15]

The Evangelist makes use of the hymn and in doing so alters its meaning in two ways.[16] First, by placing vv. 6-9 (the original opening?) between the second and third strophes he has transformed the original *sophia* speculation so that vv. 10-12 now refer to the incarnate *logos* and vv. 14 and 16 become a further exploration of that claim. The explanatory expansions also serve to direct the reader/listener to major themes in the rest of the gospel: v. 13 asserts what it means to be God's children, that is, to believe in his name (20:31) which includes being begotten of God (3:3, 5); v. 15 asserts the major theme of the pre-existence *(ēn)* of the Son that runs throughout the gospel; the same verse is repeated on the lips of John the Baptist at 1:30; v. 17 asserts the significance of "love in place of love" by contrasting the Law given through Moses and the "enduring love" through Jesus Christ (throughout the gospel Jesus is pictured as replacing the Temple and the Jewish feasts); v. 18 contrasts the claim that Moses (Exod 33:18) and Isaiah (Isa 6:5) had seen God with the assertion that it is "God the only Son, the one who is in the bosom of the Father, who has made him known." It is worth noting that of the threefold activity of God *ad extra* creation is mentioned only in the hymn. The rest of the gospel is concerned with Jesus as the Son who reveals the Father and leads us into eternal life (= salvation: 1:29; 3:16-17; 4:21-26, 42; etc.).

The second and more important use of the hymn therefore is that it serves as an overture to the rest of the gospel. As Dunn puts it, the author has conflated the *logos* christology of the hymn (ideal pre-existence) with a Son of God christology (historical sending of the Son) so that there is a clear image of the *logos*-Son pre-existing as a divine personal being who has been sent down *(katabainō)* from heaven and will re-ascend *(anabainō)* there again. The *logos* who is divine (v. 1: *theos*) and who became flesh (v. 14: *sarx*) is thus in a full and appropriate sense proclaimed as God's only or unique Son (v. 18: *monogenēs theos*). As

Dunn concludes,[17] it is only with John that we have a clear and unambiguous affirmation of the Son's personal, that is, real pre-existence and so a clear and unambiguous doctrine of incarnation. Dunn articulates the challenge of John's christology on three levels. First it prevents Christians from settling for a more accommodating faith that would see Jesus either as merely a human being, even if the eschatological prophet sent by God (ebionitism), or as a divine being who merely appeared to be human (docetism, gnosticism). Second it changes the concept of God by on the one hand resolving the Jewish tension between transcendence and immanence (1:18; 12:45; 14:9) and on the other creating a new Christian tension: the *logos* incarnate as a new person in God. Third, as a consequence it set the terms for subsequent (post-biblical) christological development: on the one hand ruling out modalism because the Son is truly distinct from the Father and on the other raising in acute form the relation between the Father and the Son and hence the very nature of God as triune (including the Spirit). The texts most often cited in later controversies were 10:30; 14:9, 10 (on the identity and equality of Father and Son) and 14:28 (on the superiority of the Father to the Son). "In a real sense the history of christological controversy is the history of the church's attempt to come to terms with John's christology—first to accept it and then to understand and re-express it. The latter task will never end."[18]

Three questions arise as we try to understand this process. First, can we understand John's intention from the kind of language he employs? Was his language primarily metaphorical or conceptual? That is, was he primarily concerned to tell the story of Jesus, a story that has metaphoric impact even as it raises questions for conceptual understanding? Do problems arise because we have overly literalized language that was intended to be metaphorical? How do we interpret the fact that for John it is Jesus, the human, earthly Jesus from Nazareth, who pre-exists with the Father so that the gospel can be characterized as "a projection of an eternal relation . . . upon the field of time"?[19] We will seek to answer this first set of questions in our conclusion.

The second question concerns the way in which the biblical confessions of faith in Christ were developed and understood on the more popular level, especially in the practice of catechesis and baptism. In this connection Frances Young refers to "catch-phrases" that come mostly but not entirely from Scripture. The third question concerns the way in which these same scriptural sources, and above all the Gospel of John, were employed in the more intellectualist tradition of the Church Fathers as they struggled with challenges to the faith and so developed the creeds as we usually think of them. We will consider these latter two questions sequentially.

The emergence of creeds from baptismal experience. Before we think of the creeds as fixed in their present form or as "rules" or "tests" of orthodoxy we must recognize their emergence from the concretely lived experience of local communities and the resultant diversity of both form and function.[20] Perhaps the most fundamental experience that would lie at the origin of the creeds we know is doxology, the praise of God on the basis of the divine deeds. Such praise evokes and so is inseparable from telling the story. The people of Israel know of such narrative celebrations (see Deut 26:1-11; Josh 24:1-28; Pss 44; 78; 105; 106). Liturgical celebrations embodying the story of God's saving actions are what gave the people their identity. The same is true of the Christian Scriptures with their memory of the "great deed" of Jesus' death and resurrection. The hymns celebrate and evoke the story of what God has done in Christ. They originated in oral proclamation and, though eventually written down, were meant to serve the oral memory of the communities where they were formulated. For these communities the principal liturgical celebrations would be the Lord's Supper (1 Cor 11:23-26; Acts 2:42) and the reception of "those who were being saved" (Acts 2:47) in baptism (Matt 28:19; Gal 3:27; 1 Cor 12:13; Rom 6:3; Acts 2:38-41; 8:35-39; 10:44-48; *Didache* 7).

In what way did the creeds in the technical sense take their rise in connection with the rite of baptism?[21] Kelly shows that the closest connection with the actual rite was a personal profession of faith in response to the minister's triple set of questions in relation to the Father, the Son, and the Holy Spirit (Matt 28:19). Analyzing evidence from the first three centuries, especially Justin, Tertullian, Hippolytus, Cyprian, et al., he concludes: "The striking fact has been brought to light that for the first few centuries at any rate the only creed, if creed is the right designation for it, directly connected with baptism was the baptizand's assent to the minister's questions regarding his beliefs; even when they found their niche within the liturgy, the function of declaratory creeds proper long remained secondary."[22] This leads to the real issue, which is that the development of the creeds proper belongs not so much to the actual rite of baptism as to the catechetical preparation for it. The fourth century and beyond evidences the following process of catechesis: toward the end of Lent the bishop would hand over a creed in declaratory form *(traditio symboli)*. He would comment on it clause by clause and the catechumens would memorize it as a synopsis of their profession of faith. On the eve of their baptism and so prior to the actual rite the catechumens were expected to give it back *(redditio symboli)* by memory as a sign of their grounding in the faith and their unity with the community of faith. "Declaratory creeds may therefore be regarded as a by-product of the Church's fully developed catechetical system."[23] Nonetheless their close connection to baptism must not be forgotten nor, in connection with the practice of baptism, their preservation of trinitarian rather than simply bipartite or single formulas of faith.

The term *symbolum,* which did not come into regular use until the fifth century, is important for what it signifies. The Greek verb *symballein* means

. . . to fall together, to cast together. The background to the word's etymology is an ancient usage: two corresponding halves of a ring, a staff, or a tablet were used as tokens of identity for guests, messengers or partners to a treaty. Possession of the corresponding piece entitled the holder to receive a thing or simply to hospitality. A *symbolum* is something which points to its complementary other half and thus creates mutual recognition and unity. It is the expression and means of unity.[24]

Thus the identity, the unity, the completeness of Christian faith (precisely as communal) is powerfully evoked when the two halves fall together, i.e., when the bishop's handing over of the *symbolum* is reciprocated with the baptizand's memorized profession of faith.

However this "movement towards fixity" (Kelly's chapter 3) was a gradual development that tended toward fixed forms only in the fourth century. The first three centuries are best characterized as creative and diverse, that is, as manifesting a variety of forms and functions. The Apostolic Fathers (*Didache, 1 Clement, Shepherd of Hermas,* Ignatius of Antioch, Polycarp of Smyrna), who remain close to the New Testament, give us fragments of confessional formulae that are simple as well as trinitarian and reflect various possible situations (baptism, catechesis, liturgy, polemic). Justin Martyr (d. 165), who wrote at Rome, "provides the earliest direct evidence we possess for the emergence of relatively fixed credal questions at baptism; and he illustrates the continued existence of one-clause, purely Christological confessions alongside the Trinitarian ones employed at baptism and on other occasions."[25]

Irenaeus of Lyons (d. ca. 200), who manifests concern for the "canon of truth" or "rule of faith," has been called the first biblical theologian because of his systematic use of Scripture, especially Paul and John. Kelly points out the frequent use of 1 Cor 8:6 in his creedal statements. Yet he does not develop strong anti-heretical motifs in these kinds of texts despite his strong anti-gnostic polemic elsewhere. He knew a short baptismal creed with a threefold interrogation. He combined a traditional Christ-kerygma with bipartite and tripartite formulae. He drew upon summaries of Christian faith that were not strictly creeds but more or less stereotyped formulae.[26] Likewise Tertullian (d. ca. 225), who refers to baptismal questions and answers and emphasizes a "rule of faith" with polemical overtones, does not appear to know any single authoritative creed but "was drawing on formulae which had attained a fair measure of fixity."[27]

Finally with the *Apostolic Tradition* (ca. 217) of Hippolytus (d. 235) at Rome we have "the first document which shows us what appears to be a fixed creed in its integrity."[28] While this is a formal, fixed creed there is still question whether it was the official creed of the Roman Church (cf. the "Old Roman Creed" in Kelly's chapters 4 and 5) and how much room there still was for variation. Kelly draws a number of conclusions from his analysis.[29] The movement toward fixity was a gradual process. There were many "creeds" in "the looser, less exact sense of the word" existing independently of one another in the second and third centuries with tripartite, bipartite, and simple clauses. Declaratory creeds, "stereotyped in form and officially sanctioned by local church authorities," had no currency but interrogatory creeds because of their close connection to the liturgy of baptism tended to move more quickly toward verbal fixity and official local recognition. In all of this it is important to remember that the development of creeds had less to do with anti-heretical motives than with fidelity to the "deposit of doctrine" handed down from the beginning as the canon or rule of faith. Thus the first three centuries witness to an emerging, vital, and varied communitarian faith that was tied to local communities and especially to their practice of baptism.

The Old Roman Creed, which Kelly dates as early as the late second century (ca. 197?) presumably in interrogatory form, and characterizes as a conflation of an earlier short trinitarian formula and an originally independent christo-logical summary, is described as "nothing more nor less than a compendium of popular theology, all the more fascinating to us because we can still discern, crystallized in its clauses, the faith and hope of the primitive Church."[30] While some of the clauses in the christological insertion may be intended to exclude heresy, the primary motive throughout is to ensure solid catechetical instruc-tion by invoking "the primitive kerygma of the apostolic age."[31] All the creeds treated so far are Western but as Kelly notes (chapter 6, "Creeds Western and Eastern"), with the exception of the peculiar position of the Roman church and the fact that the Old Roman Creed is the direct ancestor of all other Western baptismal creeds (including the later "Apostles' Creed"), the Eastern creeds developed in a manner closely analogous to the Western creeds. The earlier interrogatory creeds developed into declaratory creeds in the third century with the elaboration of the catechumenate and the baptismal rite itself. The only common origin between Eastern and Western creeds would be the observance of Matt 28:19 and the baptismal act that then developed in distinc-tive ways in the local churches. Of note is a theological difference: ". . . in Western creeds the centre of interest is the primitive kerygma about the Saviour, whereas in Eastern creeds the cosmic setting of the drama obtrudes itself more obviously."[32] Indicative of the latter would be the emphasis in the first article on the oneness of God and on the Father as Creator "of all things visible and invisible"; in the second on the Father's pre-cosmic begetting of the Son and the Son's agency in the work of creation.

The purpose of this brief and summary review of the early development of creeds has been to emphasize the point that the primary function of creeds is personal and communal profession of faith. This can take shape as doxology, as a hymnlike evocation of the story of Jesus, as a catechetical handing over and rendering back of the *symbolum* that just prior to baptism and in connection with it is the memorable moment of each person's supreme commitment. Frequently in the controversies of the early Church appeal is made to what one professed at baptism as the touchstone of what one truly believes and professes.[33] The final purpose of this review, then, is to highlight by way of contrast the strikingly different character of the "Nicene Creed." Berard Marthaler calls it "a dramatic change in the function of the creed."[34] Whereas before the motive of testing orthodoxy (correct belief) was exceptional and subordinate to the baptismal purpose, it would become primary in the first ecumenical council that could claim universal and not just local authority in a legal sense. Yet it must be remembered that the Nicene creed was not intended to displace the ancient baptismal creeds of the local churches. Kelly puts it nicely:

> The Nicene symbol, it is correctly pointed out, was first and foremost a definition of orthodox faith for bishops. It was propounded to smooth over a particular crisis in the Church. No one intended it, in the first instance at any rate, to supersede the existing baptismal confessions. Bristling with anti-Arian clauses and armed at the tail with polemical anathemas, it was hardly suited to be the solemn formula in which the catechumen would avow his adhesion to the Christian revelation.[35]

The Nicene creed was a creed for bishops who had pastoral care and concern for the universal Church. But the selection of details was determined by specific challenges to Christian self-understanding among an intellectual elite (mostly bishops themselves). And so we turn to our third question, the way in which the Church Fathers came to formulate the creeds as we know them, above all by their interpretation of the scriptural sources, the principal one being the Gospel of John.

The development of creeds as expressions of wisdom theology. The image of Jesus as the pre-existent Son of God in John's gospel has had a transformative effect on the understanding of God's Word *(logos)* in both the Hebraic wisdom tradition (Wisdom, Word, Spirit, etc., as ways of expressing the divine immanence) and the Greek philosophical tradition *(logos* as the ordering principle of the cosmos). Neither of these speculative approaches will prove adequate to the orthodox understanding of Jesus as embodying the fullness of divinity and humanity. The creedal confession of the God-man subsumes into itself and reinterprets on a higher level what is true in the "Alexandrian" *logos-sarx* (Word-flesh) approach and in the "Antiochene" *logos-anthrōpos* (Word-human being) approach. Neither is completely wrong but neither is adequate. The key to what finally emerges as the orthodox view is the maintenance of the Gospel of John, i.e., the *whole story* of Jesus, over against any attempt to disengage the *logos* from that story. Thus as we have been urging throughout, abstract speculations and conceptualizations, as important as they are, must always give way to the primacy of story.

At the same time the development of wisdom theology among the Church Fathers was itself a narrative quest. It grew out of the crisis of *hairesis,* especially in the form of gnostic speculations, and the corresponding move toward confessional unity and continuity as assuring both individual and communal identity. As a drive for wisdom it was experienced concretely in the mystical ascent of the soul to God, a journey of interiority whose intended goal or outcome was a cosmic vision of the whole as known only in contemplation of the divine. Thus for all the speculative overtones the intent was eminently practical and real: salvation through knowledge *(gnōsis)* of the divine. The image of Jesus that encapsulates this quest is that of John's gospel: the pre-existent Son of God in an eternal relation to the Father who has descended into this world in order to enable us to ascend with him back to the Father. Perhaps no author better embodies this quest than Origen of Alexandria (d. 254) who has been called "the first great theologian."[36]

If the crisis was Gnosticism, the key issue was creation, i.e., the relationship between God and the world. The Christian doctrine of creation gave shape to the understanding of incarnation, resurrection, and sacraments, and was especially connected to the reality of salvation.[37] That Christian doctrine depended on the authority of tradition. Irenaeus in his five-volume work against Gnosticism *(Adversus haereses)* employs "two basic approaches" to meet the crisis. The first was to develop a coherent system mainly out of biblical sources that would affirm the goodness of this world as God's world. The second was to appeal to the authority of Scripture by tracing those books that could be accepted as "a rule of faith" back to the apostles and their preservation to the apostles' successors, the bishops.[38] It was Irenaeus's "masterly use" of John to refute Gnosticism that most probably led to the acceptance of the Fourth Gospel in the canon. There seems to have been widespread use of Johannine imagery and motifs in the piety and devotion of Christians in the early second century but no citation of John in orthodox writing until toward the end of the same century. This was probably because of early gnostic use of the gospel (cf. *The Gospel of Truth* and *Pap. Egerton* 2). The first commentary was written by the gnostic Heracleon and some believed the gospel itself was written by the gnostic Cerinthus. Theophilus of Antioch (ca. 170?) was the first Christian writer to attribute the gospel to John and the first to quote from it.[39] But it was Irenaeus who, as the first biblical theologian, employed Pauline and Johannine themes to achieve his masterful synthesis of the biblical story in the image of Jesus Christ, the Son of God, as the recapitulation of God's creative, revelatory, and redemptive activity in the world. In so doing Irenaeus does not disengage the *logos* from the story and indulge in abstract speculations. Can the same be said for Origen?

The second century saw the rise of Christian apologists like Justin Martyr who entered into philosophical dialogue with the "pagan detractors" of Christianity and pastors like Ignatius of Antioch and Irenaeus who sought "to proclaim the gospel to the faithful and to protect them from gnostic perversions of the faith."[40] The acceptance of John by the end of the century, principally through the work of Irenaeus, provided both a terminology that resonated with contemporary thought (especially *logos*) and a weapon to confront the syncretic power of Gnosticism. This twofold task, apologetic and pastoral, continued in the third century but it took different directions in the West (northern Africa and Rome) which simply opposed Christian tradition ("the rule of faith") to Gnosticism and in the East (principally Alexandria) which sought to demonstrate that Christianity is the true *gnōsis*.

> This difference in attitude towards gnosticism is due largely to a difference in environment. Western theologians lived in an atmosphere that was practical rather than speculative, more interested in law and action than in philosophy; the only philosophy which had any lasting influence on the life and culture of the west was Stoicism with its strongly ethical and practical emphasis. Alexandria, on the other hand, was a centre of cosmopolitan culture, where any and every philosophy and religion could gain a hearing and gather a following.[41]

The critical issue in the third century revolved around what Pollard calls "two varieties of Monarchianism," both of which were concerned to preserve biblical monotheism (Deut 6:4). The Western temptation would prove to be toward "modalistic monarchianism" that denies the real distinction between Father, Son, and Spirit, seeing them only as successive manifestations of the one God. The Eastern temptation (especially after Origen) would be toward "dynamic monarchianism" that denies the full divinity of the Son, asserting rather that he was raised to divinity by adoption. Western theologians of the third century like Hippolytus, Tertullian, and Novatian refuted both approaches by avoiding *logos* speculation as inadequate and focusing instead on systematic exposition of John (the main texts were 10:30; 14:9, 10, 28) that affirms both the identity and the distinction of Father and Son. "This they did so successfully that the great trinitarian controversies of the fourth century and the christological controversies of the late fourth and early fifth centuries appear to have had little impact on the Western church."[42] Eastern theologians, on the other hand, divided over the understanding of the *logos* in the light of middle-Platonic speculation (the "Alexandrian" tendency) or in the light of the Hebraic wisdom tradition (the "Antiochene" tendency). The most interesting figure in this period and the most illustrative of our theme of "narrative quest" is Origen, so we will focus on him for purposes of illustration and then jump to Athanasius of Alexandria (d. 373) whom Pollard calls a "neo-Alexandrian" (close to the Western tradition) and who represents the most important contrast to Origen.

The pre-existence of the soul, i.e., prior to the creation of this material world and so enjoying a natural affinity with the spiritual world of the divine or eternal forms, is a Platonic idea. It offers an answer to the vexed question of the origin of the soul. Origen espoused this as a way of answering two interrelated questions: the relationship of the One (God) to the Many (creation) and the relationship of divine providence (as good in opposition to Marcion) to human freedom (as the source of inequalities in opposition to the Gnostics Basilides and Valentinus). In doing so he combined Hellenistic thought with scriptural and theological concerns. Yet all of this is in service of mystical union of the soul with God.[43] He could distinguish the common people as "more simple" than the educated elite (usually because of overly literalistic interpretations of Scripture) and still be concerned to affirm against Celsus that Christianity served the good of all. Nonetheless there were higher and lower levels of participation in divine things. Thus he was attracted to a rather esoteric allegorical exegesis of Scripture (following Philo) in order to resolve conflicts both within Scripture itself and between Scripture and contemporary philosophy. His guiding criterion of truth, however, was always the ecclesial and apostolic rule of faith: ". . . we maintain that that only is to be believed as the truth which in no way conflicts with the tradition of the church and the apostles."[44]

Nonetheless, as Aloys Grillmeier remarks, "Origen is, above all, the theologian of the soul of Christ."[45] What follows is a brief summary of his theology. God the Father *(ho theos)* is the absolutely transcendent and incomprehensible One *(monad* or *henad)* who eternally generates the Word *(logos = theos)* as the intermediary between God (One) and creation (Many), subordinate to the Father insofar as the Father alone is unbegotten *(agenētos)* and superior to the rest of reality as created *(genēta)* because uniquely Son by nature *(monogenēs)*. The Son is the total and substantial image of the Father because the Father *(ho theos)* communicates the divinity in a whole or complete way to the Son *(monogenēs theos)*. The influence of John is evident throughout not only in the use of Johannine terminology but in the fact that Origen conceives this relationship as dynamic and dialogic by connecting image with vision and ultimately revelation. "For a proper understanding of Origen, one must also consider that for him an intimate bond exists between image and vision. For in Origen's thought 'being-an-image' is a dynamic reality, and a vision is a total dedication to the one beheld, a loving and lucid spiritual assimilation."[46]

How we come to participate in this relationship depends on Origen's understanding of the pre-existence of spiritual "beings" or "intelligences." For Origen, God is eternal and immutable, therefore eternally and immutably Creator. Spiritual beings ("intelligences") exist eternally with God as Creator insofar as they are present in the uniquely begotten Son who is Wisdom. The truth of faith is that

> . . . God the Father always existed, and that he always had an only-begotten Son, who at the same time, according to the explanation we have given

above, is called Wisdom. This is that Wisdom in whom God delighted when
the world was finished, in order that we might understand from this that God
ever rejoices. In this Wisdom, therefore, who ever existed with the Father,
the Creation was always present in form and outline, and there was never a
time when the prefiguration of those things which hereafter were to be did
not exist in Wisdom.[47]

However, these spiritual "beings" or "intelligences" are created prior to the
material universe as originally equal among themselves. Differentiations and
inequalities are the result of a pre-cosmic fall away from that original unity
and equality. This is explained in terms of the spiritual life as a certain boredom (*koros* = *satietas*) of contemplation, one of the great temptations of
monastic life, or as a growing cold in fervor and charity (*psychē* as associated
with *psychos* = cold).

> God is fire and warmth. Moving further away from God the intelligences
> got cold and became souls. So we are talking about a decline in fervour
> and charity. The reduction from intelligence into soul is a matter of degree,
> for not all fell to the same level. Hence the diversity of rational creatures
> in their different orders, angels, men, demons, and within each order a
> continuous diversity. The original fall is thus not the immediate cause, but
> the motive for the diversity of the perceptible world which God created
> after it.[48]

All those intelligences (except God) have a kind of ethereal corporality before
the fall that is retained by angels and demons after the fall and is regained by
humans at the resurrection (1 Cor 15:44: *sōma pneumatikon,* but interpreted
with the term *eidos* = form or outward appearance, as the body's principle of
continuity). After the fall the type of body one has depends upon the degree
of fallenness with consequent locations: in heaven (angels), on earth (humans),
in Gehenna (demons). Thus this material creation (earth) was created by a
loving and providential God as good (against Gnostic dualism) but as a locus
of divine pedagogy to reeducate fallen souls with regard to the locus of true
reality (= the divine) and so to reintegrate souls into the divine unity of truth
(vision) and goodness (love). Only the *logos* united with a human soul can do
this.

Here we come to Origen's most distinctive teaching. All spiritual "beings"
or "intelligences" have fallen away to some degree except the soul of the
logos[49] which is thus unique among all created spiritual beings.

> But that soul of which Jesus said, "No man will take my soul from me" [John
> 10:18], that soul, from the beginning of its creation and after, clung insepa-
> rably and persistently to him, to the Wisdom and Logos of God, the truth and
> the true light. It received, as a whole, the whole [of the Logos]. It entered
> itself into his light and his glory. So it was made, in the proper sense, one

spirit with him—just as the apostle promises, to those called to imitate this soul, that one "who joins himself to the Lord is one spirit" [1 Cor 6:17].[50]

This raises the question whether the soul of the *logos* is the same in nature as human souls. In any event for Origen the reality of this soul is to mediate between God and the flesh, so that the soul attached in love and adoration to the *logos* makes it possible for the *logos* to become flesh (John 1:14). Thus we have a descending hierarchy from God *(ho theos)* to *logos (theos)* to the soul of the *logos* (variously but appropriately named together with the flesh it had assumed "Son of God and Power of God, Christ, and Wisdom of God" as well as "Son of Man"; cf. *De Princ.* 2.6.3) to the unity of "one flesh" that can be transfigured by the glory of the *logos*-soul.

This descending hierarchy has a purpose, our salvation: to bring souls back to their original unity with the divine by reversing the process in ascending order from body *(sōma)* to soul *(psychē:* lower [tendencies toward flesh]; higher: *nous* or *hegemonikon* ["governing faculty"]) to spirit *(pneuma* as God's gift in Christ, that is, the pedagogue of the higher soul training it in virtue and knowledge of God). Thus we are called to participate fully in the true image of God, the *logos*.[51] The biblical history of salvation seen as the strategy of divine pedagogy can be schematized into "shadow" (Old Testament to John the Baptist), "image" (the incarnate life, passion and resurrection of Jesus as the "temporal" gospel), and finally "reality" (the fullness of life in the vision of God as the "eternal" gospel).[52] Salvation is a journey of interiority whereby Jesus as teacher of wisdom and model of virtue brings souls back to the real world of the divine. Some will make only limited progress but for those who are given the higher gifts the end of the journey is a cosmic vision of the whole as known only in contemplation of the divine reality. For Origen the supreme virtue is wisdom; thus in his hierarchy of the attributes *(epinoiai)* of the *monogenēs theos* wisdom is first, followed by word, life, light, and so on.[53] In the eternal generation of the Son creation is present both as wisdom (= "ideas" in the Platonic sense), the model for created reality and as word (= *logos* in the Stoic sense of the ordering principle of the cosmos) that is the agent or instrument of the one divine creativity. Thus the end of all our journeying is to return to the place from which we started and to know it for the first time (to paraphrase T. S. Eliot). This is salvation: to know the Father through, with, and in the Son. "Our salvation therefore consists in our climbing up to the Father by means of the steps of Jesus' bodiliness, of his interior and divine Sonship. Our Redeemer is thus all the steps himself *(Comm. Jo.* XIX. 6, 38-39); he continually adapts himself to the capacities of those who are his: for some, milk; for others, a healing herb; for the perfect, solid food *(C. Celsum* IV. 18)."[54]

Origen is a fascinating and fertile thinker, "the first great theologian," in whose writings later thinkers, both orthodox and heretical, will find inspiration and support.[55] What is of greatest interest to the thesis of this book is that his view of the pre-existent soul of Christ attached in love and adoration to the eternal *logos,* thus a divine-human reality prior to the creation of this material world, affords a viable and insightful interpretation of the Jesus in John's gospel who can pray for the glory he had with the Father before the foundation of the world (John 17:5). Indeed Origen should be seen as an ecclesial theologian whose principal purpose was to maintain "the rule of faith." Most of his writings consist of commentaries and homilies based on the Scriptures. One of the most extensive is his thirty-two book commentary on John that Crouzel considers his "masterpiece." While he may seem attracted to Platonic and Stoic speculation, like Irenaeus he is more concerned to answer "pagan" critics from without and most importantly to maintain the continuity of faith from within the Church's tradition. His narrative quest may involve a move from this world to the world of the divine, a journey that employs a descending-ascending motif, i.e., the mystical ascent of the soul to God through the salvific power of the *logos,* but it is a journey he takes in company with John.[56]

It is not Origen but Arius who represents a speculation of the *logos* disengaged from the biblical story of Jesus. For Origen the eternal generation of the Son from the Father is key to maintaining their unity and distinction within the one divine life. This would be central to the orthodox understanding at Nicea. Yet his descending hierarchy from the *monad* to the *logos* to the soul to the body with the corresponding mediating functions of both *logos* and soul (as well as body) would appeal to Greek philosophical speculation on the *logos* as mediating between the One and the Many, participating in both but clearly subordinate and inferior to the absolute *monad.* Does this mean that the *logos* is truly and fully God or at best a kind of "second god" in strict subordination to the Father as "the only true God" (John 17:3)? If the *logos* is fully God, can there be any real distinction between Father and Son (modalism)? If a "second god," in what sense if any can the *logos* be called divine (subordinationism)? Arius, who was as much influenced by his teacher Lucian of Antioch as by the "elite" at Alexandria, pressed the logic of subordination to its ultimate conclusion. His views or modifications of the ideas of the semi-Arians would seem to have been the more popular and natural understanding in the Greek-speaking East. "The fact is that once the dispute between Arius and his bishop became more than local, the majority of Eastern church leaders felt greater sympathy for moderate Arian views than for the anti-Arian position adopted at the Council of Nicaea and backed by Athanasius and the West."[57]

The issue for Arius, as for many of his contemporaries, was monotheism, whether based in the Platonic notion of the *monad* or in the Hebrew idea of the one God (Deut 6:4). The Father alone is God in the strict sense *(monad).* The Son can be called divine but only as begotten *(gennētos)* by God and so created *(genētos:* the two words were understood to come to the same thing).

The Son is the perfect creature of God, begotten "before the ages" and so the one through whom God has created all things (Col 1:15-18a). Although Arius himself may have been a "biblical literalist"[58] his views did appeal to those interested in and influenced by Greek philosophical speculation on the *logos*. Unlike the Hebrew images of wisdom, word, spirit, etcetera that are intended to express the divine immanence (= God alive, active, present in this world) while maintaining the absoluteness of the divine transcendence, the Greek problem revolved around maintaining the divine transcendence over against any involvement in this world; hence the need for intermediary beings between God and the world. If it can be said in any realistic sense that "the Word became flesh" (John 1:14), the Word cannot be divine in the same way that the *monad* is divine.

Although individuals differed in their understanding of how to do so, the intent of both "Alexandrian" and "Antiochene" developments as a reaction to Arianism in the fourth century was to preserve the divinity of the *logos*. The "Alexandrian" tendency was to suppress the full humanity in favor of the hegemonic superiority of the *logos*. This is sometimes called *logos-sarx* christology. The extreme form of this came to be known as monophysitism, the absorption of the humanity into the one divine nature. The "Antiochene" tendency was to stress the full humanity and full divinity in such a way that it became difficult to know who was the acting subject in Jesus. This is sometimes called *logos-anthrōpos* christology. The extreme form of this came to be known as Nestorianism. It effectively separated the humanity and the divinity because of an inadequate understanding of the unity of the subject. While both these schools stress important truths—unity of subject on one side and fullness of divine and human natures on the other—neither was adequate for the orthodox affirmation of creedal faith. For this it was necessary to interpret the Gospel of John in the light of its primary concern, the salvation of human beings, rather than in the light of either Greek cosmological speculations on the *logos* or Hebrew wisdom speculations on the Word.[59] The reason is that John's view of Jesus as incarnate *logos* has radically transformed both understandings.

Athanasius, who became bishop of Alexandria three years after Nicea in 328, has been called "the beacon of Nicene orthodoxy."[60] For our purposes (to give a context for understanding the creedal confessions of Nicea and Constantinople I) it will suffice to mention three areas in which Athanasius' work has had and continues to have much influence. These are first, the primacy of soteriology over cosmological speculation; second, the strong differentiation of the inner divine life from the act of creation; and third, the effective use of John's gospel as a weapon against the Arians.

As does the Gospel of John, Athanasius gives primacy of place to the salvific role of the *logos*-Son over the creative and revelatory roles. He is credited with reviving Irenaeus's "exchange theory" (but without the motif of recapitulation) as a *theological* argument for both the full divinity and the full humanity of Jesus.[61] The argument for the divinity (against Arius) is that only the Creator (the divine Self as personally and immediately involved) can recreate us. The argument for the *full* humanity (that which in principle essentially constitutes our human nature: soul and body) is that only what is united with the divine is saved. This became a commonplace among the orthodox Fathers. In Athanasius, despite a certain obscurity about the soul of Christ, what is notable is the stress on the moment of the incarnation (John 1:14 is one of his major points of reference) with the consequent difficulty in assessing positively the human activity of Jesus from birth to death. The divine Son is active and the humanity passive. In fact the focus of his human life, after the incarnation, is upon his death as a sacrifice that redeems our debt of death. Yet what dies (rather than who) is his body that alone is capable of death and in which as his temple and instrument the incorruptible *logos* dwells (*De Incarnatione* 9). Thus the impression is given that he was born and died, but he never lived!—or at least his human life and activity *qua* human is of little importance.

Associated with this is the severing of the close connection Origen made between the divine nature and the divine creativity. Frances Young articulates the contrast well: "The fundamental conception with which Origen works is that the oneness of God and the multiplicity of creation is united in the Saviour." Origen seeks to link the One and the Many through the notion of mediation, the principal thrust of which is "the re-integration of all things and their restoration to their original perfection, through the union of God and his creation in the Mediator Christ." On the other hand: "For Athanasius, the Logos of God cannot be a mediating being, for he constitutes the transcendent Absolute embracing all absolutes, and is therefore truly one with God and on the divine side of a clear line between the Creator and creatures."[62] Athanasius does take from Origen the notion of human salvation as involving a restoration of the image of God through the saving power of the *logos*. "He became human that we might become divine" (*De Incarnatione* 54). But he makes a much sharper distinction between the inner divine life and the creative, revelatory, and salvific activity of God *ad extra*. Pollard sees their positions, both starting with the *logos* concept of John's Prologue, as proposing a radical alternative: cosmology or soteriology.

> Origen interprets the Prologue as cosmology, while Athanasius interprets it as a statement of the nature of God and of his activity towards mankind. They differ in their view of the relation of God to the world. For Origen, it belongs to God's nature to create; not only is the generation of the Logos an eternal process, but so also is the creation of spiritual beings. The life of God consists in the activity of creating. For Athanasius, on the other hand, God lives in himself, transcending his creatures of whom he has no need; "his life

surpasses them, and it is not the creation of the world but the begetting of the Logos which constitutes the divine life."[63]

While I would agree with Crouzel over against Pollard that for Origen the only "eternal" part of the creative process is the eternal generation of the Son in whom and through whom the divine creativity takes place, I think there is a significant difference between seeing the divine nature and life as inherently and inseparably creative and separating such creativity from the inner divine life where "God lives in himself, transcending his creatures of whom he has no need." Ironically, it is precisely this conceptual separation of the inner divine life ("immanent trinity") and the divine involvement in the creative process ("economic trinity") that has led subsequent theologians to very abstruse and abstract speculations on the inner workings of the triune divine life.

Finally, as the third point, all of this is heavily dependent on the exegesis of John's gospel.[64] As we have noted before, John's image of Jesus that conflates the *logos* of the Prologue with the Son of God in the rest of the gospel has had a transformative effect not only on the Hebrew understanding of Wisdom (or Word) but also, in the patristic period, on the Greek understanding of *logos* as a subordinate or second god. In other words if one takes John's gospel literally as affirming the concretely existing reality of Jesus, he has always existed *as the God-man* in a relationship of oneness yet distinctness. The Jesus who speaks in John is the incarnate *logos* (1:14), God the only Son (1:18). Paradoxically this image of Jesus is what the tradition denies by conceptually separating the inner life of God from the incarnate life. This came to its official, creedal expression at the councils of Nicea (325) and Constantinople I (381), to which we now turn.

2. A Multivalent Reading of Nicea and Constantinople I

Doxology, the praise of God on the basis of God's deeds, evokes the story of what God has done. For the professing community it establishes both continuity with the past, bringing it into the present and ensuring the future, and identity as a community united in the same faith by telling the same story. Thus as we have already asserted, while the primary function of a creed may be considered to be doxological this proves to be a multivalent function that includes a narrative of faith, a profession of faith, a celebration of faith, and an orthodox "test" of faith. All these readings imply a narrative quest but clearly priority is given to the narrative itself as the foundational reality. For Nicea and Constantinople I that narrative is inseparable from the Gospel of John. We will consider each of these readings in turn, principally at Nicea which marks the critical shift from earlier creeds for catechumens to creeds for bishops.

A narrative of faith. "So, then, the Fathers of Nicaea took up a baptismal creed—a fact which was thought in the fifth century to be an advantage which the first council enjoyed over against Chalcedon—and inserted into it their clauses directed against Arius. Their intention was to exclude any equivocation in the kerygma of the church and its creed."[65] But as Grillmeier also notes their primary intention was to remain faithful to "the rule of faith" as found primarily in the biblical witness. The creed of Nicea, like all the creeds, is a selective summary of Scripture that is intended to communicate the basic story centered around "the three 'characters'" (Young) but in a form determined by specific concerns or issues. The concern for monotheism is manifest in the very first phrase: "We believe in *one* God," but this one God is then described as Father, Son, and Holy Spirit. Both East and West affirm that the Father is almighty, maker of heaven and earth (cf. the "Apostles' Creed") but the Eastern creeds add: "maker of all things visible and invisible." This indicates the greater "cosmic" concern of the East, but it is much clearer in the affirmations about the eternal generation of the Son from the very being of the Father (absent in the Western creeds). We will return to this below under the rubric of a "test" of orthodoxy, but for now the most important issue is the close employment of the Gospel of John in the affirmations about the Son. The Holy Spirit is only mentioned at Nicea but is the main new development of Constantinople I.

"And in one Lord Jesus Christ, the Son of God" is notable for the use of the major christological titles from Scripture and for the absence of the term *logos*. "Son of God" is pervasive in the New Testament and certainly the central image of Jesus in John.[66] What follows is the sequence of phrases in the creed of Nicea and their biblical parallels.

(1) "Begotten from the Father": 1 John 5:18 has "begotten from God";

(2) "Uniquely"[67] or "only Son" *(monogenēs):* John 1:14; 1:18 has *monogenēs theos;* 3:16, 18 and 1 John 4:9 have *monogenēs huios;*

(3) "That is, from the very being *(ousia)* of the Father": *ousia* is nonbiblical, but the image of Jesus coming from God *(ek tou theou)* is found at John 8:42; 16:28; 1 John 5:18; cf. Heb 1:3 = "the exact imprint of God's very being" *(hypostasis);*

(4) "God from God": John 1:1; 20:28;

(5) "Light from Light": "God *(ho theos)* is light" at 1 John 1:5, but Jesus is called "the true light" at John 1:9 and "the light of the world" at John 8:12;

(6) "True God from true God": the Father is called "the only true God" at John 17:3 but the adjective "true" is frequently applied to Jesus, e.g., at John 1:9; 6:32; 15:1;

(7) "Begotten, not made": anti-Arian, but repeats (1) above;

(8) "Of the same being (or substance: *homoousion*) with the Father": anti-Arian, but controverted (see below);

(9) "Through whom all things were made": John 1:3;

(10) "Both those in heaven and those on earth": Col 1:16.

This concludes the first paragraph on the Son. It includes all the anti-Arian phrases we will analyze below but more importantly it draws almost exclusively on the language and thought of John. However the sequence, influenced as it is by anti-Arian concerns, is important. The creedal statement first secures the consubstantial oneness of the Son with the Father before it speaks of the Son's relation to creation (by conflating John 1:3 and Col 1:16). Only then, in the second paragraph, does it turn to the story of our salvation.

The focus on Jesus as our savior is the primary concern of the Western creeds. Nicea presents a very abbreviated version of it that is much more developed at Constantinople I. The language is much less Johannine and reflects more a general summary of the biblical story. The sequence is as follows.

(1) "Who for us humans *(anthrōpous)* and for our salvation": this is more Pauline than Johannine; the only occurrence of "salvation" in John is at 4:22;

(2) "Came down": John uses the word for "descending" *(katabainō)*, e.g., at 3:17; 5:7; 6:33; etc., but the idea of "coming down" *(katelthonta)* is certainly Johannine in spirit;

(3) "And was made flesh": while the verb *(sarkōthenta)* is non-biblical it certainly resonates with John 1:14;

(4) "Became human": another non-biblical word, but combined with "coming down" it is most important as emphasizing a full God-man christology as opposed to either the truncation of humanity *(logos-sarx)* or the truncation of divinity *(logos-anthrōpos);*

(5) "Suffered, and raised on the third day, and ascended into the heavens, coming to judge the living and the dead": the summary manner in which the creed states the rest of salvation history indicates where the true interest of this creed lies, but it also indicates the creedal impulse to tell the whole story, however summary and selective the manner of doing so. Hence however much this creed may give rise to subsequent speculation it is first and foremost a summary of the basic Christian story as found in Scripture.

A profession of faith and a celebration of faith. As we have seen, the origin of creeds lies in kerygmatic (oral proclamation) and didactic (catechesis) concerns, principally in the preparation of catechumens for baptism. Thus they were intended as professions of faith of local churches and as vehicles to communicate that faith, basically the story of salvation in Christ, to prospective members of that same community of faith. Their purpose was integrative: both to integrate individuals into the community through personal acceptance at baptism (first in interrogatory form and later in the declaratory form of the *redditio symboli*) and to celebrate the ongoing faith of the community in ritual worship (first at the celebration of baptism and eventually at the Eucharist). We have treated this already but it is important to remind ourselves of these more fundamental and popular functions as we make the transition to the understanding of creeds as "tests" of orthodoxy. As Kelly[68] notes, the creed formulated at Nicea was intended to address a particular crisis. It was not intended to supersede or replace the existing baptismal confessions of local churches. In fact he points to three "disconcerting phenomena" after 325: new creeds were formulated with no reference to Nicea; Athanasius seems to neglect Nicea, especially the *homoousios,* until ca. 350; and the West seems to be ignorant of Nicea until Hilary of Poitiers made it more widely known around 355. Some have proposed that Nicea was "a purely political formula," but while the influence of Constantine was important the "irreproachable faith of the 318 holy Fathers" (Chalcedon: *DS* 300) did become the ultimate test of orthodoxy. It is to that function of the creed that we now turn.

An orthodox "test" of faith. The creed of Nicea would never have been formulated had it not been for the Arian crisis coupled with Constantine's interest in the unity of the empire. The coupling is important. The concern for orthodoxy (= correct or true belief) goes back to Paul's conflicts with the communities at Corinth, Galatia, and elsewhere and is manifest in the emerging questions, especially surrounding Gnosticism, of the second and third centuries. Precedents for synodal actions regarding orthodoxy can be found in the acts of the two synods of Antioch of 268 and 325. Kelly calls the latter "the forerunner of all synodal creeds."[69] But the significance of Nicea is that it was the emperor who summoned the bishops to the council (as would be the case for all seven ecumenical councils from 325 to 787). Constantine was concerned to maintain the unity of the empire and he increasingly found that the unity of Christian faith could be a useful means to that end and its disunity a threat. He had found the structure of synods (comparable to the Roman senate) useful in the Donatist controversy and so in ongoing church-state relations. However, as Davis notes,

> One important element of procedure saved the relative autonomy of the bishops in doctrinal matters: the emperor though present never had the right to vote in the Senate. Constantine took an active part in its debates, but there is no evidence of his voting at the Council of Nicaea; he only confirmed the decisions of the bishops and made them binding under Roman law. Conciliar procedure thus modeled on that of the Senate enabled the Church to safeguard a certain independence in all matters of doctrine by encouraging the emperor to work through assemblies of bishops to achieve unity of belief.[70]

Thus Constantine by calling the council and then promulgating its decisions as binding in law ensured the truly ecumenical character of Nicea, that is, the universal authority of the bishops' decisions in a legal sense.[71]

The definition of orthodoxy is most clear in the four elements inserted into the original baptismal creed to refute the Arian views. And it is precisely these four elements, the first and last using non-biblical language and the second and third giving a particular interpretation of texts that might more naturally be understood otherwise, that have laid the foundations for what modern theology terms "dogma."[72] Following the enumeration of the sequence of phrases given above, the first that is anti-Arian (3) employs the non-biblical word *ousia* to insure the appropriate interpretation of "begotten" *(gennēthenta)* and "only begotten" *(monogenēs)*. The uniqueness of Jesus as the Son lies not simply in being begotten, but in being begotten from the very being or essence of the Father. "What we have here is a deliberately formulated counter-blast to the principal tenet of Arianism, that the Son had been created out of nothing and had no community of being with the Father. The Arians had been perfectly willing to acquiesce in the description 'begotten from the Father,' so long as they were at liberty to interpret it in a sense consistent with their theory of the Son's origin by a creative fiat of the Godhead."[73] The move beyond biblical language was made necessary by the ability of the Arians to give their own interpretation to every biblical text proposed, for example that Jesus "came from God" (John 8:42) or "from the Father" (John 16:28) or was "begotten from God" (1 John 5:18). The *ek tēs ousias tou patros* was meant to counter the Arian phrase *ek tou mē ontos* ("from that which was not").

The next anti-Arian phrase, "true God from true God" (6), is a direct refutation of one of the Arians' strongest biblical arguments, namely that Jesus himself refers to the Father as "the only true God" (John 17:3). The Arians could accept the affirmations "God from God" and "Light from Light," even "God from true God" insofar as the Son is "god" through the communication of grace. What Nicea has done is interpret John 17:3 in a nonrestrictive way. The third anti-Arian phrase, "begotten, not made" (7: *gennēthenta ou poiēthenta*) denies the Arian interpretation that "to be begotten" necessarily implies being created. Origen's understanding of the eternal generation of the Son is the necessary background here. Yet even in John the natural interpretation of *gennaō* is either literal birth (John 3:4, 6; 8:41; 9:2, 34; 16:21; 18:37) or metaphorical (John 1:13; 3:3-8 = those born "from above" or "from the Spirit"; cf. 1 John 2:29; 3:9; 4:7; 5:1, 4, and even v. 18!).

The most famous anti-Arian phrase, "of the same being (or substance) with the Father" (8), employed a word *(homoousios)* that was somewhat ambiguous and open to heterodox interpretations. But the main argument against it was that it, along with *ousia,* "was not to be found in Holy Scripture, and thus the tradition that the binding formulae contained in the Church's creeds should be expressed in inspired language was violated."[74] Nonetheless it was intended to communicate the orthodox interpretation of Scripture over against Arianism, that is, the full divinity of the Son as eternally and immutably sharing in the very being or substance of the Father by way of generation. That interpretation would have to be won, as Arianism especially through the offices of Eusebius of Nicomedia continued to influence Constantine in his desire to establish the unity of the empire. Imperial favor for Arianism would reach its height once Constantius, one of Constantine's sons, became sole emperor in 350. Athanasius about this time (350–354) wrote his defense of Nicea, *De decretis Nicaenae synodi,* but Arianism would not be defeated until Theodosius I outlawed it in 380.[75] However, while the arguments raged and imperial power shifted the principle of employing a creed as a test of orthodoxy for the whole Church was established and this creed along with that of Constantinople I would be recognized as such at the Council of Chalcedon in 451.

Before turning to the implications of orthodoxy we will take a brief look at the creed popularly known as the "Nicene Creed" but formulated at Constantinople in 381 and recognized at Chalcedon as "the faith of the 150 Fathers." Its importance is underlined by Kelly: "Of all existing creeds it is the only one for which ecumenicity, or universal acceptance, can be plausibly claimed. Unlike the purely Western Apostles' Creed, it was admitted as authoritative in East and West alike from 451 onwards, and it has retained that position, with one significant variation in its text, right down to the present day."[76] Although as Kelly argues it was a completely new text (of its 178 words, only 33 can be derived from Nicea) and followed the same pattern of taking an already existing creed and interpolating new elements into it, it certainly was concerned to ratify in a new creed the faith of Nicea. We will look briefly at some of the distinctive elements.

In reference to the Father, as noted above, it has in common with the West the phrase "maker of heaven and earth." With regard to the Son the first paragraph is the one that reaffirms Nicea but with some interesting changes. It places "only Son" *(ton monogenē)* in apposition to Son of God and follows that with "begotten from the Father before all ages." "Before all ages" is new but up to this point what is asserted would be an acceptable Arian position, especially since the creed omits the clarifying Nicene phrase "that is, from the very being *(ousia)* of the Father." However the creed goes on to repeat three anti-Arian phrases found in Nicea: "true God from true God," "begotten not made," "of the same substance *(homoousion)* with the Father" and then concludes the first paragraph with the Son's relation to creation: "through whom all things were created" (John 1:3, omitting the reference to Col 1:16).

The second paragraph on the Son is of interest because it gives a fuller account of the story of salvation, especially in reference to Jesus' birth and death: "having come down from the heavens and having become enfleshed from the Holy Spirit and from Mary the Virgin and having become human" reflects the tendency to tie the affirmations of the creed more concretely to their scriptural source. In this case the two rather abstract and non-biblical terms from Nicea *(sarkōthenta enanthrōpēsanta)* are interpreted with the interpolated words "from the Holy Spirit and from Mary the Virgin" which clearly call to mind the infancy narratives in Matthew and Luke. Similarly "crucified for us under Pontius Pilate" calls to mind the passion narratives and gives concrete, historical shape to the simple "having suffered" *(pathonta)* of Nicea. The specifications of "buried" and "according to the Scriptures" have the same effect in reference to "raised on the third day." The expansions "sitting on the right of the Father" and coming again "with glory" also give a fuller biblical picture. Finally "of whose kingdom there is no end" (Luke 1:33) is aimed at theologians like Marcellus of Ancyra (d. 374) and Photinus, his more radical disciple, "who taught that the Word is a transitory projection of an energy of the Father for the purpose of redemption and would be absorbed again into the Father after the final judgment."[77]

It was clearly the intent of Constantinople in formulating a new and fuller creed to give a more expanded biblical account of the story of salvation than was present in the creed of Nicea. This is also evident in the third section on the Holy Spirit, which avoids the term *homoousios* and stays close to biblical images. The great contribution of this creed is the definition of the divinity of the Holy Spirit against the "Macedonians" or "Spirit-fighters." The language is almost entirely biblical: "the Lord" = 2 Cor 3:17; "and Giver of life" = Rom 8: 2; 2 Cor 3:6; John 6:63; "proceeding from the Father" = 1 Cor 2:12; John 15:26; "who spoke through the prophets" = 2 Pet 1:21. The phrase just before this last is liturgical and pastoral: "who with the Father and the Son is co-worshipped and co-glorified" is the language of the Cappadocians, especially Basil the Great.[78] Thus the intent was to affirm the full divinity of the Holy Spirit in biblical and liturgical language that might provide an avenue of conciliation with those who saw the Spirit as subordinate to the Son, as the Son to the Father (the semi-Arian position). The final list of things to be believed in this last section is, as Kelly says, made up of "perfectly normal constituents of the third article of Eastern baptismal formularies," i.e., Church, baptism, remission of sins, and the life of the world to come.

How is it that this creed has become the only one universally accepted in the whole *oikumenē?* While it clearly functions as an orthodox "test" of faith as first recognized at Chalcedon, it is clear that it is a narrative of faith in a much fuller sense than Nicea (evidenced mainly by its fuller use of biblical images) and that, as such, it will prove most compatible and useful as a profession of faith at baptism and a celebration of faith at the Eucharist. Kelly argues that it was probably used for baptism at Constantinople soon after the council. In any event it was used for baptism in all the Eastern churches and even in some Western churches from the sixth century on. It was also used at the Eucharist (an innovation) to combat heresies (for example, in the East monophysite bishops used it to combat Chalcedon [!] in 511; in the West the third council of Toledo mandated it to combat Arianism in 589) but it was not accepted for such use in Rome until mandated by Henry II (1014) because Rome, it was said, had never been tainted by heresy, and also because Rome had a problem with the popular and widespread addition of *filioque* as tampering with the authorized text.[79] Thus the creed was clearly perceived in subsequent history as an orthodox "test" of faith, but as we move now to our concluding reflections on the implications of the creedal image of Jesus we must keep in mind these multivalent readings and the foundational priority of the story that the creed tells.

3. The Pre-Existent Son

If the image of Jesus as "Beloved Son" in Mark is the image of one who freely and obediently enters into the awesome power of death and so transforms its meaning, the image of Jesus in John is the image of one who eternally transcends the limitations of the flesh and the threatening power of death. "For this reason the Father loves me, because I lay down my life in order to take it up again. No one takes it from me, but I lay it down of my own accord. I have power to lay it down, and I have power to take it up again. I have received this command from my Father" (John 10:17-18, NRSV). The controlling image is Jesus' eternal relation to the Father. Yet he does lay down his life. Both Mark and John communicate the significance of Jesus by telling the story of his way to the cross. Mark focuses on that way as a way of suffering, rejection, humiliation, and abandonment. The paradox is that God is alive, active, present (symbolically "the mystery of the kingdom of God") precisely in the suffering and death of *this man* Jesus who is God's Son (Mark 15:29). John focuses on that way as a way of truth (revelation of the Father) that leads to eternal life (= salvation). As Jesus, "God the only Son" *(monogenēs theos),* is intimately and dynamically in the bosom of the Father (John 1:18: *ho ōn eis ton kolpon tou patros*), so we as disciples (symbolized by the "beloved disciple") are invited to find our rest in the bosom of Jesus (John 13:23: *en tō kolpō tou Iēsou*). But the way, whether the focus be on humiliation or on exaltation, is a way that cannot ignore or evade the concretely lived experience of the human and historical Jesus.

In a similar way the creedal statements of faith at Nicea and Constantinople I cannot be disengaged from the story that is their foundation and context of meaning. Even as "tests" of orthodoxy in the face of the Arian crisis they are not intended to develop a new faith but to be faithful to the biblical witness. They are, then, interpretations of Scripture and must always be understood and contextualized by the prior and foundational reality of Scripture, even as their particular non-biblical language is intended to engage the legitimate concerns of their own time and culture. Yet it must be recognized that the creed of Nicea, followed by Constantinople, made a crucial step that has greatly influenced subsequent theology and has given rise to much abstract conceptualization and speculation. In effect the creeds separate conceptually the eternal relation of Jesus to the Father from his concrete existence in time as mediator of God's creative, revelatory, and salvific activity. The image that embodies this move symbolically is that of the "pre-existent Son."

This means that "an epoch-making paradigm shift has taken place between scripture and Nicaea; the same message of Jesus as Son of God appears in a completely different 'thought system' or interpretative system."[80] It has led to a descending form of "christology from above" that puts more stress on Jesus' divinity than on his humanity. This in turn has led to a certain dichotomy between Jesus' humanity and his pre-existence as the divine Word that is not found in the biblical texts.

> This dichotomy in turn cuts the theology of the godhead loose from its Christian moorings in the human life, death and destiny of Jesus of Nazareth, the only genuine Christian source for our knowledge of divinity. If we do not find concrete meaning for the terms Father and Son in the life of Jesus, the terms will gradually be drained of all meaning as we drive them back and back and gradually lose them in the lithophanic eternity of pre-existence.[81]

A similar criticism could be leveled at contemporary "christologies from below" insofar as they would cut the human, historical life of Jesus loose from its Christian moorings in the very life of God. The biblical witness, especially John, does not know of pre-existence as a speculative theme isolated from or independent of the concrete reality of Jesus. Neither does it know of the concrete reality of Jesus isolated from or independent of the Father who sent him and the Spirit who anointed him (Mark 1:10-11; John 1:32-34). The Gospel of John, like the entire New Testament, was written in the light of resurrection faith. The affirmations of the creed are dependent on that fact. If we forget or ignore the centrality of the resurrection in all that we say about Jesus we are in danger of dichotomizing the root-metaphor of biblical faith, namely that the absolutely transcendent God is the same God who is alive, active, present (i.e., immanent) within human history and especially within the experience of life and death.[82] What we know of Jesus in his life, death, and resurrection reveals to us the truth about God as Father, Son, and Spirit, but with John we know this as mediated to us by the *incarnate logos,* that is, by one who is not separated or alienated from the universal human experience of a journey or story that begins in birth and ends in death.[83]

In Mark, Matthew, Luke, and John we have four accounts of this journey and each of them is distinctive. Yet each of them is first and foremost a story, a story that has metaphoric impact because each in its own way maintains the root metaphor of biblical faith, that is, the identification (A = B) of the absolutely transcendent God with the God who is completely and fully immanent. Indeed the paradox is that only a God who is absolutely transcendent can be fully immanent, completely present to the whole, without being reduced to any part of created reality. The genius of John was to bring this to its most

acute expression while maintaining the primary mode of divine self-communication, the story of a God who walks with God's people. Like every great
poetic artist he roots this metaphoric experience in the reality of existence: "I
am" (Exod 3:14; John 4:26; 6:35; 8:12, 24, 28, 58; 10:7, 9, 11; 11:25; 14:6;
15:1; 18:5).

In terms of narrative the *plot* is a temporal cause-effect sequence that
logically moves from pre-existence to incarnation to exaltation (on the
cross: John 3:14-15; 8:28; 12:32-33), but the *atmosphere* breaks all boundaries because the one who speaks exists in an eternal relation to the one
who sent him (John 8:14-19, 23-29, 42, 54-58). Jesus embodies the very
reality of God and thus breaks the narrative boundaries of time. Christ, in
the resurrection, has broken through all such boundaries and so John, aware
of the risen Jesus' eternal relation to the Father in the power of the Spirit,
places that eternal relationship in a narrative setting that moves from birth
to death.

> The pneumatic, present Christ is no longer limited by time but is released
> from the limits of time; he is no longer bound by time but free from time; he
> is no longer determined by a before, now and afterwards, but by a contem-
> poraneity which is above time. Existing in the mode of God, that of the
> Spirit, Jesus is now equally present to all times. So the origin of Johannine
> christology is not pre-existence, but the Easter experience of the pneumatic,
> present Christ, as was the case with the Synoptic Gospels, Paul and the
> Deutero-Paulines. The Gospel itself gives us indications that Easter plays the
> crucial role here: "His disciples did not understand this at first; but when
> Jesus was glorified, then they remembered that this had been written of him
> and had been done to him" (12.16).[84]

The *tone,* as with Mark, is that of the omniscient narrator who presents
God's point of view. As narrator John has carried the logic of resurrection
to its ultimate conclusion: the transcendent God appears as a *character* in
a literary form, the timeless in time, the spaceless in space, the inexpress-
ible in concrete images. The chief "character" or protagonist in the history
of Israel, YHWH, now emerges in the full Christian faith experience as
Father, Son, and Spirit. This is the same story that the creed celebrates in
its own poetic way. What, after all, is the creed based on if not a particular
interpretation of a biblical image in opposition to Arius's interpretation?
Subsequent theologizing, however legitimate its attempts at greater precision
in language and conceptualization, must never forget that its foundation
and context of meaning lie in God's primary mode of self-communication,
the telling of the story. With this proviso the image of the pre-existent Son
has great power in our lives because it calls us on a journey of ever deeper
interiority, a journey into the very life of God. "I will not leave you orphaned;
I am coming to you. In a little while the world will no longer see me, but

you will see me; because I live, you also will live. On that day you will know that I am in my Father, and you in me, and I in you" (John 14:18-20, NRSV).

Notes: Chapter Three

[1] James D. G. Dunn, *Christology in the Making. A New Testament Inquiry into the Origins of the Doctrine of the Incarnation* (Philadelphia: Westminster, 1980) 258 (emphasis in original).

[2] James M. Robinson, ed., *The Nag Hammadi Library* (San Francisco: Harper & Row, 1977).

[3] Frances M. Young, *The Making of the Creeds* (London and Philadelphia: SCM Press and Trinity Press International, 1991) 5–6.

[4] Ibid., 5, 12.

[5] J. N. D. Kelly, *Early Christian Creeds* (3rd ed. London: Longman, 1972) 24.

[6] Ibid., 10–11.

[7] Reginald Fuller, *The Foundations of New Testament Christology* (London: Collins, 1965) proposes a three-stage pattern of pre-existence/incarnation/exaltation to be found explicitly or implicitly in six christological hymns. Thus he says that the phrase "in the form of God" (Phil 2:6) "is to be interpreted not from *demûth* ("image") or *şelem* ("likeness") in Gen 1:26, but in the light of the parallel phrase in the immediate context, *einai isa theō,* "to be equal with God." To be in the "form" of God means to exist in a state of equality with God" (p. 208). He is rejecting the thesis of Oscar Cullmann, *The Christology of the New Testament* (rev. ed. Philadelphia: Westminster, 1963) 174–181, that Phil 2:6 must be interpreted in light of Gen 1:26. Cullmann, however, tries to establish pre-existence by associating "Son of Man" with Paul's notion of Christ as the "image of God" and "the last Adam": ". . . by the 'form' of God in which Jesus Christ existed at the very beginning is meant precisely the form of the Heavenly Man, who alone is the true image of God. . . . Because Christ is the Son of Man, he is the pre-existent Heavenly Man, the pre-existent pure image of God, the God-man already in his pre-existence" (p. 177). I would agree with Dunn, *Christology* 113ff., that the hymn is not concerned with temporal questions of pre-existence or prehistory but with the comparison and contrast of an archetypal choice: "The Philippian hymn does not intend to affirm that Jesus was as historical or as prehistorical as Adam, but that the *choice* confronting Christ was as *archetypal* and determinative for mankind as was Adam's; whether the choice was made by the pre-existent Christ or the historical Jesus is immaterial to the Philippian hymn" (p. 120, emphasis in original).

[8] Paul's focus is always upon the eschatological event of Jesus' death and resurrection. Ideas of pre-existence are imported from elsewhere and applied to Paul by interpreters, for example in the language of God sending his Son (Rom 8:3) or Christ though he was rich becoming poor for our sakes (2 Cor 8:9). Such language of itself does not bespeak pre-existence any more than the language of Christ as the wisdom of God (1 Cor 1:24, 30) or the spiritual rock (1 Cor 10:4) or the one in heaven to be brought down (Rom 10:6), all of which again interpret the death and resurrection of

Jesus. Even 1 Cor 8:6 can be understood in this context as an affirmation of the "one Lord Jesus Christ" not as a pre-existent being but as the one who "embodies the creative power of God" (Dunn, *Christology* 182).

⁹ Ibid., 212 (emphasis in original).

¹⁰ Raymond E. Brown, *The Semitic Background of the Term "Mystery" in the New Testament* (Philadelphia: Fortress, 1968). The prevalent notion of mystery in the New Testament is God's wisdom, or will, hidden in God, revealed in Christ, and announced in the gospel, that is, made known to the whole of creation through the Church.

¹¹ This follows the proposal of Raymond E. Brown, *The Gospel According to John I-XII* (New York: Doubleday, 1966) 3–37.

¹² Dunn, *Christology* 219. On pp. 164–165 Dunn affirms the wisdom background, citing among others Brown, *John* 519–524. The following are the hymns to Wisdom in the Jewish Scriptures usually considered to provide this wisdom background: Job 28:23-28; Proverbs 1–9, especially 8:22-31; Bar 3:9–4:4; Sirach 1; 4:11-19; 6:18-31; 14:20–15:10; 24:3-22; Wis 6:12–11:1, plus the apocryphal 1 Enoch 42.

¹³ T. E. Pollard, *Johannine Christology and the Early Church* (New York: Cambridge University Press, 1970) 14–15.

¹⁴ Dunn, *Christology* 243 (emphasis in original).

¹⁵ Pollard, *Johannine Christology* 13. On p. 7 he cites Floyd V. Filson to the same effect.

¹⁶ Dunn, *Christology* 244–245.

¹⁷ Ibid., 248–250, 256–258.

¹⁸ Ibid., 250.

¹⁹ C. H. Dodd, *The Interpretation of the Fourth Gospel* (New York: Cambridge University Press, 1953) 262; cited by Dunn, *Christology* 57.

²⁰ Berard Marthaler, "Introduction: Forms and Functions of the Ancient Creeds," in *The Creed. The Apostolic Faith in Contemporary Theology* (rev. ed. Mystic, Conn.: Twenty-Third Publications, 1993) 1–15. Ronald Modras, "The Functions and Limitations of Creedal Statements," in Hans Küng and Jürgen Moltmann, eds., *An Ecumenical Confession of Faith? Concilium* 118 (New York: Seabury, 1979) 36–44, lists the following functions: confessional, doxological, catechetical, kerygmatic, apologetic, and integrative (into the community of faith).

²¹ This is the question of ch. 2, "Creeds and Baptism," in Kelly, *Creeds* 30–61.

²² Ibid., 50.

²³ Ibid., 51.

²⁴ Joseph Cardinal Ratzinger, *Introduction to Christianity* (San Francisco: Ignatius Press, 1990 [original English translation 1969]) 62. Kelly, *Creeds* 52–61, discusses various possible meanings in the first three centuries. Ratzinger's view fits the later practice of *traditio symboli* and *redditio symboli* of declaratory creeds.

²⁵ Kelly, *Creeds* 75.

²⁶ Ibid., 76–81.

²⁷ Ibid., 88.

²⁸ Ibid., 89.

²⁹ Ibid., 94–99.

³⁰ Ibid., 131.

³¹ Ibid., 166: "The clearest proof of the authenticity of the Old Roman Creed lies in the way in which, while some of its clauses have received a sharper definition and others

a heightened emphasis from the controversial atmosphere of the second century, they one and all hark back to the primitive kerygma of the apostolic age."

[32] Ibid., 194.

[33] For example, Marcellus of Ancyra at Rome in 340 (ibid., 102–104) and Eusebius of Caesarea at Nicea in 325 (ibid., 181–183, 220–226). For a summary of other examples see ibid., 206–207.

[34] Marthaler, *Creed* 10.

[35] Kelly, *Creeds* 255.

[36] Henri Crouzel, *Origen. The Life and Thought of the First Great Theologian* (San Francisco: Harper & Row, 1989).

[37] Young, *Creeds* xi.

[38] Ibid., 16–25 for a good summary of Gnosticism and Irenaeus's response.

[39] Pollard, *Johannine* 40. For a good review of the use of John in the second century see ch. 2, "The Development of Christology in the Second Century," 23–48.

[40] Ibid., 49. The summary of the third century is indebted to ch. 3, "Christology in the Third Century," 49–116.

[41] Ibid., 50. Pollard continues: "Valentinus and Basilides, founders of the two leading gnostic systems, were Alexandrians, while as early as the first century a brilliant attempt had been made by Philo Judaeus to reconcile or harmonise Judaism with current philosophy. In the first half of the third century Neo-Platonism was to be developed there at the very time when Clement and Origen were trying to achieve a reconciliation of the church's faith with Middle-Platonism and Alexandrian Judaism."

[42] Ibid., 75.

[43] Aloys Grillmeier, *Christ in Christian Tradition* (2nd ed. Atlanta: John Knox Press, 1975) 141, makes this point strongly: "Origen, however, is not primarily interested in the ontological constitution of Christ. He sees Christ above all as mediator of the mystical union of the soul with the hidden God, as mediator between church and God, and all this from the viewpoint of the union in knowledge and in love. Logos, soul of Christ, the humanity of the Lord, are seen in the service of that movement in which God goes out from himself and returns to himself." Also Crouzel, *Origen* 99: "The only kind of knowledge that really interests Origen is the kind that he calls 'mystical': *mystikos* being the adjective that corresponds to *mysterion,* mystery." And further: "The analysis of the act of knowing shows it to consist of an activity of an order decidedly mystical: knowledge is a vision or a direct contact, it is participation in its object, better still it is union, 'mingling' with its object, and love. In the state of blessedness, we repeat, the saved will have been taken, as it were, into the Son, yet without pantheism, for they will see God with the very eyes of the Son" (p. 116). In ch. 7 (pp. 121–133) he develops "the mystical themes" in Origen.

[44] *De Princ., pref.,* 2, from Origen, *On First Principles,* edited and translated by G. W. Butterworth (Harper Torchbooks, 1966 [London: S.P.C.K., 1936]) 2. Origen follows this in parr. 3–9 with a statement of faith that affirms the basic story of Jesus in creedal form yet recognizes that many things still stand in need of investigation by those with "the higher gifts of the Spirit" (par. 3), especially wisdom.

[45] Grillmeier, *Christ* 146.

[46] Piet Smulders, *The Fathers on Christology* (De Pere, Wis.: St. Norbert Abbey Press, 1968) 44.

[47] *De Princ.* 1.4.4, translated in Origen, *On First Principles* 42. In *De Princ.* 4.9.2 Origen makes it clear that rational or spiritual beings "were made in the beginning, were made when before they did not exist. . . ." Cf. Crouzel, *Origen* 189–190 for a strong refutation of Methodius' interpretation of Origen as teaching that "pre-existent intellects" were coeternal with God.

[48] Crouzel, *Origen* 210.

[49] Ibid., 211 cites certain passages from *De Princ.* 1.5.5; 1.6.2; 1.8.4; 2.9.6; 4.2.7 as suggesting that "some intelligences escaped the fall."

[50] *De Princ.* 2.6.3, translated in Richard A. Norris, Jr., *The Christological Controversy* (Philadelphia: Fortress Press, 1980) 76. Origen employs the analogy of an iron kept always in a fire to explain the union of the soul with the *logos*. "In this fashion, therefore, that soul which, like the iron in the fire, has been abidingly placed in the Logos, in Wisdom, in God, is God in all its acting, all its feeling, and all its understanding. Consequently, it cannot be called changeable or mutable. It possesses unchangeability because it is unceasingly fired by its unity with God's Logos." *De Princ.* 2.6.6 in ibid., 79.

[51] On the "trichotomic scheme" of Origen's anthropology and the corresponding participation in the image of God see Crouzel, *Origen* 89–98. He concludes: "The theology of the image of God, at the root of the possibility of knowing God, is the foundation of the whole of Origen's mysticism" (p. 98).

[52] Ibid., 104–112.

[53] Ibid., 189–190.

[54] Smulders, *Fathers* 43.

[55] Ibid., 44: "Origen's synthesis forms the starting point of the later christological debates. All the errors as well as all the great orthodox teachers will claim to find support in him." Smulders goes on (pp. 48–52) to enumerate elements in Origen's thought that because of a lack of later technical terminology on Origen's part or a failure on the part of both opponents and advocates to maintain the delicate balance and genius of his whole *opus* could and did lead to the heretical positions of Arius (d. 336), Eusebius of Caesarea (d. 339), Marcellus of Ancyra (d. 374), Apollinaris of Laodicea (d. 390), as well as later monophysitism and Nestorianism. Crouzel is concerned throughout his book to defend Origen against later use of his work and condemnation of it as an anachronistic failure to consider the totality of his work and the qualifications he himself makes concerning views that are more open to speculation. For a convenient anthology of Origen's writings with a good introduction see Hans Urs von Balthasar, *Origen. Spirit and Fire. A Thematic Anthology of His Writings,* translated by Robert J. Daly (Washington, D.C.: The Catholic University of America Press, 1984). The translator also offers a helpful foreword and epilogue.

[56] Pollard, *Johannine Christology* 98, maintains against Maurice Wiles *(The Spiritual Gospel)* and Henri Crouzel *(Theologie de l'image de Dieu)* that in spite of his "methodological principle" of interpreting the *logos* by the Son and not vice versa Origen in fact "is unable to transpose his interpretation of the gospel [of John] from the philosophical key into the more specifically biblical and religious key." But is his use of *logos* and his "doctrine of the eternal [!] pre-existence of spiritual beings" (p. 99) as nonbiblical as Pollard assumes? As interpreted by Crouzel both would seem to have good foundation in the Hebrew wisdom tradition and in the image of Jesus as presented in John's gospel.

[57] Young, *Creeds* 45.

[58] Ibid., 46.

[59] Pollard, *Johannine Christology* 316–318, outlines four different methods for interpreting John: (1) Arius: "metaphysical monotheism" that stresses cosmology over soteriology; selective use of Scripture, including John; (2) Marcellus of Ancyra: "biblical monotheism" that stresses salvation history, the Word as expressive of God's creative and revelatory power, but fails to appreciate John's distinction between Son and Father; (3) Eusebius of Caesarea: Greek subordinationism that stresses the Son as a "second God" or "demigod" who as subordinate mediates between God and the world: a "cosmological function, derived by reading into the Prologue of St. John presuppositions which have come from extrabiblical sources . . ." (p. 317); (4) Pseudo-Athanasius (the author of *IV Oratio contra Arianos:* Athanasius or his disciple?): soteriology, i.e., "the knowledge that God has acted in Jesus Christ for the salvation of mankind is central and regulative for every thought concerning his relation to the godhead on the one hand, and to humanity on the other" (p. 318). This is the adequate and true interpretation of John already in the West and would become the common faith of East and West at Nicea.

[60] Smulders, *Fathers* 71: "For almost half a century [after the definition of Nicea] Athanasius, who became bishop of Alexandria in 328, had to lead an uninterrupted and often lonely struggle against the united power of the Arians and other opponents of Nicaea. In this controversy, Athanasius became the beacon of Nicene orthodoxy and for succeeding generations her oracle. The various ways in which he treated of the doctrine of redemption and Christology in this debate thus came to exercise a widespread influence."

[61] Ibid., 72–79 and the texts cited there from *De Incarnatione* (before Nicea?), *Contra Arianos,* and the *Tomus ad Antiochenos* (362). Grillmeier, *Christ* 308–328, discusses in detail the problem of the soul of Christ in Athanasius. From a Stoic-Alexandrian notion of the *logos* as the "force from which all life and all movement comes" it would be natural to understand the *logos* as supplanting the soul psychologically: "where the original itself appears with all its power, the copy, with its secondary and derived power, must at least surrender its function, even if it does not give place altogether. Athanasius probably assigned to the human soul as such a substance of its own, and maintained its immortality. When he considers the being of Christ, however, his attention is immediately caught by the Logos and his relationship to the body of Christ. This relationship is regarded as being quite analogous to the other, that of Logos-world, soul-body" (p. 311). Thus what is decisive for salvation (activity) is assigned to the *logos* and both soul and body become necessary only in the passive sense of what is assumed by the *logos*.

[62] Young, *Creeds* 84, 85, 86.

[63] Pollard, *Johannine Christology* 131. The citation is from Louis Bouyer, *L'incarnation et l'église-corps du Christ dans la théologie de Saint Athanase* (Paris, 1943) 48.

[64] Pollard in two very fine chapters, ch. 7. "Athanasius' Refutation of the Arians" and ch. 8, "The Controversy over Marcellus of Ancyra," which includes Marcellus' refutation of the Arians, Eusebius of Caesarea's refutation of Marcellus, and Pseudo-Athanasius' *(IV Oratio contra Arianos)* refutation of Marcellus, shows effectively how central was exegesis of John to these disputes. He has high praise for Pseudo-Athanasius as having grasped the Johannine paradoxes of oneness and distinctness.

[65] Grillmeier, *Christ* 266. The "318 Fathers" had the examples of the synods at Antioch in 268 (against Paul of Samosata) and 325 (against Arius) that also took an existing creed and incorporated new elements into it. Grillmeier notes that there is still no agreement whether the baptismal creed used at Nicea was the creed of Caesarea presented at the council by Eusebius or a creed of Jerusalem or a creed from elsewhere in Palestine or Syria. Kelly, *Creeds* 229, concludes: "We are left with the meagre conclusion that N consists of some local baptismal creed, of Syro-Palestinian provenance, into which the Nicene keywords were somewhat awkwardly interpolated." It seems likely that many bishops presented the confessions of faith of their own local churches.

[66] Pollard, *Johannine Christology* 177. He gives a list of the Johannine texts.

[67] "By placing *monogenē* after 'begotten from the Father', and by following it immediately with the explanatory phrase 'that is from the essence of the Father' the Creed emphasises that the Son's uniqueness lies in his relation to the Father, not simply as 'only-*begotten* Son' but as the Son who alone is begotten 'from the essence of the Father.'" Hence "uniquely" is a better translation than "the traditional, but erroneous, phrase 'only-begotten.'" Ibid., 179 (emphasis in original).

[68] Kelly, *Creeds* 254–262, for the whole discussion of "After Nicaea."

[69] Ibid., 210–211. Leo Donald Davis, *The First Seven Ecumenical Councils (325-787). Their History and Theology* (Wilmington, Del.: Michael Glazier, 1987) 55: "Under Ossius' direction, the bishops introduced an innovation in ecclesiastical practice: they issued a creedal statement. Hitherto, creeds were for catechumens; this one was designed for bishops."

[70] Davis, *The First Seven* 57. For the reference to Constantine's involvement in the Donatist controversy, see ibid., 30–31.

[71] Kelly, *Creeds* 205–207, notes that the transition from local to conciliar creeds means that the motive of testing orthodoxy became primary, whereas before it was exceptional to the baptismal purpose. "The creed of Nicaea was the first formula to be published by an ecumenical synod: consequently it was the first which could claim universal authority in a legal sense. Its anathemas excommunicating, in the name of the Catholic Church, those who dissented from its definitions sounded a new note in the history of the Church as an institution" (p. 207). Young, *Creeds* 13, summarizes the shift as follows: "Bishops had met in Council before to deal with members of their own number who failed to teach what their consensus demanded. Excommunication had been used before, and false teachers anathematized. The new elements lay in using a creed to define orthodoxy, and in the availability of imperial power to enforce the decisions of the Council and provide the bishops with greater effectiveness in exercising their authority on earth."

[72] Davis, *The First Seven* 69–71, analyzes the "real significance" of Nicea in accordance with Bernard Lonergan, *The Way to Nicaea* (Philadelphia: Westminster, 1976): "Bernard Lonergan appears to me to have best described the real meaning and importance of the Council. He argues that within the dialectic of the pre-Nicaean speculation about the Trinity there was operative a twofold movement which reached its goal at Nicaea. Trinitarian and Christological doctrines were evolving explicitly, but implicitly the very notion of dogma was evolving as well" (p. 69). The key is the move from the multivalent character of Scripture to a single intellectual truth as foundational. This is a move, subjectively, from undifferentiated to differentiated consciousness, on the assumption that dogmas are clearer than Scripture. While the assertions of

truth in creedal statements are important, my concern is to maintain that they can possibly be distorted if disengaged from the scriptural story that is their foundation and context of meaning.

[73] Kelly, *Creeds* 235.

[74] Ibid., 238–239. Kelly lists four objections: (1) the term connotes a materialistic conception of God; (2) it connotes Sabellianism (modalism); (3) it was already condemned at the Synod of Antioch in 268 against Paul of Samosata; (4) it is non-scriptural. Pollard, *Johannine Christology,* in the "Appendix. The *word* Homoousios" (pp. 320–322), sees the only real objection at the time of Nicea to be the scriptural one. Numbers 2 and 3 came much later. Before Nicea, Arius objected to the term because it was used by the Manichees in a materialistic sense (No. 1).

[75] For a readable summary of this history see Davis, *The First Seven* 75–79, 81–119.

[76] Kelly, *Creeds* 296. The significant variation is the addition of *filioque* in the West, an addition that was widespread by the beginning of the ninth century but was never included in the creed at Rome until 1014. For a contemporary appraisal of the creed by various authors see Küng and Moltmann, eds., *An Ecumenical Confession of Faith?*

[77] Davis, *The First Seven* 124.

[78] Kelly, *Creeds* 341–343 provides the biblical references as well as references to Basil and Athanasius. The other Cappadocians besides Basil the Great are Gregory Nazianzus and Gregory of Nyssa.

[79] Ibid., 344–367 for historical arguments on the development of both baptismal and eucharistic use of the creed, as well as the insertion of *filioque* in the West.

[80] Karl-Josef Kuschel, *Born Before All Time? The Dispute over Christ's Origin* (New York: Crossroad, 1992) 503. This book is an interesting and encyclopedic exploration of the question. His basic orientation is expressed as follows: "It is my conviction that the hiatus between exegesis and dogmatics, about which there are so many complaints, can be overcome only if dogmatics understands itself as consistent exegesis" (p. 489). See my review in *Horizons* 21/1 (Spring 1994) 197–198.

[81] James P. Mackey, "The Holy Spirit: Relativizing the Divergent Approaches of East and West," *The Irish Theological Quarterly* "Special Issue to Commemorate the Sixteenth Centenary of the First Council of Constantinople [381]" 48/3, 4 (1981) 266. In the same issue Joseph S. O'Leary, "Has the Nicene Creed Become Inaccessible?" 240–255 emphasizes the *logos* as event and story known in the movement of the Spirit: "If there is a Logos in history we know it only as Pneuma, blowing in and out of the edifices of the past, with a critical, prophetic breath that can tear down and build up. Thus we can have concepts of eternity, but no eternal concepts, because the transcendent can be adequately thought of only in constant adjustment to the movement of the Spirit" (p. 251). Both authors thus represent the greater stress in contemporary theology on a biblically based historical consciousness that takes account of cultural shifts.

[82] For a fuller account see my article, "Revelation as Metaphoric Process," *TS* 47 (1986) 388–411. "The great discovery of Israel is that the absolutely transcendent God—from whom there is no flight, for He is Creator of all—is also immanent, intimately involved in and profoundly affected by the historical journey and suffering of His chosen people. . . . God seems to be saying to Moses and the people [at Exod 3:14]: 'You will only discover who or what I am (my Name) in the actual unfolding of our story together, i.e. as I journey with you in your many trials'. YHWH is the God of their fathers who is known in the story of the Exodus through all generations" (p. 396).

[83] Bernard J. Cooke, *The Distancing of God. The Ambiguity of Symbol in History and Theology* (Minneapolis: Fortress, 1990) precisely critiques the Christian tradition, especially the Platonic notion of participation as an ascent away from this world to God, as alienating us from ordinary, everyday human experience and so distancing us from God. "The link of Christians to God through grace and revelation came to be considered in abstract terms of ontological participation rather than in terms of experienced personal relationship" (p. 266). Elizabeth A. Johnson, *She Who Is. The Mystery of God in Feminist Theological Discourse* (New York: Crossroad, 1992) seeks to show that trinitarian orthodoxy is rooted in fidelity to experience. She offers a striking instance from female experience that should affect the exclusive use of male metaphors: "Such exclusive use of male metaphors is a blatant anomaly because to be so structured that you have room inside yourself for another to dwell is quintessentially a female experience. To have another actually living and moving and having being in yourself is likewise the province of women. So too is the experience of contraction as a condition for bringing others to life in their own integrity" (p. 234).

[84] Kuschel, *Born Before all Time* 385–386.

CHAPTER 4

A Systematic Image: "The Incarnate Word" in the *Summa Theologiae* of Thomas Aquinas

"Alone upon the earth, and lifted and liberated from all the wheels and whirlpools of the earth, stands up the faith of St. Thomas; weighted and balanced indeed with more than Oriental metaphysics and more than Pagan pomp and pageantry; but vitally and vividly alone in declaring that life is a living story, with a great beginning and a great close; rooted in the primeval joy of God and finding its fruition in the final happiness of humanity; opening with the colossal chorus in which the sons of God shouted for joy, and ending in that mystical comradeship, shown in a shadowy fashion in those ancient words that move like an archaic dance; 'For His delight is with the sons of men.'"[1] The eloquent words of G.K. Chesterton appear to support our thesis, yet it is this chapter more than any other that will bring into focus the question of which is prior: system or story. The title of this chapter may be misleading because Thomas had "an extreme suspicion of systems" insofar as the wonder that the simple reality of existing *(esse)* evokes leads into inexhaustible knowability.[2]

Karl Rahner can conclude an essay on Thomas's understanding of truth as follows: *"Adoro te devote latens Deitas, quae sub his figuris latitas.* Everything is a parable—*figura*—of God, who is constantly being unveiled yet at the same time constantly concealed in the parable."[3]

For Thomas one could say that all drama, both human and divine, originates within the divine life that according to Christian faith is a triune life of dynamic relationships. Yet he is clearly interested in employing the tools of philosophy, especially those provided by *"the* philosopher" Aristotle, in order to offer as coherent and systematic an explanation of Christian faith as is possible for the human mind. Faith and reason were never separated in the work of Thomas. Indeed, as Josef Pieper points out, "It may, then, be said with complete accuracy that this formal unity of philosophy and theology is the structural principle of St. Thomas's *summas,* especially his *Summa theo-logica.*"[4] But does the fact that Thomas "always speaks in a formal way" (Cajetan) and so seems to banish metaphorical language in favor of clarity, precision, and "austere conciseness"[5] mean that for him primacy must be given to system over story?

To explore this question we will once again follow our threefold rubric of the world behind the text, the world of the text, and the world before the text. As in the previous chapter the first engages the dynamics of "narrative quest" in Thomas's own life: (1) the foundational move occasioned by the new "science" of the recently rediscovered Aristotle with a corresponding crisis over "Augustinism"; (2) the basic motivation of the drive for sure knowledge *(scientia)* propelled by the academic professionalism of the university; and (3) the decisive orientation as a passionate quest for the final integration of faith and reason in the science of theology. In the light of this context we will then engage in a limited and focused reading of a text of Thomas, namely the *Tertia Pars* of the *Summa theologiae.* Finally we will conclude with a reflection upon "the incarnate Word" as the key integrating image of the whole *Summa* and the image that has had greatest impact on subsequent generations.

1. From *Sapientia* (Augustine) to *Scientia* (Aristotle)

The fact that Thomas could embrace and "baptize" Aristotle, indeed could truly raise him from the dead, is proved in three ways according to Chesterton: by "his huge and solid orthodoxy" that could support so much that seemed unorthodox; by "the new Christian *motive"* of humility, that is, beginning always with the lowly and the earthly; and, supporting all, by the central Christian *truth* of the incarnation, i.e., of the definitive affirmation of the human body, its senses and its connection to the material universe. "When once Christ had risen, it was inevitable that Aristotle should rise again."[6] Add to this the "general tone and temper of Aquinas . . . that *positive* position of his mind, which is filled and soaked as with sunshine with the warmth of the wonder of created things,"[7] and one begins to get some understanding of the extraordinary achievement that he represents.

To capture this achievement as a narrative quest we will consider three factors that contributed to the writing of the *Summa theologiae:* first the importance of "authorities" *(auctoritates),* which include the Scriptures, the creeds and councils, the Church fathers, especially Augustine and pseudo-Dionysius, and Aristotle; second the cultural conditions of his time, with special focus on the academic professionalism of the university; and finally the amazing power of the human intellect in its quest for truth as pure being, that is, as whole and integrated—the goal of all true *scientia.*

The importance of "authorities." Thomas Aquinas (1224/25–1274) has almost from the moment of his death been known as *doctor communis*. What made him such is surely "the assimilative powers which excluded nothing, omitted nothing, which insisted that everything that is, 'belongs'—for example, both the Bible and the metaphysics of Aristotle."[8] Thomas's ability to demonstrate the inherent compatibility between two forces—the radical evangelical perfection of voluntary poverty represented by the new mendicant orders (Franciscans and Dominicans) and the urge to make use of the work of Aristotle to investigate reality on the level of "pure natural philosophy"—is the main theme of Josef Pieper's very fine book on Aquinas. But Thomas drew on many authoritative sources from a rich Christian heritage and while the Bible and Aristotle are key to understanding him such figures as Augustine, John Damascene, Boethius, Pseudo-Dionysius, and Peter Lombard, not to mention the creeds and councils, were ever present to and influential in his thinking and writing. We will look first at the importance of Scripture.

"To approach the flowering of medieval theology in the thirteenth century through nothing more than a study of the great summas, the *questiones disputatae,* and the commentaries on Boethius or Pseudo-Dionysius is automatically to neglect a key element of medieval scholasticism, the extensive commentary on the Bible."[9] As with Origen and the other great Fathers of the Church, Scripture is the heart and soul of all sound theology—a tradition recently reaffirmed at Vatican II. This was no less true in the time of Thomas. For him personally there were two reasons for this: his membership in the Dominican order and his position as a "regent master in theology" at the University of Paris. The ideal of the newly founded mendicant orders was a return to the gospel, the living of an evangelically inspired life as the "poor of Christ." As M. D. Chenu strongly emphasizes, "it was not the rediscovery of the Aristotelian texts that brought about the life-giving sap, but rather the reawakening of a faith that fed on sacred texts."[10] This corresponded well with Thomas's vocation as a *magister in theologia* which meant first and foremost that one was a *magister in sacra pagina*.[11] The basic duties of a *magister* were *legere, disputare,* and *praedicare:* that is, the first and foundational step was to *read* (lecture) an authoritative text, then to engage questions that might arise from the text and resolve them, and finally to preach, normally in the form of university sermons. Clearly such duties revolved around the Scriptures as the primary text.

Thomas's commentaries on the Bible merit a study in themselves but for our purposes it is more important to note how the Scriptures are integrated into the *Summa theologiae.* "It is true that in the history of Thomism the *Summa theologiae* has monopolized everyone's attention and commentaries; but therein precisely lies a grave problem, and to understand and solve it, the first condition is to avoid obliterating the fact that the *Summa* is embedded in an evangelical soil."[12] It is also true, as Chenu carefully notes, that "scholastic exegesis" represents a gradual evolution from a pastoral reading of the sacred text to a scientific discipline. While respecting the figurative and allegorical tradition of patristic exegesis, Thomas was concerned to offer a literal, or historical, interpretation that would serve the science of theological explanation (cf. *S.T.* I, q. 1, a. 10, ad 1um). The objective was not so much spiritual edification as intellectual insight. This includes taking the *text* seriously in terms of its own internal order, adhering to the letter *(littera)* of the text, emphasizing definitions of terms and their categories, searching constantly for causes *(rationes),* and passing spontaneously from exegesis (*expositio* of the biblical text) to theology (*quaestiones* that the text raises).[13] The move was from *lectio divina* to *doctrina sacra,* but for Thomas especially in the *Summa theologiae* his theology remains a "biblical theology."[14]

Closely connected to the authority of Scripture, and indeed its authoritative interpretation, is Church tradition, especially that embodied in ecumenical councils and creeds. As James Weisheipl observes, "The turning point in the development of Aquinas's theology was his labor on the continuous gloss on the four Gospels. Eschmann even calls it a turning point in 'the history of Catholic dogma.'"[15] This gloss came to be known as the *Catena aurea* ("golden chain") and consists of citations from the Church Fathers (twenty-two Latin Fathers and fifty-seven Greek Fathers). It was particularly the research into Greek theological sources, including conciliar documents, that marked the turning point for Aquinas and for subsequent theology. Thomas discovered the acts and proceedings of the first five ecumenical councils (from Nicea in 325 to Constantinople II in 553) some time between 1260 and 1263 and he was the first among medieval scholastics to employ them verbatim, which he did in the *Catena aurea* (1262–67) and in the *Summa theologiae* (1266–73).[16] Prior to this discovery the principal sources for such knowledge included Boethius (d. ca. 524) and John Damascene (d. 749).

There are two important implications for Thomas's theological method in this turn to conciliar texts. The first is that verbatim citations allowed him to use their authority as conclusive proof in an argument, e.g., *S.T.* III, q. 2, a. 1, *sed contra* employs Chalcedon to assert two natures (against Eutyches) and a. 2, *sed contra* to assert one person (against Nestorius). Second, while Thomas recognizes the centrality of the Nicene–Constantinopolitan creed his emphasis on the texts of Ephesus, Chalcedon, and Constantinople II indicates his recognition of a certain progress in doctrine from the implicit to the explicit (which can be done either in a council or by the Pope alone[17]) and his own preference for more linguistic clarity via philosophical argumentation (as in Cyril of Alexandria and Pope Leo I).

Of the individual authors Thomas cites, two stand out as the most influential on his thinking. Both (Dionysius and Augustine) were influenced in turn by neo-Platonic thought. "Of all the Greek theologians, the one who most influenced Thomas and indeed all of his contemporaries was Pseudo-Dionysius the Areopagite, a man purporting to be the disciple of St. Paul mentioned in the Acts of the Apostles 17:34."[18] In his commentaries Thomas is concerned to elicit the literal meaning of the text that he understands to contain the intention of the author. Yet he pursues such sources primarily for the sake of the truth, as is manifest in the use of authorities in his more personal works such as the *Summa*. In the case of Dionysius this is done almost in spite of the great distance between the two approaches. "From the standpoint of his literal commentary . . . we must note the internal resistance he experienced, to the point of expressing it bluntly (a thing he rarely does), as regards the style, the way of thinking, in brief the mentality of the Areopagite—a man for whom symbolism is the key to the understanding of the universe, and therefore the privileged form of thought."[19]

Of all the Latin theologians none can be considered more influential than the great Augustine (d. 430). The increasing importance of the newly discovered texts of Aristotle led to a crisis over the nature and use of authorities from the past, particularly the "Christian" Augustine vis-à-vis the "pagan" Aristotle. "The fact is that in the West the name of Augustine stood for the highest and purest type of Christianity, just as his spirit represented what was the most religious in the basic sense of that term."[20] Augustine embodied what was deepest and best in Christianity both intellectually and spiritually and was perceived to ensure the "Latin" character of theology over against a "Greek" theological influence that was increasingly rejected (an irony since Augustine was so heavily influenced by Platonic thought himself). The influence of Augustine is best seen in Peter Lombard's *Liber sententiarum,* "a modest but clever compilation of Augustinian thoughts and texts—from which, however, the barbs had been eliminated—with the result that they were pressed into service to the benefit of a classical theology."[21] What Thomas took from Augustine was a passionate focus on God as the source and goal of all human wisdom *(sapientia)*. But as with all of his sources he integrated the Augustinian heritage into his own original vision of things, a vision that owed a great debt to Aristotle.

"It was the rise of Aristotelianism, a sensational event in the rediscovery of Antiquity, that was to be the determining factor, both material and spiritual, of the development of the work of Saint Thomas."[22] As is well known, Aristotle's work on logic had been influential in the schools since Boethius but in the twelfth century Arabic translations from the Greek, which were then translated into Latin, gave access to Aristotle's works on natural philosophy, metaphysics, ethics, the human soul, and more. As Pieper remarks, "This meant a good deal more than the addition of a few books to the curriculum. Suddenly a totally new, rounded, coherent view of the world was pitted against another more or less coherent traditional view."[23] What Thomas took from Aristotle was that quality of mind that Chesterton characterizes as "humility" (closeness to the earth) and that enables us to recognize in him "a man of science" *(scientia)*. "His Aristotelianism simply meant that the study of the humblest fact will lead to the study of the highest truth."[24] Or as Pieper eloquently puts it,

> We find Thomas giving us ever new shades of the fundamental Aristotelian position. Aristotle, he says, refuses to withdraw from the realities present to the senses, refuses to be distracted from those things that are evident to the eyes. And Thomas himself emphatically accepted this principle. Here was the decisive turn to concreteness, to the empirical reality of the world. Those things evident to the senses, which can now be seen, heard, tasted, smelled, and touched, are to be taken as realities in their own right, standing on their own ground—not as mere reflections, shadows, not as mere symbols of something else, something invisible, spiritual, otherworldly. The visible, and sight itself, the perceptions of the senses and the power of perception—all that is now affirmed and acknowledged to be valid in itself. Which means that the physical world of material reality, *within* man himself also, the body, the senses and what the senses grasp—is all to be taken seriously in a manner hitherto unknown.[25]

If the influence of the patristic period can be said to stretch to the end of the twelfth century and to be characterized as "spiritualistic symbolism," that is, as the Platonic tendency to move away from the material things of natural reality to a more spiritual level of reality (e.g., eternal forms), the thirteenth century as embodied in Thomas and his use of Aristotle represented a turn to "the concrete reality beneath this world of symbols," to a "hearty worldliness" that was in essence a *theological* move as an acceptance and affirmation of "things as God created them" in their intrinsic goodness. "In all the work of St. Thomas the world of positive creation is perpetually present."[26] In a word, as Chesterton states emphatically, he saved the *human* element in Christian theology.

Thomas's intent was always to remain true to the gospel and his use of Aristotle was a means to do so, but this was not evident to many of his contemporaries. The crisis over Aristotle was really twofold: on the one hand "Latin Averroism" was a crisis over the correct interpretation and use of Aristotle; on the other hand "Scholastic Augustinism" was a crisis over the legitimacy of using the "pagan" Aristotle at all. "Probably there would not have been a thirteenth-century Augustinism if there had not developed on the scene a Latin Averroism derived from Aristotle. There certainly would not have been a thirteenth-century Augustinism if Thomas had not used the pagan Aristotle in the service of his theology."[27]

"Latin Averroism" refers to the use made of the commentaries of Averroes on Aristotle by certain members of the arts faculty at the University of Paris, particularly Siger of Brabant. Chesterton characterizes Thomas's famous

reply to Siger in 1270 as "his one moment of personal passion." More fundamental than the critical doctrines involved (the questions of the unicity of the
intellect, free will, divine providence, and the eternity of the world) was the
dualistic assumption that one could totally separate scientific and theological
truth. "St. Thomas was willing to allow the one truth to be approached by two
paths, precisely *because* he was sure there was only one truth."[28] He insisted
that the arguments must be based on "the reasons and statements of the
philosophers themselves" and it was most probably to supply an adequate
interpretation of Aristotle for teachers and students, as Weisheipl observes,
that he embarked on his extensive commentaries on Aristotle, all of which
were written between 1268 and 1273.

The other side of the debate, which Weisheipl calls "Scholastic Augustinism," questioned whether Aristotle should be used at all, especially in theology. This resistance was motivated principally by the Franciscan masters
(especially Bonaventure and John Pecham) who "claimed a tradition of orthodoxy loyal to the real or imagined authority of Augustine."[29] While this
issue was not resolved during his lifetime it is a sign of Thomas's great genius
that he could incorporate both Aristotle and Augustine into his writings "as
witnesses for the truth which revealed itself through them. . . ."[30] Thomas
examines the *texts* of both, as well as his other authorities, in order that the
truth might prevail, but the one text he treats differently because of its
supreme authority is the word of God as set forth in Scripture.

This brief summary of the importance of Thomas's authorities and the
crisis that arose because of the use of Aristotle cannot be understood apart
from the cultural conditions of his time. If the foundational move for Thomas
was the use of the recently rediscovered Aristotle to afford fresh and creative
interpretations of the tradition, the basic motivation was the drive for sure
knowledge *(scientia)*. The matrix that would sustain this drive as a concretely
lived experience was the academic professionalism of the university.

The academic professionalism of the university. "The drama that went on
in his mind and in his religious life, and on which the fate of Christian
thought hung in the balance, had its causes and produced its effects right
at the University—a university, it is true, in which all the ingredients of a civilization in full bloom were massed together, to which, moreover, Christian
faith had, deliberately and authoritatively, committed its doctrine and spirit.
It is, then, right at the University that Saint Thomas found, not only the technical conditions for drawing up his work, not only the polemic occasions for
turning it out, but also the enveloping and penetrating spiritual milieu needed
for it."[31] To understand how this was so we need to consider three factors: the
cultural conditions that gave rise to the university, the professionalism that
this promoted, and the importance of the mendicant orders for its success. As
to the first Robert Schreiter summarizes three commonly observed cultural

conditions that enabled theology to develop as *scientia:* the rediscovery of Roman law in the West, the rise of towns and cities, and the development of the western university.

The rediscovery of Roman law, dated to Gratian in the eleventh century, gave the kind of order to society that could allow the emergence of cities and is reflected in Anselm's work on redemption that saw order as an ideal for society. The rise of towns and cities evidences a shift from a more feudal, rural economy to a more bureaucratic, complex urban economy that carried with it the emergence of the guilds as marking a greater division of labor. This latter helped the university to develop insofar as the teachers of this more complex society, organized now into guilds, had moved from rural monasteries to urban centers. "The development of the Western university is perhaps the most significant factor for theology as sure knowledge. It provided a new environment and offered the protection of the guild to the magistri."[32] For Thomas personally this cultural shift was experienced when he left the feudally constituted abbey of Monte Cassino in 1239 (his father had left him there as an oblate in 1230) and entered into the university life at Naples, a life that would be the principal context for his work until his death.

The new "schoolmen" were now centered in such great cities as Paris, Bologna, Oxford, and Cologne but for Thomas no doubt Paris was "his natural home," as Chenu puts it. Established around 1200, the University of Paris became the intellectual center of the West. There were certainly a variety of reasons for this, but one stands out: ". . . the University of Paris became the most representative of the medieval universities because, among other things, it was founded in the purest and most radical way upon those branches of knowledge which are 'universal' by their own nature: theology and philosophy."[33] These universities stood in the current of urban life and intended to reach out and embrace the whole *(universitas)* of Christian thought. The most important new factor was academic professionalism signaled by the doctrinal authority of the *magistri.* As many authors note, the universities were not incorporated into the ecclesiastical hierarchy but formed a relatively autonomous "guild" of teachers and students concerned with the whole of the sciences (theology, philosophy ["arts"], medicine, and law). This does not mean that they were totally independent of ecclesial control since they were founded to serve the Church, but that they had a certain independence and exemption from older structures represented by rural monks and bishops. They had a new authoritative status ("office") based on their academic training, their intellectual astuteness in resolving disputed questions, and their sense of corporateness within the university setting.

> Intellectual corporation of the city, the university was at the same time an official body of the Church, with its own proper "office," and with rights and liberties that it enjoyed pursuant to charters granted by authority of the

collective Christianity it meant to serve. . . . Quite obviously, it was the faculty of theology that formed the soul of the University and that supplied the *raison d'etre* of the Church's jurisdiction. Here, again, was something new: that a body of authorized professors invested with a *licentia docendi* should be given in the Church charge and authority of expounding the revealed truths of faith.[34]

Thomas first went to Paris in 1245 to study under Albert the Great. He was probably there from 1245 to 1248 and thence moved with Albert to Cologne. He returned in 1252 to prepare himself to lecture on the *Sentences* of Peter Lombard (1252–56) after which he became a master in theology and taught there (1256–59). This first period saw him embroiled in the anti-mendicant controversy (1252–57). He returned for a second Parisian regency (1269–72) probably because of new attacks on the mendicants but he immediately encountered the controversy over "Latin Averroism." We will return to the mendicant controversy but first a word on Thomas himself as the most striking embodiment of academic professionalism.

"There are numerous tokens by which Thomas considered the spirit of the *disputatio* equivalent to the spirit of the university itself."[35] That spirit, as Josef Pieper indicates, was one of conversation or dialogue, close to the ideal of the Platonic dialogue, in which one truly listens to one's interlocutor, repeating an opposing position before responding to it, that is, seeking to make one's own the position to be refuted, and above all respecting the dignity of the interlocutor. Why? Because we are on a quest for the truth, a quest that is a communal process of learning involving both teacher and student, a quest in which gratitude for the honesty of fellow seekers and readiness to participate in the quest by taking a stand and answering for it are paramount. The genius of Thomas surely revolves around his ability to formulate and focus upon the question *(quaestio)*. He even appears to have invented the *quaestio de quolibet* as a way of engaging in free and open discussion on anything whatsoever.[36] He certainly engaged in its development, apparently with enthusiasm, and this reveals his spirit of free and open inquiry since the *magister* could no longer control the agenda.

The importance of the *quaestio* lies precisely in the *quest* for truth. The structure and language of this quest embraced the ideals of clarity and consistency. The structure or "procedures of exposition"[37] included the *lectio,* the *quaestio,* the *disputatio,* and (in the *summas*) the *articulus.* The *lectio* refers to the reading of written texts considered to be authoritative. Laboring over such texts and interpreting them with the use of grammatical analysis and dialectical reasoning was at the very heart of the professionalism of the university *qua scientia.* This entailed in the time of Thomas a veritable rebirth of ancient learning. Thomas himself was very anxious to have the best available texts and was frustrated when unable to do so. His mastery even when the best texts were not available is evident in his commentaries on Aristotle that transformed the intellectual outlook of the West. "Thomas had an infallible scent for the real meaning of Aristotle, even when the text before him was unclear or distorted."[38] Such reading inevitably gives rise to the *quaestio,* which refers to the use of reason to call into question the subject-matter, for example whether God exists, in order to provide an explanation through intelligible causes *(rationes).* "In these very terms Saint Thomas, in his famous fourth *Quodlibet* (a. 18), defined the working status of the theologian, as of one whose task it is, once he has taken possession of the datum of revelation, to build up into a 'science' the intelligibility of his faith."[39] In the *summas* the focus on the *quaestio* was far more important than maintaining a thesis as in later Scholasticism. From the *quaestio* evolves the *disputatio,* which was the university exercise *par excellence.* It has been described as "academic jousts that passionately absorbed the contemporary mind."[40] Thomas was literally a master in this regard as only the master could give the final *determinatio,* or authoritative formulation, of a disputed question. The written form of these *quaestiones disputatae* was the report of the master's *determinatio.*

While we will look at the structure of the *Summa theologiae* later, it is important to note that the *articulus* developed in the collections of disputed questions and in the *summas* reflects the spirit of the *disputatio.* Thomas simplifies it to the four steps of formulating a question, addressing opinions, offering a systematic answer, and responding to objections. The language that served this drive for clarity, consistency, and conciseness was medieval Latin, which was the living language of worship honed to be a perfect tool for sure knowledge, an *instrumentum conjunctum* to Thomas's extraordinary and questing mind. "Thomas speaks the Latin of the university, of the schools, of scholasticism at its apogee. His was the language of teaching, and hence a language directed primarily toward clarification, toward lucidity, toward preventing misunderstandings."[41]

Thus we see embodied in Thomas the truest and best ideal of medieval *scientia,* a full-time, trained professional *(magister)* whose intellectual discipline embraced the spiritual wisdom of the ecclesial tradition and the truth of new knowledge opened up by the greatest human minds whether Christian or "pagan." The audience became the students and colleagues in the university setting but the goal is well expressed in the Dominican slogan *contemplata aliis tradere,* which was accomplished through study, teaching, and preaching. Understanding Thomas's break with Monte Cassino in 1239 and his joining the Dominican Friars in 1244 despite the opposition of his family is integral to comprehending the success of his quest. The word "mendicant" contained the roots of controversy, for it was the intention of both Francis of Assisi and Dominic de Gúzman that their friars exercise "evangelical poverty" by going out into the world to preach and teach and at the same time to earn their bread by begging. Through papal protection they also had a new kind of freedom as they were "exempt" from the control of the old order (local bishops and monks) in their preaching and care of souls. In addition it was of great concern to Dominic that his friars have an excellent education especially in philosophy and theology so as to be able to engage the intellectual questions and disputes of the day. Within such a group Thomas found the ideal environment for the development and exercise of his talents. The anti-mendicant controversies, the first concerning teaching positions at the University of Paris (1252–57) and the second attacking even more forcefully the very notion of mendicant orders (during Thomas's second Parisian regency of 1269–72),[42] surely engaged Thomas's talents for disputation as well as his passion for the way of life he had chosen. But it was the latter that insured and sustained his remarkable career as an academic professional, a man of true *scientia*.

The quest for truth as pure being. We have characterized the decisive orientation of Thomas's quest as logical and grammatical *consistency*. This is true, but as such it is a quest for what utterly transcends us and yet captivates us by its beauty: being itself, that which is the cause of all things and so grounds the scientific certitude of explanatory systems. Here faith and reason, metaphorical and literal speech, while distinct, intertwine in the search for and expression of truth. Thomas inherited from the twelfth century a certain tension between "a striking recovery of appreciation for the reality of the sensible world" and a continuing "symbolist mentality" based on a somewhat confused mix of the diverse symbolic understandings of Augustine and Pseudo-Dionysius, each in turn influenced by neo-Platonic notions of participation as ascent to the real world of the divine.[43] His genius was to employ the metaphysics of Aristotle to offer a new and creative interpretation that would affirm the reality and goodness of this world as inseparably grounded in the divine causality. The amazing power of the human intellect is that knowledge of this world brings with it knowledge of the divine.

"The most marvelous of all the things a being can do is: *to be.*"[44] It is a commonplace to say that Thomas's whole theology hinges on the ineluctable insight that in God essence and existence are identical whereas in creatures they are really distinct. God *is* God's actuality or, in a quite literal sense, God is real precisely as active *(actus purus)*. Since God confers existence by creating, we can say metaphorically with Scripture that we breathe the very breath of God (Gen 2:7) and literally with Thomas that God is in all things most intimately *(S.T.* I, q. 8, a. 1) and thus constitutes each and every created reality as not only good but *holy*. "Platonic thinking makes much of the conception of an ascent to God by way of the hierarchic ladder of essences, of a gradual approximation to the immutable Being of God. Thomas, on the other hand, says: Every existing thing—whether alive or not, whether material or spiritual, whether perfected or wretched, and in fact whether good or evil—everything that has existence, confronts us in the most direct way with the primal reality of God."[45]

As we emphasized in Chapter One what roots or grounds genuine metaphor and the true poet's mastery of it is the insight that what is, *is* or, as Chesterton puts it, that "eggs are eggs." This humble fact leads to the highest truth. The root metaphor of the Hebrew Scriptures expressed as Abraham's faith at Gen 14:22 is that YHWH is God Most High *(El-Elyōn),* which in turn is based on the central revelatory text of Exod 3:14: *ᶜehyeh ᶜasher ᶜehyeh,* which can be rather literally translated as "I will be who (or what) I will be." Rather than a name this seems to be an invitation to journey together in order to discover who or what this God of Abraham, Isaac, and Jacob really is. It is in telling the story of the Exodus that we have a context to interpret the significance of the metaphor, namely that the absolutely transcendent and free God *is* immanent (alive, active, present) in the midst of God's people. Yet it is a natural and necessary move to see this metaphor rooted in the mystery of existence. Thus if God has a name in any proper sense it would be *egō eimi ho ōn,* which is the Septuagint translation of Exod 3:14 and means "I am the One who is." Thomas's theological enterprise is centered around just such literal, being-centered interpretation of revelation. And it is just this insight into reality *(ens)* that, in turn, makes all great art possible. As Chesterton puts it in his droll way: "He very specially possessed the philosophy that inspires poetry; as he did so largely inspire Dante's poetry. And poetry without philosophy has only inspiration or, in vulgar language, only wind."[46]

Thus the passionate focus on God carries with it an equally passionate focus on the goodness and holiness of creation. Faith and reason, theology and philosophy are so conjoined in Thomas that while one may distinguish them one should never separate them as later Scholasticism tended to do. What makes Thomas attractive is his appreciation, indeed reverence, for this world in all its concrete particularity and his common sense with regard to the ordinary use of language. The goal of grammatical and logical consistency is achieved through close attention to experience. Yet the central and decisive experience is the one only God can give, the divine self-communication in revelation that is received in faith. This begins in creation, deepens in covenant, and culminates in incarnation. It is in the person of Jesus, the Word Incarnate, that the fullness of Wisdom is revealed.

2. A Reading of the *Summa Theologiae, Tertia Pars*

The *Summa theologiae* of Thomas is more like a model in Ian Barbour's terms, that is, a systematically developed reflection on the living myths that communities transmit, in this case the Christian community centered in Rome. "A model represents the enduring structural components which myths dramatize in narrative form. . . . [Models] are neither literal pictures of reality nor useful fictions. They lead to conceptually formulated, systematic, coherent, religious beliefs which can be critically analyzed and evaluated."[47] Yet we propose here once again, with Thomas's *Summa* as the most acute test of our thesis, that all our human attempts at systematic conceptualization and formulation have their originating ground in stories that have metaphoric impact and must constantly return to these stories as the only adequate context for meaning.

Thomas started the *Summa theologiae* in 1267 and continued to work on it until his death in 1274. He thus left it unfinished at *Tertia Pars,* q. 90, in the middle of the treatise on penance. He wanted to write a work that was encyclopedic in its completeness, synthetic in its organization, and reflective of "sound educational method" (*secundum ordinem disciplinae:* I, *prologus*). It was written for "beginners" (*incipientes*) who are frequently hampered, partly by the multiplication of useless questions, articles, and arguments, partly by the complexities of textual commentaries and disputed questions, and partly by a repetitiousness that leads to boredom and confusion. Thus his purpose is to offer as clear and concise an account of the science of theology (*sacra doctrina*) as possible. This raises three issues that we will touch on briefly: the "scientific" character of the *Summa,* the order or plan (structure) employed, and the style and tone of the author.

In a fine section entitled "Sacred History and the *Ordo Disciplinae"* Chenu articulates the basic problem: "to transform a sacred history into an organized science."[48] Revelation as it comes to us through Scripture is primarily a sacred narrative that includes historical and so contingent events. Science as it comes to us through Aristotelian categories is primarily an organized knowledge of causes that are metaphysical and so necessary principles of being. "If there is a discipline that the Aristotelian classification of the sciences excludes from its orbit, surely it is history!"[49] In the very first question of the *Summa* Thomas addresses the issue of *sacra doctrina,* its necessity in relation to philosophical studies (that is, for salvation [a. 1]), its character and greater worth as a science (aa. 2–5), its simple superiority as wisdom because of its knowledge of the highest cause, God (a. 6), its subject matter that again is God (a. 7), its foundational premise based on the authority of God's revelation as known in Scripture (a. 8), and how the language of that Scripture is to be interpreted (aa. 9–10). But the central insight that gives a magisterial order to Thomas's teaching in the *Summa* is his employment of the neo-Platonic schema of emanation and return *(exitus et reditus)* shorn of its necessary emanationism and located in the context of divine and human freedom. "Thus is broken asunder what appears to be a paradox—that of inserting and expounding a sacred history within a representation of the universe which, more than any other one, right at its source, rules out all history."[50]

Chenu among others has focused on this insight, but Romanus Cessario offers a modified version of it that is helpful in understanding the design or plan of the *Summa* as a whole. Many have compared the *Summa* to a cathedral, as Chenu notes, but that may be too static. Certainly the parts in relation to the whole must be seen as arranged "in a circular diagram, in a ring returning back upon itself: the outpouring of reality out of the divine Source, which by necessity contains within its initial stages the state of being on the way back to the same Source, with the Creator Who in Christ has become one with the Creation revealing Himself as the Way of this return."[51] This is comparable to Mark's concentric or ring structure and like Mark, Thomas's *Summa* can perhaps be imaged not so much as a cathedral or even a tapestry but as a fugue that repeats key themes as it moves toward a dramatic climax. That dramatic climax is the way back to God that may always have existed in principle but was only realized and so assured in the gracious, free, contingent coming of the incarnate Word.

Cessario along with Chenu and others poses the question of theological method as already mentioned; that is, how can the Aristotelian canon of scientific knowing as articulated in the *Analytica Posteriora,* i.e., of universal and necessary knowledge through causes, be serviceable in giving an account of salvation history as articulated in the biblical accounts: a divine–human dialogue that is "contingent, free, gracious, and historical"?[52] Cessario's modification of the *exitus–reditus* schema is to see it "not as a singular circular movement (thus, Chenu) but rather in terms of concentric circles, each possessed of its own degree of necessity."[53] There are three necessities that are interlocking and as such unfold the divine drama that is the origin and goal of all drama and every story. The structure is as follows:

(1) *Prima Pars,* qq. 2–43. The first circle is of divine necessity: the intra-Trinitarian drama of the Father uttering a Word and together with that Word breathing forth "the force of loving recoil," the personal bond of Love.

(2) *Prima Pars,* qq. 44–119 + *Prima Secundae,* qq. 1–114 + *Secunda Secundae,* qq. 1–189. The second circle is of hypothetical necessity: given the fact that God has freely chosen to create the world as it is the works of the Trinity *ad extra* (nature) find their intrinsic intelligibility as constituted by God in their dynamic return to their divine Source (the beatific vision).

(3) *Tertia Pars,* qq. 1–59 + qq. 60–??. The third circle is of a more tenuous necessity, viz., salvific: the fact that God has freely chosen to recreate or restore the image of God by the incarnation of the Son (= Word) confers "the necessity of an unsurpassable exemplar and final causality upon salvation-history as enacted in the personal history of Jesus of Nazareth" who comes forth and returns as the perfect image of the Father. "Jesus comes forth and returns as the perfect and consummate historical agent in a personal history; he realizes human nature in its historically unsurpassable concrete shape; he enacts human nature as a perfect history."

Thus the foundational reality upon which everything depends is the eternal drama of the divine *perichoresis* of Father, Son, and Spirit. As Thomas himself has outlined the *Summa* the clear and simple division treats first of God as one, as triune, and as creator *(Prima Pars)*, then of human nature in its journey toward God *(Secunda Pars)*, and finally of Christ and the sacraments as the full realization of human nature and the only way back to God *(Tertia Pars)*. But I think Cessario has a valid insight that underlying this surface structure is the dynamic of God's own inner life. The divine necessity of the intra-Trinitarian *perichoresis* is what gives intelligibility and consistency to nature and to salvation history. Thus in the *Prima Pars* the very essence of God, which is "to be" (qq. 2–26), is as given in revelation an internally dynamic "to-be-related" (qq. 27–43).[54] This should not be understood as a mere speculation about God's inner being but as a dramatic vision of the dynamism of all things as related to God (I, q. 1, a. 7). Everything comes from God and everything returns to God who alone is identical with God's existence *qua* relational. Thus it may be more appropriate to characterize the *Summa* as theocentric rather than christocentric, but this would be an artificial distinction insofar as what constitutes Christ is primarily his eternal relation to the Father.

The tone of the *Summa,* then, is to view everything *sub ratione Dei.* "All things are treated in theology *[sacra doctrina]* from the viewpoint of God *[sub ratione Dei]*, either because they are God himself or because they have a relationship *[ordinem]* to God as to their origin and end. Whence it follows that God is truly the subject-matter of this science" (I, q. 1, a. 7).[55] Everything is framed between God as efficient cause *(Prima Pars)* and God as final cause *(Secunda Pars),* with the incarnate Word as the exemplar and instrumental cause *(Tertia Pars)*. But if the proper subject matter of theology is God in God's very reality, the method and style must be consistent with the limitations of our human condition. According to Thomas theology uses metaphorical or symbolic language not for delight, as in poetry, but "on account of their necessity and usefulness" (I, q. 1, a. 9, ad 1um).[56] At the same time theology seeks always the literal or historical sense of the Scriptures that their author, God, intended, ". . . for nothing necessary for faith is contained under the spiritual sense [= allegorical, tropological, anagogical] that is not openly conveyed through the literal sense elsewhere" (I, q. 1, a. 10, ad 1um). The literal sense (ad 2um) includes history (facts), etiology (causes), and analogy (which makes a judgment based on what is non-contradictory in diverse passages).

Speaking analogously *(analogice loquendo)* for Thomas is a matter of judgment as to what is appropriate, consistent, and logical within the parameters of normal language use. As David Burrell notes, instead of understanding as a kind of seeing involving concept formation (as in John Duns Scotus), Thomas's approach is more akin to an ongoing inquiry using examples and so involving dialectic, discovery, and recognition. Thomas offers no theory of analogical predication but rather assumes the common experience that "our

ordinary talk trades on many kinds of similarities."[57] If God is outside any
genus and unknowable as such he insists that God must be improperly knowable
(ana-logos). His focus is on the dynamics of *esse*. Since "to be" or "to exist"
does not behave like an ordinary predicate the mind is led on from the senses
to some understanding of the divine in the power of judgment. This kind of
judgment is not contained in a concept. A theological use of analogy focuses
"on the manner in which whatever is said can be cast so as not to mislead."[58]
For example, *"to be God is to be"* is the only way to speak properly of God
which, according to Burrell, is to say what cannot be said, that is, that God is
not a thing. Yet what cannot be said can be shown inadequately but truly when
we use analogous terms. Thus we say that God is good, just, creative, forgiving,
loving, compassionate, and so on based on our human experience of such
realities. Such language is metaphorical. To repeat a conclusion from Chapter
One, independent, literal speech about God, for example that God is real and
active, derives from embodied-selves-in-a-world who continually probe the
richness and potential of human experience in metaphorical language based
on analogy. Thomas does not deny this, for the literal sense is that intended by
the author, that in Scripture will most often be metaphorical or parabolic or
ironic (cf. I, q. 13). His concern for literal interpretation is set in contradis-
tinction to the spiritual senses of Scripture because he seeks precision and
clarity for the sake of argumentation. Still he knows in the *Tertia Pars* that
whatever necessary conclusions he may draw, however logical and consistent
they may be, come from what is freely given in Christ. When he turns to that free
gift he speaks of fittingness or appropriateness. This calls for a discriminating
quality of mind that elicits a texture of assent conditioned by the limitations
of human judgment.

   At this point it would be impossible to read Thomas's work as a narrative
as in the other chapters. His concern is to address in the form of questions
those issues for human understanding that arise from the story. Yet the story
remains the originating context for the questions and the final arbiter of their
meaning. Does Thomas remain true to the story? I would say in essence, yes;
in particulars, it depends on which story is being told—that of Mark or that of
the Creed based in John. Thomas is the spiritual heir of Athanasius who, as
was developed in the preceding chapter, focuses on the eternal begetting of the
logos within the divine life and sees salvation as a restoration of the image of
God through the saving power of the *logos*.[59] The structure of the *Tertia Pars*
is indicative of how much Thomas has been influenced by the development of
the Nicene–Constantinopolitan Creed and its subsequent interpretation at
Ephesus and Chalcedon, not to mention the neo-Chalcedonian stress on the
divinity that resulted in Constantinople II (553).

   "The transition from the *IIa* to the *IIIa Pars* is a passage from the order of
the necessary to the order of the historical, from an account of structures to
the actual story of God's gifts."[60] Contrary to those who object that Christ only

appears now and perhaps as an afterthought or appendix, I would hold that the key image of "the incarnate Word" is intended to sublate the entire preceding discussion of the divine and the human into the one reality that alone can integrate and explain everything in the prior articles. The procedure and its corresponding structure remain grounded in the divine necessity of efficient, final, and exemplary causality, however contingently and freely given in its actuation (III, qq. 1–26), and moves thence to the actual account of salvation history in Scripture (III, qq. 27–59). Thus Scripture is integrated into the christological scheme but only after a number of related questions have been addressed that may seem overly speculative to us but were integral to the concerns of Thomas and his contemporaries. With Cessario one could say in more personalist terms that Thomas concentrates first on the dignity of Christ's person and then on the intensity of his love as manifest in his life, death, and resurrection. "Aquinas does not expound the details of Christ's life simply for the purpose of presenting a complete narration of his earthly mission. The Scriptures themselves accomplish that commission. Aquinas, on the other hand, performs the task of a theologian."[61]

This task in the *Tertia Pars* is both historical and speculative. "His theology reaches its most concrete and existential level, as his thinking becomes dominated by the facts witnessed to by the Gospel and the tradition of Church belief and practice. At the same time the *Tertia Pars* is profoundly speculative, because it calls into play and synthesizes the theological, metaphysical, anthropological and ethical principles that have been elaborated earlier in the *Summa.*"[62] The section on christology (qq. 1–59) can be outlined as follows: (1) qq. 1–3: the union of the incarnate Word; (2) qq. 4–15: the humanity of the incarnate Word, which can be subdivided into a consideration of the human nature assumed (qq. 4–6) and the contingent features (both perfections and defects) of the human nature assumed (qq. 7–15); (3) qq. 16–26: the consequences of the union, both logically necessary (qq. 16–17) and revealed (qq. 18–26); (4) qq. 27–37: the mother of Christ and his childhood; (5) qq. 38–45: the public life of Christ; (6) qq. 46–52: the passion and death of Christ; (7) qq. 53–59: the resurrection of Christ. According to the *prologus* of the *Tertia Pars* the treatment of the Savior himself (qq. 1–59) was to be followed by a treatment of the sacraments as the means of our salvation (which Thomas completed up to q. 90), and of our final end, immortal life, which we attain through Christ by our own resurrection (never written).

In sum the *Tertia Pars* is concerned with the consummation of the whole theological enterprise *(ad consummationem totius theologici negotii)* by considering the Savior of all in his own person and in his benefits for the human race. As Cessario rightly points out the pivotal point in the christological section proper, short as it is, comes at q. 26 on Christ as mediator. Thomas implicitly invokes John 14:6 ("I am the way, the truth, and the life") in the *prologus:* ". . . our Savior . . . demonstrated the way of truth to us in himself . . ." (. . . *Salvator noster . . . viam veritatis nobis in seipso demonstravit . . .).* The first half (qq. 1–26) explores how he is the way of truth *in himself;* the second (qq. 27–59) how he actually realized that mediation *in his life, death, and resurrection.* Since the first half determines how the second half is to be read we will confine ourselves to three issues that arise from the structure of qq. 1–26. First *theology:* how is Christ seen from the point of view of God (qq. 1–3)? Second *anthropology:* how is Christ seen from the point of view of human nature (qq. 4–15)? Third *methodology:* how is Scripture to be read in the light of the incarnate Word (qq. 16–17, 18–26)?

The whole *Summa* is about God, about how everything comes forth from the bounteous goodness of God and returns to that same goodness. It is inevitable, then, that the *Tertia Pars* begin by seeing Christ first in terms of God's intention and goodness and only then in terms of the human need for salvation. Thus q. 1 asks whether the incarnation is fitting *(de convenientia incarnationis).* The first two articles connect divine goodness and human need for restoration. "It pertains . . . to the meaning of the good that it communicate itself to others. . . . Wherefore it pertains to the meaning of the highest good that it communicate itself to a creature in the highest way" (a. 1).[63] This involves no change in God's eternal existence (ad 1um) nor does it imply the assumption of a nature subject to moral fault *(malum culpae),* however much subject to the effects of sin *(malum poenae:* ad 3um). The second article turns to the necessity of the incarnation for the restoration of the human race. There is no absolute necessity since God could have attained the end in other ways but there is a kind of necessity that is "better" and more "fitting" *(melius et convenientius)* for the attainment of the end (a. 2). Thomas offers both positive and negative arguments. First for the promotion of human beings in good *(ad promotionem hominis in bono)* he mentions faith, hope, charity, right living, and in what seems the most important and culminating argument full participation in the divinity that is the true happiness and end of human life. Similarly for the removal of evil *(ad remotionem mali)* he mentions instruction in the wiles of the devil, the dignity of human nature that is sullied by sin, human presumption, human pride, and again as the most important and culminating argument the liberation of humankind from enslavement, which is achieved by Christ making satisfaction for us, something a mere human could not do and something God ought not do. "It was fitting, then, for Jesus Christ to be both God and man" (a. 2).

Although the two sets of arguments are perfectly balanced the weight of the argument would seem to fall on what is always primary in Thomas's mind: the final end of humankind which is full participation in the divine life. In Cessario's terms "image-perfection" (the Word as the perfect image of the Father) is the absolute precondition for "image-restoration" (the incarnate Word who alone can offer perfect satisfaction because of the infinite worth of the one acting: a. 2, ad 2um). Thus it is a drama played out between God the

Father and God the Son from which every merely human attempt at satisfaction receives its efficacy (a. 2, ad 2um). The incarnation reveals what God was willing to do for us because we humans corrupted by sin were rendered incapable of restoring God's image. The third article points this out as the motive for the incarnation. Although anything is theoretically possible from the perspective of God's power everything in Scripture indicates that sin is the reason for the incarnation. This is not to deny that God's one and only purpose in the incarnation is to communicate the divine goodness, but it is to say that that purpose has been conditioned by the history of human sinfulness that has its origins in the sin of Adam and Eve.

The rest of the articles in q. 1 treat the related issues of the remedy for actual sins vis-à-vis original sin (a. 4) and the appropriate "moment" of the incarnation in "the fullness of time" (aa. 5 and 6). Thus in this first question Thomas has laid out the basic perspective that controls his entire christology, that is, that only God can save us and that God does so by becoming one of us so that we might become divine. In his fifth positive reason for the incarnation Thomas cites Augustine: *Factus est Deus homo ut homo fieret Deus* (a. 2). This is a tradition that can be traced back to Irenaeus and was strongly invoked by Athanasius. Hence Thomas's starting point is squarely within the traditional patristic and conciliar understanding. Indeed, his purpose is not to create something new but rather to address all the related questions that the tradition raises for his contemporaries. Yet as already indicated his approach from an anthropological point of view has been influenced by the rediscovery of Aristotle, especially the principle of causal influence within the same genus that the most perfect representative exercises on all the rest.

Question 2 focuses on the manner of union of the incarnate Word considered in itself and is in effect a review of all the major heretical positions during the patristic period and the conciliar responses. Thomas cites in particular those councils that had to work out the theoretical implications of the Nicene–Constantinopolitan Creed: Ephesus (431), Chalcedon (451), and Constantinople II (553). Key to his treatment is Boethius's (d. ca. 521) definition of person: *rationalis naturae individua substantia,* combined with Aristotelian hylomorphism in reference to the understanding of nature. The basic insight is expressed as follows: "Consequently, all that is present in any person, whether belonging to his nature or not, is united to him in person. If, then, the human nature is not united to the Word in person, it would not be united at all. To hold that would be to abolish belief in the Incarnation and to undermine the entire Christian faith" (a. 2). The human nature of Christ exists in a more perfect reality, the person of the Word.

Question 3 describes the manner of the union from the viewpoint of the person assuming, with aa. 1, 2, and 8 focusing on fittingness *(utrum conveniat)* and aa. 3–7 on various hypothetical possibilities *(utrum possit).* A useful distinction is made between the principle of an act and its term. It is fitting for a divine person to assume a human nature (a. 1) because a person is both the principle (this action is properly attributed only to a person) and the term (the union takes place in the person). Moreover it is more fitting for the Son rather than the Father or the Spirit (a. 8) to be incarnated because of the nature of the union as well as its purpose (adoption) and its effect (true wisdom). The first argument on the nature of the union focuses on the consummated perfection of humankind: ". . . the Word, God's eternal conception, is the exemplar *[similitudo exemplaris]* for all creation. Creatures are first established, though changeably, in their proper kinds by a sharing in that likeness; similarly, it is fitting that creatures be restored to their eternal and changeless perfection through the Word's being united, not participatively, but in person with the creature" (a. 8).

Questions 2–3 and 4–15 are concerned to employ philosophical principles as adumbrated earlier in the *Summa,* especially those of Aristotle, to interpret the biblical and conciliar data of God's self-gift in Christ. When Thomas turns to a consideration of the human nature assumed he divides it into those things that are assumed (q. 4: the nature; q. 5: the parts; q. 6: the order of assuming them) and those things that are co-assumed (qq. 7–13 = perfections; qq. 7–8: grace; qq. 9–12: knowledge; q. 13: power; and qq. 14–15 = defects: q. 14: defects of body; q. 15: defects of soul). Throughout Thomas wishes to safeguard the truth of Christ's full humanity but at times he makes rather elaborate claims especially about Christ's knowledge, based on *"a priori* deduction from a certain view of what it is to be truly and perfectly human."[64] Liam Walsh links these anthropological presuppositions to three theological principles that flow from Thomas's treatment of the incarnation (qq. 1–3) and prepare for his treatment of salvation.

First "the *principle of perfection:* because Christ is the incarnate Son of God he must, in his human condition, have the maximum human perfection of grace, knowledge, power, and sensibility." This corresponds to the orientation of the whole *Summa* to see everything *sub ratione Dei,* especially the divine goodness and love that in Christ communicates in an eminent and universal way the perfection of the image to be restored. Yet the work of redemption calls for a second principle, *"the principle of economy:* in order to carry out the work of [humanity's] redemption on earth, Christ had to accept certain limitations and disabilities." This makes sense only for those defects of body (hunger, thirst, death) and soul (physical and emotional pain) that are reconcilable with perfect knowledge and grace and so essential to the purpose of making satisfaction for the sin of the human race (q. 14, a. 4 and q. 15, aa. 4–9). Thus the principle of perfection prevails unless qualified by needs essential to the economy of redemption. Finally the third principle is *"the principle of credibility."* If we are to believe in him as fully human Christ must show himself in a credibly human way. This appeals to the contemporary concern to give full weight to the human, historical experience of Jesus. Yet for Thomas it is a very subordinate principle insofar as it serves, along with the principle of economy, to qualify the primary principle of perfection. Walsh comments, "The classical method followed by St. Thomas has the advantage of measuring Christ by the bounty of God rather than by the needs of men. And if one believes that man's needs and possibilities transcend his own awareness of them, because they have been expanded by the gift of God, one may be persuaded that St. Thomas's approach is ultimately more revealing."[65]

This is true in principle but the contemporary objection is whether Thomas's view, which is in line with the classical patristic approach, does not rob Jesus of his full humanness in the sense of his lived, experiential solidarity with the human experiences of struggle, anguish, temptation, and the challenge to make a free human decision to remain faithful in the face of everything that seems to contradict such trust. Was he truly like us in all things except sin (Heb 4:15; cited at Chalcedon)? Thomas's view is that Christ does for us what we in our sin cannot do for ourselves but his appeal to instrumental causality seems to preserve the humanness of Jesus more as a matter of philosophical principle than concretely lived, personal experience. This brings us to the third point: how Scripture is to be read in the light of the incarnate Word as developed in qq. 1–15.

"In the *Tertia Pars* an idea that is used frequently and effectively is that of instrumental causality. This, which is found in Aristotle, is applied to Christology by St. John Damascene. An instrumental cause brings about an effect superior to itself precisely as it is moved and applied by a higher or principal cause."[66] For Thomas a single effect is produced by ordered causes. The humanity of Christ is an instrument of the divinity not as separated but as conjoined in the unity of hypostasis (q. 2, a. 6, ad 4um) in such a way as to be "a living instrument with a spiritual soul, which itself acts even when it is being acted upon" (q. 7, a. 1, ad 3um) and which can give grace as an instrumental cause acting efficiently through the power of the divinity (q. 8, a. 1, ad 1um). The basic principle is set forth at q. 19, a. 1, ad 3um: "While activity is to be attributed to the subsisting subject, it is nevertheless determined by the form and nature, in the sense that it is from this that the activity receives its determinate character. Consequently, diversity of forms or natures results in diverse kinds of activity; the unity of the subsisting subject, on the other hand, ensures the numerical unity of the specifically determinate action." Thus the subject (*hypostasis* or *persona*) is the one who acts but as specified by the nature, which as instrumental cause is the human nature in Christ. Yet, as instrument of the divinity for our salvation, the saving action of the humanity and divinity is one and the same: ". . . the activity of his human nature, in so far as that nature is the instrument of the divinity, is not distinct from the activity of the divinity; for it is one and the same saving action by which his humanity and his divinity save us. At the same time, Christ's human nature, as a nature, possessed its own activity distinct from the divine activity, as has already been noted" (q. 19, a. 1, ad 2um).

For Thomas, Christ's human will enjoyed a certain independence, that is, with regard to any choice of normal human means as long as such choices did not conflict with the higher or principal cause, God's use of this instrument to achieve the final end. Everything Thomas has to say in qq. 7–15 on the contingent features of the human nature assumed, and especially his use of Scripture, is controlled by his understanding of human perfection as necessary for the effective use of this instrument in achieving salvation. He sums it up in the paradoxical formula *simul viator et comprehensor* (q. 15, a. 10). Christ has all those perfections suitable to one who is the incarnate Word, such as fullness of grace, beatific vision, etcetera, and only those defects of soul and body necessary for the economy of salvation and the credibility of being fully human. Walsh offers two critical cautions on Thomas's use of Scripture:

> Firstly, he sometimes claims information about the earthly condition of Jesus from texts which, to an exegete, are primarily reflections of the Church's faith in the risen Christ. Secondly, he tends to read texts in the light of his own anthropology, when an exegete would require that Semitic patterns of thought and language should be used to disclose the meaning of the text and discover the underlying facts. One could, of course, claim that these texts had, by the time St. Thomas wrote, become vehicles of a constantly evolving Christian tradition, and that he was entitled to appeal to the authority of that tradition as it was carried and expressed by the scriptural text. But since the tradition must always be submitted to the critique of the original biblical meaning, one has to ask whether his anthropology so distorts the biblical data that his theological portrait of the human condition of Christ falsifies the Christ of the Gospel.[67]

When Thomas moves from the ontological structure of Christ (qq. 1–15) to the consequences of the union (qq. 16–26) he seeks to be logically consistent with the philosophical principles already established and at the same time to show how they can be harmonized with the biblical and ecclesial teachings. After treating the logic inherent in statements that touch on the truth of Christ's *esse* and *fieri* (q. 16) and his unity of *esse* (q. 17) he turns to the questions raised and finally resolved at Constantinople III (680–81) of the unity of Christ's will (q. 18) and activity (q. 19) and finally to a series of questions raised primarily by the biblical data: John 14:28 = Christ's subjection to the Father (q. 20); Luke 6:12 = Christ's need to pray (q. 21); Heb 4:14 = Christ's priesthood (q. 22); Eph 1:5 = Christ's adoption as Son (q. 23); Rom 1:4 = Christ's predestination (q. 24); John 5:23 = adoration of Christ (q. 25); 1 Tim 2:5 = Christ as sole mediator between God and humans (q. 26). Although I have selected only one text as example in each case (usually from the *sed contra* of the first article) these questions are permeated with biblical citations, e.g., q. 22 has fifty-five citations from Scripture. But as one reads the text of Thomas (including qq. 27–59 that follow) one is impressed by the fact that such citations, while integral to the argument, are really occasions for raising speculative questions that are resolved on the basis of the philosophical principles of the *Summa* rather than on a reading of the scriptural texts in their various contexts. The main sources for the interpretation of Scripture are themselves interpretations, namely the recently rediscovered conciliar texts that Thomas uses with great skill. One cannot fault Thomas for this. He gives us a brilliantly conceived synthesis of what might be called the traditional image of Jesus. But one can ask how that image should be qualified by contemporary advances in biblical scholarship and related analyses (philosophical, psychological, sociological, cultural, and historical) of the human condition. We address this now by evoking the impact on Christian self-identity of Thomas's image of Christ as a transition to a contemporary image that lays greater stress on social transformation.

3. The Incarnate Word

If the intention of the creedal statements of faith at Nicea and Constantinople I was not to develop a new faith but to be faithful to the biblical witness in changed cultural and historical circumstances, Thomas's intention was surely to remain in continuity with that creedal faith within the academic professionalism of the university characterized by the drive for sure knowledge *(scientia)*. The key integrating image of his narrative quest (the world behind the text) as set forth in the *Summa* (the world of the text) is the incarnate Word. The synthetic clarity of this image and its fruitfulness in resolving puzzling questions has had a profound impact on all subsequent generations (the world before the text).

Until very recent times the most pervasive and popular image of Jesus (at least among those Christians influenced by western European thought modes) has been that of Jesus as the eternal Word of God who descended into flesh (John 1:14), died for our sins, and ascended back into eternal glory with the Father. He did this so that those who believe in him "may not perish but may have eternal life" (John 3:16). Thomas is the theologian *par excellence* of this image. In his drive for sure knowledge he has built an incredibly subtle and complex system that has given the world "the most exacting account possible of Christian faith as it relates to reality."[68] That reality for Thomas included the professionalism of the university, the centrality of the biblical and conciliar tradition, and the analytical power of the recently rediscovered Aristotle. This kind of theology, reaching its apex in Aquinas, has dominated the western (largely European) theological scene from the twelfth to the twentieth centuries. It has functioned best within cultural conditions that are urban, pluralistic, highly intellectual and academic so that high value is placed on analysis and explanation, something that normally takes place within the professional environment of the university.

Within this context Thomas's image of Christ as the incarnate Word has had great power. It is the power of existence itself *(ipsum esse subsistens)* overflowing with bountiful and infinite goodness into the concrete, particular, historical reality of a single human life. It is the communication of that goodness in all its perfection, as the perfect image of the Father, to this single human life so that all human life might finally be restored to the image and likeness of God. It is a dramatic image of God reaching out and embracing human life with the effective power of love *(caritas),* a love that brings the human nature of Jesus into effective communion with the divine intention so that as a man he is both exemplar and instrumental cause of our restoration in the image and likeness of God. For Thomas the drama is played out in one who alone can fulfill in an appropriate and fitting way all the conditions necessary for such a restoration, that is, one who is a divine Person acting within the full potential but inevitable limitations of a fully free human nature.

The power and truth in all this lies in the image of Jesus as the eternal Word in an eternal relation to the Father, already presented in the Gospel of John and affirmed in the Nicene–Constantinopolitan Creed. The weakness here as there is that—no matter how much the full humanness of Jesus is affirmed in principle—he is not truly one of us but only *appears* to be like us because he *decides* to do things that will make such an appearance credible. The transformation of our human condition is thus achieved by God alone who decides to use a human nature to achieve the end although God might have chosen to use other means for the same end. It is at least an open question whether such a transformation is a true *inner* transformation of our human condition.[69] Would this not seem to require one who had to struggle to overcome the disobedience of Adam (Phil 2:6-8; 1 Cor 15:20-22, 44-49; Rom 5:12-21; 8:3; Heb 4:15; 5:7-10), one who "although he was Son, learned obedience through what he suffered" (Heb 5:8)? Thomas explains these texts in terms of his overarching system, and rightly so. But today we seek to reconnect the Johannine and creedal image of the pre-existent Son with the story that is its origin, foundation, and context of meaning. That story is the concrete, personal reality of Jesus from Nazareth, a man anointed by the Spirit and sent by the Father to proclaim the good news of God's salvific will, a man who is God's beloved Son so that his story is indeed God's own story, a man who is indeed the very Word of God incarnated in human history and human experience—but not known apart from that history and that experience.

Finally that story is inseparable from the story of the poor and oppressed. Indeed, to read the story from the viewpoint of the poor and oppressed is to read it with new eyes and new ears. Thus we turn now from the image of Jesus as the "Word become flesh," the incarnate Word that has given rise to much philosophical speculation from Thomas's day to our own, to the "God become poor" *(Dios hecho pobre),* the rejected prophet who struggled to remain faithful to us even while we were his enemies (Rom 5:8).

Notes: Chapter Four

[1] G. K. Chesterton, *Saint Thomas Aquinas. "The Dumb Ox"* (New York: Doubleday Image Books, 1956) 115–116.

[2] Josef Pieper, *Guide to Thomas Aquinas* (San Francisco: Ignatius Press, 1991) 158–160. He cites a review by Aymé Forest as affirming Thomas's suspicion of systems.

[3] Karl Rahner, "Thomas Aquinas on Truth" in *Theological Investigations* 13 (New York: Seabury, 1975) 31. See also his essay "On Recognizing the Importance of Thomas Aquinas" in the same volume, 3–12.

[4] Pieper, *Guide* 157.

[5] M. D. Chenu, *Toward Understanding Saint Thomas* (Chicago: Henry Regnery Company, 1964) 117ff: "In a word, Saint Thomas scissored out anything resembling literary garb. His was a language of austere conciseness that takes a long time to become accustomed to, but then it makes one find some otherwise excellent writers to be intolerable praters. In soberness of this sort the *imperatoria brevitas* of Latin is reached, and many of the formulas chiseled out by Saint Thomas remain forever in philosophy itself" (p. 119).

[6] Chesterton, *Aquinas* 119. The discussion summarized in the text is on 116–119.

[7] Ibid. (emphasis in original).

[8] Pieper, *Guide* 22.

[9] Bernard J. Cooke, *The Distancing of God. The Ambiguity of Symbol in History and Theology* (Minneapolis: Fortress Press, 1990) 157. The eventual neglect of biblical commentaries took its toll: "Central as the *explicatio sacrae paginae* was to theological education in the first half of the thirteenth century, the emphasis on Scripture study could not withstand the growing prominence of systematized theology. It tells us something about the course of late medieval and early modern theology and religion that the summas rather than the biblical commentaries of Aquinas become the object of explanation and academic formation, and that the biblical commentaries of Peter Lombard were all but forgotten in the centuries that saw his *Sentences* function as Europe's common theological textbook" (p. 160).

[10] Chenu, *Understanding* 46. "In Saint Thomas, the Friar Preacher, inspiration rooted in the Gospel became the soul of a theology stocked with the wisdom of the Ancients." Chenu develops this evangelical basis more fully on 234–242. To describe the renewal of Scripture study between 1179 and 1215 he draws on the work of Beryl Smalley, *The Study of the Bible in the Middle Ages* (2d ed. Oxford: Clarendon Press, 1952).

[11] James A. Weisheipl, *Friar Thomas D'Aquino. His Life, Thought, and Work* (New York: Doubleday, 1974) 110ff. brings out the fact that for a regent master in theology at Paris the authority of the Bible was primary, then patristic and ecclesiastical sources, and last the use of philosophical reasoning. Commentaries on the *Sentences* of Peter Lombard were very secondary except for the brief period between 1223 and 1235.

[12] Chenu, *Understanding* 233. This is the purpose of his chapter 7, "The Commentaries on the Bible," 233–263. He lists the commentaries with notes about their composition on 245–249. Cf. Weisheipl, *Friar Thomas* 116–123.

[13] Chenu, *Understanding* 249–253.

[14] Ibid., 259: "Roughly speaking, the *Summa* contains three sections wherein there is a direct elaboration of Holy Scripture: of *Genesis,* in the treatise on creation (*Ia Pars,* q. 65–74), of the books on the Law, in the treatise on ancient Law (*Ia-IIae,* q. 98–105), finally of the Gospels, in the treatise on the life of Christ (*IIIa Pars,* q. 27–59). These three sections the speculative trend of modern theology will gradually eliminate, or push aside to a preliminary, and no longer integrant, zone of study."

[15] Weisheipl, *Friar Thomas* 171.

[16] Ibid., 164. "Later writings of Thomas, such as the *QQ. de potentia, Catena aurea,* the commentaries on John and the first letter of Paul to the Corinthians, as well as *De rationibus fidei* and other works that discuss the Incarnation, utilize verbatim the texts of the early councils. Geenen claims to have located about thirty passages throughout twenty-two works of Aquinas that explicitly use the text of Chalcedon in discussing the error of Eutyches. The profoundest impact of the conciliar texts, however, is to be found in the third part of the *Summa theologiae,* where Thomas discusses the Incarnation; one might say that the intricate problems of fifth-century theology are relived in the objections, replies, and 'sed contra' of the *Summa"* (p. 168). The reference is to Gottfried Geenen, "En marge du Concile de Chalcédone: Les textes du Quatrième Concile dans les oeuvres de saint Thomas," *Angelicum* 29 (1952) 43–59. See also G. Geenen, "The Council of Chalcedon in the Theology of St. Thomas" in *From An Abundant Spring,* edited by the staff of *The Thomist* (New York: P. J. Kenedy & Sons, 1952) 172–217.

[17] Geenen, "The Council of Chalcedon" 198–209 gives an example of how Thomas sees such progress in the addition of the *filioque* to the Creed. Instructive of how Thomas can adapt his methods to the different situation of catechetical instruction for adults is Nicholas Ayo, translator and editor, *The Sermon-Conferences of St. Thomas Aquinas on the Apostles' Creed* (Notre Dame: University of Notre Dame Press, 1988). In this particular work Thomas cites the Bible about three hundred times (especially the Psalms and John) and the Fathers only eleven times (Ayo, *The Sermon-Conferences* 10).

[18] Weisheipl, *Friar Thomas* 173. "The author of the *Corpus* is still unknown; he seems to have been an early sixth-century author, who was perhaps a Monophysite, trying to pass his works off as contemporary with St. Paul. The alleged antiquity of the *Corpus* gave it an authority second only to the canonical books of Scripture" (p. 174). Thomas cites Dionysius more than 1,700 times according to Chenu.

[19] Chenu, *Understanding* 228. See the citations in n. 50 on Thomas's difficulty with the obscure metaphorical language of Dionysius. On Thomas's intention in writing commentaries, see 206–214.

[20] Ibid., 53.

[21] Ibid., 52. Chenu continues, "The *Book of Sentences* became the manual universally used and the basic matter being taught in the universities. The unheard-of success it enjoyed at the Lateran council of 1215 served to determine once and for all the school tradition that would exist within the framework of Western theology and would bar any rival attempts seeking to reinforce their positions with help from the Greek doctors."

[22] Ibid., 31–32. Perhaps "Aristotelian*ism*" is not the right word to apply to Thomas's work since he can disagree with Aristotle (e. g., in his interpretation of Plato) and does not affirm Aristotle as an authority in the same sense as divine revelation. His interest lies in the *truth* of what Aristotle affirms, not in his authority as such. Cf. Pieper, *Guide* 50–54.

[23] Pieper, *Guide* 40.

[24] Chesterton, *Aquinas* 89.

[25] Pieper, *Guide* 44–45 (emphasis in original).

[26] Chesterton, *Aquinas* 84. For the contrast between "spiritualistic symbolism" and "hearty worldliness" see Pieper, *Guide* 44–49.

[27] Weisheipl, *Friar Thomas* 285.

[28] Chesterton, *Aquinas* 93 (emphasis in original).

[29] Weisheipl, *Friar Thomas* 285.

[30] Pieper, *Guide* 54.

[31] Chenu, *Understanding* 13.

[32] Robert J. Schreiter, *Constructing Local Theologies* (Maryknoll: Orbis Books, 1985) 89.

[33] Pieper, *Guide* 62.

[34] Chenu, *Understanding* 19–20.

[35] Pieper, *Guide* 87.

[36] Ibid., 81–82. Chenu, *Understanding* 91–93.

[37] Chenu, *Understanding* 80–98 offers an excellent analysis of these procedures.

[38] Pieper, *Guide* 57. There was, as Pieper notes, a certain "connatural" knowledge between Thomas and Aristotle.

[39] Chenu, *Understanding* 87.

[40] P. Mandonnet, "Chronologie des questions disputées de saint Thomas d'Aquin," *Revue thomiste* 23 (1928) 267–269; text cited by Chenu, *Understanding* 90–91.

[41] Pieper, *Guide* 106. He offers a fine discussion of Thomas's use of language on 102–117. In the course of it he notes Christine Mohrmann's conclusion that medieval Latin was a living language without being the language of an ethnic community (p. 104; see Christine Mohrmann, "Le dualisme de la Latinité medievale," *Revue des Etudes Latines* 29 [1951] 338). See also Chenu, *Understanding* 100–125.

[42] For a clear presentation of the two "antimendicant controversies" see Weisheipl, *Friar Thomas* 80–92 (for that of 1252–57) and 263–272 (for that of 1266–71). See also Pieper, *Guide* 63–75 and Chesterton, *Aquinas* 72–76.

[43] Cooke, *The Distancing of God* 143ff. Parallel to the more intellectual quest of the academic professionals in the universities was the great interest in other "quests" as seen in the Arthurian legends as applied to Christ the King, concretely expressed in pilgrimages and crusades, and the devotion to the human Jesus in the crib and on the cross promoted especially by Franciscan spirituality. For the "symbolist mentality" Cooke refers to M. D. Chenu, *Nature, Man, and Society in the Twelfth Century* (Chicago: University of Chicago Press, 1968) 99–145.

[44] Etienne Gilson, *The Christian Philosophy of Thomas Aquinas* (London: Gollancz, 1957) 83, cited by Pieper, *Guide* 136 (emphasis in original).

[45] Pieper, *Guide* 142. His whole discussion of "a theologically founded worldliness" as grounded in "St. Thomas's all-embracing reverence for all existing things" is articulated in a clear and excellent manner on 134–143.

[46] Chesterton, *Aquinas* 152–153.

[47] See Chapter One above, pp. 39–49.

[48] Chenu, *Understanding* 302. See the whole discussion on 301–310.

[49] Ibid., 303.

[50] Ibid., 306.

[51] Pieper, *Guide* 102. He goes on to cite Thomas's early work *In I Sent.,* d. 14, q. 2, a. 2: "In the emergence of creatures from their first Source is revealed a kind of circulation, *quaedam circulatio vel regiratio,* in which all things return, as to their end, back to the very place from which they had their origin in the beginning." This text is also cited by Chenu, *Understanding* 311, n. 14.

[52] Romanus Cessario, *The Godly Image. Christ and Salvation in Catholic Thought from Anselm to Aquinas* (Petersham, Mass.: St. Bede's Publications, 1990) 10. This book is a revision of his earlier *Christian Satisfaction in Aquinas. Towards a Personalist Understanding* (Washington: University Press of America, 1982).

[53] Ibid., 11. The structure of the *Summa* that follows in the text is from Cessario's work.

[54] See the analysis by Catherine M. LaCugna, "The Relational God: Aquinas and Beyond," *TS* 46 (1985) 647–663.

[55] My translation. In general, for the text of Thomas I am using the Latin text and English translation of the Blackfriars' edition: St. Thomas Aquinas, *Summa theologiae.* 60 vols. (London: Eyre & Spottiswoode; New York: McGraw-Hill, 1964). I follow their translation unless otherwise indicated as my own.

[56] My translation.

[57] David Burrell, *Analogy and Philosophical Language* (New Haven: Yale University Press, 1973) 125.

[58] Ibid., 237.

[59] Cessario, *The Godly Image* seeks to show a development from a more juridical to a more personalist model in Thomas's use of the "satisfaction model" to explain salvation. He concludes, "He who in the depths of the divine reality is the perfect image expressed by the Father and who together with the Father breathes forth personal love as the bond of fellowship, replicates this divine communion within the medium of his humanity and his human history for our sakes" (p. 205). And again, "The perfect mesh of the Father's loving initiative to save humankind and of Christ's human response is a crucial feature of Christ's satisfactory work, according to St. Thomas. For in that communion of loves our own imaging communion with the Trinity is restored" (p. 206).

[60] Chenu, *Understanding* 315.

[61] Cessario, *The Godly Image* 151.

[62] Liam G. Walsh in the introduction to St. Thomas Aquinas, *Summa theologiae.* 49: *The Grace of Christ (3a. 7–15)* (Blackfriars ed., 1974) xvii.

[63] My translation.

[64] Walsh, *The Grace of Christ,* xxii.

[65] Ibid., xxiv (emphasis in original). The discussion of the three principles is on xxii–xxiv.

[66] R. J. Hennessey in the introduction to St. Thomas Aquinas, *Summa theologiae.* 48: *The Incarnate Word (3a. 1–6)* (Blackfriars ed., 1976) xix.

[67] Walsh, *The Grace of Christ* xix.

⁶⁸ Schreiter, *Constructing Local Theologies* 88.

⁶⁹ The difference in approaches, evidenced in contemporary theologians, is well laid out by Paul E. Ritt, "The Lordship of Jesus Christ: Balthasar and Sobrino," *TS* 49 (1988) 709–729. He makes the comparison as follows: "Using the terminology set forth by Monika Hellwig ["Christology and Attitudes Toward Social Structures" in Thomas Clarke, ed., *Above Every Name: The Lordship of Christ and Social Systems* (Ramsey, N.J.: Paulist, 1980) 13–34], one could say that, for Balthasar, Jesus exercises his lordship of creation in a way that is primarily prior to and independent of human response. . . . Once again drawing on the terminology afforded by Hellwig, one could say that [for Sobrino] Jesus exercises his lordship throughout the cosmos in a way that is coconstituted by human agency" (p. 724). While the concern of this article is with Jesus' dominion over all creation it is clear that the two views flow from very different approaches to christology.

CHAPTER 5

A Social-Transformation Image: "The Rejected Prophet" in the Mexican American Experience

"Strikingly, the most certain thing we know about Jesus is that he was a storyteller and speaker of great one-liners."[1] Jesus' use of parables and aphorisms in his historical ministry is no accident. Rather the centrality of story is deeply rooted in the heritage of Israel and is continued from Jesus through the gospel narratives to the present.[2] The natural environment both then and now for the creation, the telling, and the handing on of stories is "the grass roots community. Story is a perspective close enough to the street to be the way the 'ordinary Christian' (non-professional theologians) reflects. In the parishes and neighborhoods life stories are unfolding in dialogue with each other and the larger Christian story. If the Christian peoples are to reflectively own their lives, this process must be articulated and celebrated."[3]

Story has been one of the key elements in the contemporary movement known broadly as "liberation theology." This entire book has been written as an attempt to demonstrate the centrality of narrative in Christology and so justify the return to narrative in liberation theology. Telling the story of Jesus and intertwining his story with our story is the primary way we articulate and celebrate who he is and who we are as his disciples. All our images of Jesus whether biblical, creedal, systematic, or liberative are funded by story and must return to story in order to have an adequate and appropriate context of meaning. No matter what we say by way of doctrinal formulation or moral exhortation the power to convince the mind and move the will remains in the personal self-involvement evoked by a story that grips the imagination.

This final chapter intends to demonstrate that such storytelling is central to and definitive for Christian self-understanding by exploring one specific cultural current within many streams of contemporary liberation theology, whether Latin American, Native American, African American, or others from this conti-

176

nent or Asian, African, etcetera from other continents. I have chosen the specifically Mexican American experience for a number of reasons. The first is inseparably personal and pastoral. I share the background and perspective of T. Richard Snyder who says, "This is no task for a straight Euro-American male who holds a privileged position within the professional world of theological education."[4] Yet as he insists, in spite of the suspicions we may arouse and the traps we may fall into, it is vital that Euro-American males embark on a journey of "solidarity in the struggle for liberation." He remarks sagely, "It has been stated accurately that the leadership of the liberation struggle must come from the oppressed, from those held silent and invisible by their bonds. Only those who know the tragedy of being oppressed can be trusted to lead us into a transformed world. While this is absolutely essential, the question remains whether the rest of us who would participate in liberation must watch on the sidelines or whether we have something crucial to contribute."[5]

On a pastoral level, over the past few years I have been chaplain to "La Comunidad Católica de Spokane." While our community includes people from Central and South America the majority are Mexican and Mexican American. I feel very close to these people. One of the greatest compliments I have ever received came from a Chicana while we were sharing the fiesta of *"Cinco de Mayo."* I made the comment, *"Yo soy muy gringo"* ("I'm really a gringo"), to which she responded with warmth and feeling: *"Si, tu eres gringo, pero con el corazón de un mexicano"* ("Yes, you're a *gringo* all right, but with the heart of a Mexican")! I pray that is true, and the desire to be ever more so has motivated this study. Yet however sympathetic and knowledgeable I become I will never be a Mexican nor a Chicano. Hence I agree with the further remark of Snyder: "If we listen to the voices of the oppressed, the fundamental arena of action for Euro-American males needs to be within their own communities."[6] The goal is liberation, and solidarity in the struggle is the way. One of the most oppressed groups in the United States has been Mexican Americans. I would hope to make my fellow Euro-American males aware of that in order to move this country toward fundamental structural transformation that is truly liberative.

The second reason is more academic and theological. Allen Figueroa Deck describes 1992 as the year of the "boom" for Latino theology in the United States.[7] Indeed there has been a veritable explosion of high quality Latino/Hispanic theology in recent years that makes this growing body of literature a resource of great interest to academic theologians. The similarities with and differences from Latin American liberation theology are notable and merit investigation. The mode of production within academic and professional settings constitutes an invitation to all members of the theological community (Euro-American males included) to engage in ongoing critical dialogue with the methods, claims, and results. The authors of course reflect the diversity of Hispanic/Latino origins in the United States, including Cuban, Puerto Rican, Ecuadoran, and others as well as Mexican, and also have Protestant as well as

Roman Catholic backgrounds. This chapter while focusing on the Mexican American experience will make use of these other resources as they are helpful to the argument.[8]

Finally the third reason has to do with the powerfully moving, indeed almost magical story of Guadalupe herself. This lovely bronze woman *(La Morenita)* is the mother who gives birth to this new race of *mestizos* and through them becomes the common mother of all the Americas. She embodies the compassionate care and concern of God for the least, the little ones, the poor and despised. And most importantly she has remained with her people from that day to this. I can imagine no story that better demonstrates the thesis of this book, that God communicates with us primarily through the power of story. And of course her story is inseparably the story of Jesus, her *mestizo* son, to whom she gives birth.

In order to explore the dimensions of this Mexican American experience and promise I can do no better than follow the pattern set out by Virgilio Elizondo, but with my own spin on the content. Thus this chapter will have four sections. The first, as a sort of propadeutic, will explore the return to narrative in Latin American liberation theology and the consequent continuity in terms of both identity and difference with the current "boom" in U. S. Hispanic/Latino theology. The remaining sections will follow Elizondo's pattern. The second will explore the two stories that are foundational to the Mexican American experience, namely the story of the birth of Mexican Catholicism from Guadalupe (December 12, 1531) and the story of the origins of the Mexican American struggle for identity, a "second mestizaje" in the wake of the U. S.–Mexican treaty of Guadalupe Hidalgo (February 2, 1848). The third section will explore what Elizondo calls the "Gospel matrix." But rather than seek what we may know of the historical Jesus or employ the four gospels in a harmonizing fashion I will juxtapose the Gospel of Mark as interpreted in chapter two with the Mexican American experience, for there are many parallels between them. Finally the fourth and last section will focus on the image of Jesus that seems to encapsulate best both the experience and the promise of *mestizaje,* that is, Jesus as the rejected prophet. The purpose is finally christological, to see what image of Jesus emerges from and best embodies the story. The importance and centrality of Jesus are brought out well in a recent remark of Elizondo: "What Our Lady of Guadalupe was to the birth of Mexican Catholicism, the person of Jesus is today to the birth of the new ecumenical Hispanic Church of the United States."[9]

1. The Return to Narrative in Liberation Theology

Juan Luis Segundo has written that there are really two theologies of liberation operative in Latin America.[10] The first in time came from theologians involved with university groups and intellectuals, the second from pastoral agents and theologians working among the poor. Indeed while the theological works that have come out of Latin America since 1968 strive to express and interpret the suffering, struggle, and hope of the poor and so offer strong critiques of the ideologies oppressive to the poor in both society and Church[11] they seem to be written primarily for those in positions of power who may be able to change the situation of the poor: professional colleagues in the academy, hierarchical authorities in the Church, pastoral ministers and social workers in society. Jon Sobrino in a recent book on christology says that the *locus* or setting for doing christology is not so much a question of *ubi* (whether universities, seminaries, base communities, bishops' offices, etcetera, each of which has advantages and disadvantages) but of *quid:* "Latin American christology—and specifically as christology—identifies its setting, in the sense of a real situation, as the poor of this world, and this situation is what must be present in and permeate any particular setting in which christology is done."[12] This is fair enough but if the only voice we hear is that of theologians who speak *for* the poor and so, like Oscar Romero, become the voice of the voiceless, how will the poor who are the "privileged bearers of the gospel" become "the active, historical subjects of a new understanding of faith and theology"?[13]

The voice of Christ who speaks to us from the Indians, as Bartolomé de las Casas affirmed so strikingly, must be heard. For Gustavo Gutiérrez this demands a certain "maturation of praxis" arising from a prolonged experiential movement of the people at the base, that is, the exploited sectors of society, the despised races, the marginalized cultures. Professional theologians, pastoral agents, and others function in a transitional way to enable the poor, the humiliated, the rejected of society to find their own voice. What they can offer is solidarity in the struggle for liberation. But the voice, the face, and the heart *(rostro y corazón)* of Christ already incarnate within the autochthonous pre-Columbian cultures and religions but reconstituted under the names and forms of an alien (Spanish) culture and religion must be seen and heard again. A truly indigenous christology must come from the concretely lived experience of those who have been the most exploited, despised, and marginalized.

There are two realities in Latin America that can create the conditions necessary for such a possibility: the retrieval and appreciation of popular religiosity and the liberative praxis of popular ecclesial communities *(comunidades eclesiales de base: CEB).* Taken together they constitute the two inseparable factors necessary for liberation: indigenization and conscientization.

> By indigenization I mean simply a particular people getting in touch with their own uniquely proper roots ("radicalization" in the best sense of the word) through a profound *recognition* (memory) *of themselves* in their history, their

culture, their spirituality, and their communal (ecclesial?) experience. By conscientization I mean that such a recognition, in order not to be romanticized or idealized, must be *critically appropriated* through a specific politico-communal commitment. This is an experience that remains rooted in memory but moves beyond it to imagination, i. e. to the concretely imaginative creation of a new humanity. It is a necessary move; for the experience of the people in Latin America has too often been one in which their history has been suppressed, their culture despised, their spirituality alienated, and their communal values of solidarity and co-operation devalued.[14]

While in differing contexts one or the other may receive greater emphasis, indigenization and conscientization must finally be seen as inseparable and constantly interactive within an ongoing process of liberation. At the grassroots level both are grounded in and funded by the telling of the stories: the imaginative retrieval of the past in order to open up the possibility of an authentic future. One of the distinctive differences between Latin American and U. S. Hispanic/Latino theology, it is frequently claimed,[15] is that Latin Americans put more stress on the political and economic factors that create the oppression of class while U. S. Latinos put more stress on the historical and cultural factors that create the oppression of race. The truth of this surely lies in the degree to which such emphases reflect different social locations. We will take a brief look at each in the light of our theme, the primacy of narrative, and conclude with the most fundamental and important factor in any authentic liberation movement: the lived experience of women, as told in their stories, and especially poor women of color.

The motif of liberation assumes a people in captivity who must be "ransomed" (cf. Mark 10:45). Just as for all four gospels Jesus was the only one who could bring about salvation, that is, true liberation by the free gift of himself even unto death, so the people in captivity are the only ones who can now, as the body of this same Christ, bring about their own liberation. This is what Gutiérrez means when he says that the poor themselves must become the active subjects of their own liberation. It is rooted in the pedagogy of Paulo Freire who employs a dialogical, problem-posing method that trusts the people to discover their own "generative themes" through the proverbs and stories of folk wisdom already contained in their own experience.[16] They must overcome the "cultural invasion" of the oppressor. "The oppressed, having internalized the image of the oppressor and adopted his guidelines, are fearful of freedom."[17] To realize true freedom the oppressed must engage in a critical and liberating dialogue that arises from and gives expression to their own particular experience and so opens the way to transformative action. Praxis is simply reflective participation within the concrete and particular historical situation.

In the pastoral practice of a Church that seeks to be in solidarity with the poor in their struggle for liberation an integral element is a new reading of the Bible.

"The real importance of the Bible is revealed, not by the Bible itself, nor by the traditional criteria, but by the journey of the people trying to escape from 'captivity' into the freedom God promises them."[18] This has often found its most congenial context in the development of popular ecclesial communities (*CEB*s) that Gutiérrez calls an "irruption of the poor."[19] Although originating out of the pastoral concerns of the Church and relatively small in proportion to the larger populations, they have become for many of the poor a place of consciousness raising, motivation, communal support, and political commitment.[20]

Why have Latin American theologians put so much stress on the experience of the poor and the corresponding economic and political factors that create their oppression? Simply put, because that is the overwhelming and massive reality that faces them day in and day out. For all its diversity of ethnic origin, including pre-Columbian, African, and European, "Latin" America is predominantly "Hispanic" in the sense that Spanish and Portuguese are the main languages that pervade not only South America but Mexico and Central America as well. The concrete and immediate situation that calls for committed engagement in very specific options is the plight of the economically and politically deprived, the "world of the poor." Popular religiosity has often been seen as "alienated and alienating and in need of a true *metanoia* through the praxis of liberation."[21] The agent for this is the conscientization available in the experience of popular ecclesial communities.

In the United States, unlike "Latin" America, the dominant language has become English. "The *latinoamericano mestizo* is different from the Chicano *mestizo* in that the Chicano lives in a gringo society."[22] This is key to understanding the greater emphasis on culture vis-à-vis economic and political factors among U. S. Hispanics. Cultural oppression becomes more evident and is experienced more keenly in a society where the dominant culture is other than one's own. Deck notes that "Latino theology" differentiates itself from Latin American liberation theology "not so much in method but in emphasis and tone." This is largely due to "a markedly different context, one of unusual diversity in terms of racial, ethnic, social class, and gender coordinates."[23] This pluralistic social location is reflected in four U. S. Hispanic approaches to interpreting the Bible identified by Fernando Segovia: *mujerista, barrio, mestizaje*, and *mañana*. While all four can be said to interpret the Bible and do theology from a "Hispanic" perspective[24] and so are related to each other, each also has a distinctive way of reading the Bible that comes out of the particular experience of oppression within diverse social locations: gender for *mujerista* theology, socioeconomic conditions for *barrio* theology, sociocultural rejection for *mestizaje* theology, and the sociohistorical situation of exile for *mañana* theology.[25]

In these diverse yet related theologies the fundamental and unifying cry is for life. Roberto Goizueta has offered a critical retrieval of Aristotle's notion of praxis as what is worth doing for its own sake and not as a means or instrument to achieve some extrinsic goal.

Aristotle uses the term *praxis* to denote all human activity whose end is internal rather than external to itself. He thus distinguishes praxis, activity that is an end in itself, from *poiesis,* activity that seeks some end external to the performance itself, and distinguishes both of these from *theoria.* The paradigmatic examples of praxis are political activity and moral conduct. The difference between praxis and poiesis may be rendered as that between doing and making, where the former is its own reward while the latter seeks its reward in the results of the performance; the end of praxis is the praxis itself, whereas the end of poiesis is the result left over after one has completed the task. Given this distinction, the fundamental form of praxis is nothing other than life, or living, itself; in the *Politics,* Aristotle avers that "life is action [praxis] and not production [poiesis]."[26]

The challenge to Latin American liberation theology lies in the ambiguity of the term "liberating praxis": does one become free "in the very act or process of transforming history" (Aristotle) or only *"after* one has transformed history" (Marx)? The contribution of the U. S. Hispanic experience comes in the centrality given to popular religiosity within the context of a dominant culture that is alien to Hispanic culture. "U. S. Hispanic theologians are emphasizing the inherently communal and aesthetic character of praxis, without, on the other hand, depreciating its transformative character."[27] What is important here is the sense of community as family that includes God *(Diosito),* Jesus, Mary, Joseph and other saints, *las abuelitas* (grandmothers), ancestors, as well as present and future generations. They are all "members of the family," organically one since the beginning of creation. As "inherently communal" such praxis is also "inherently celebratory" (aesthetic), continually expressing itself in music, dance, and ritual. "Insofar as praxis is an affirmation of community, it is an affirmation of community as the highest form of beauty. Popular religiosity reveals praxis as communal, aesthetic performance."[28]

The move outward toward the transformation of history and society has its source and ground in the community. The most fundamental ethical-political obligation is to survive, to defend and preserve the community with its own distinctive cultural heritage. This finds its primary expression in the "aesthetic praxis" of popular religiosity. "Popular religiosity is an anamnestic performance, or praxis, that, in reenacting the suffering of our people, simultaneously reminds us that suffering is not the last word. It is no coincidence that the Crucified Jesus and the Virgin Mary are so central to U. S. Hispanic popular religiosity."[29] Thus the very process of remembering the struggle through the praxis of popular religiosity, this way of "being in the world" *(manera de ser)* that is inseparably *en la lucha,* is liberating and life-giving.

Besides giving greater weight and value to popular religiosity, perhaps the most significant difference between Latin American liberation theology and U. S. Hispanic/Latino theology lies in the central and decisive importance given to the reality and lived experience of Latinas. Women, particularly *las abuelitas,* have been perceived as the primary bearers of the culture.[30] One of the main purposes of Goizueta's article on praxis is to overcome the dichotomous epistemologies of Cartesian and Kantian persuasion so as to recognize the "inherent rationality" of a praxis that is communal and aesthetic and so includes affect, feelings, sensuality. He sees the challenge that this represents for modern and postmodern dualisms as "more acutely visible in the experience of U. S. Hispanic women" who have been denied their intellect, that is, their rationality and so their full humanity.[31]

To avoid the kind of romanticizing that can almost inevitably accompany the retrieval through memory of an indigenous past contemporary U. S. Hispanic/Latina women are employing a method that is grounded in listening to one another's stories and celebrating them, but also moves toward clarifying the meaning of the stories, reflecting upon their implications in the context of today's world, and strategizing on the basis of their stories for the social transformation that will achieve true liberation.[32] Thus as Deck has observed the method is not so different from Latin American liberation theology but given the social location of a pluralistic and predominantly Euro-American society the emphasis and tone is. For U. S. Hispanic women this is a matter of finding and presenting to Church and society a distinctively new voice, a prophetic voice that arises from a profound affirmation of their own experience and culture. "Out of the particularity of their situation Hispanic Women have come to understand that a radical change in these structures is the only possible solution to oppression. Though differing in ways of doing it, they seek a shift in paradigm; it is not a matter of changing positions with males and with Anglos or sharing equally with them. It is a matter of bringing about a new reality; Hispanic Women believe that they have a distinct and valuable contribution to make to such a task."[33]

Hispanic women do not perceive themselves nor do they wish to be perceived as a minority that wants the "American dream" or as a marginalized group that seeks a niche for itself within the world of academe, even theological.[34] Rather they are a "remnant group" whose primary experience is the simple struggle to survive. This struggle for survival is physical and so the socioeconomic reality of Hispanic women is a fundamental consideration (though perhaps not as intensively and immediately in the United States of today as in Latin America). It is also psychological as it has to do with the struggle *to be oneself,* a struggle that has both personal and communal dimensions. But above all it is a cultural-historical struggle and so the most fundamental affirmation is that of *mestizaje,* of *la raza,* that embraces and celebrates a cultural diversity that includes Amerindian, Spanish, and African. This is the *locus theologicus* of Hispanic women's liberation theology.[35]

We will return momentarily to the centrality of narrative in this process, but first by way of conclusion to this section two points need to be emphasized: the revaluation of *syncretism* as a positive element in the Hispanic narrative quest and the recognition that this quest for a uniquely distinctive U. S. Hispanic identity is best understood as a *spirituality.*

Jeffrey Carlson proposes the thesis that "all religion is, inevitably, a form of syncretism. . . . To have a religious identity is, inevitably, to be a 'syncretic self,' the product of a process of selective appropriation, internalizing elements drawn from vastly varied pools of possibility."[36] This is particularly true of popular religiosity that more easily embraces patterns of behaviors and beliefs that escape the control of "official" religion with its normative tradition. However from a historical and cultural viewpoint Christianity whether "popular" or "official" has always been syncretic.[37] The point at issue then should not be the fact of syncretism whether on the popular or the official level but rather how the Christian community goes about discerning, in Ada María Isasi-Díaz's words, what is "true, good, and life-giving," that is, what can be "baptized" as a legitimate dimension of Christian self-understanding and what must be rejected. This is simply the process of interpretation within changing social, cultural, and historical contexts as described in the Introduction to this book. The insistence among U. S. Hispanics on the communal character of theology *(teología de conjunto)* demands this.

What is new and inescapably decisive for the process of social transformation and liberation is the voice of poor women of color arising out of their lived experience. For *mujerista* theology in the United States the socioeconomic reality (poor) and the question of sexual identity (woman) are vitally important but as included in the central question of ethnicity that includes not only race, language, country of origin, and cultural practices (as ethnicity is commonly understood) but whatever constitutes "Hispanic Women's struggle to survive." "We identify our ethnicity as a social construct *a posteriori,* that is, as a way of describing, of narrating who we are and how we live our daily lives."[38] This very process of narrating and reflecting together "through the lens of an option for and a commitment to the liberation of Latinas"[39] is itself praxis, the very experience of struggling to survive, of being *en la lucha* not as passive sufferers acted upon by the oppressors, but as active subjects bringing forth life. "An anthropology developed out of the lived-experience of Latinas centers on a subject who struggles to survive and who understands herself as one who struggles."[40]

Isasi-Díaz concludes her book with the symbol of Hispanic women's "moral truth-praxis": *mestizaje.* Hence the self-identity that is emerging for Hispanics in the United States, be they women or men, can appropriately be characterized as a "syncretic self." It is inseparably religious and cultural. Andrés Guerrero, basing himself in the Chicano oral tradition, puts the current situation well: "Chicanos with their *corazón latino* and gringo impulse

are a hope for the hemisphere and a bridge between the rich and poor nations."[41] U. S. Hispanics/Latinos/Chicanos see themselves as "a bridge"[42] who
by reason of their *mestizo* constitution and consciousness can cross borders
and give rise to the hope for a new humanity that is inclusive of all races—*la
raza cósmica.*

This quest of U. S. Hispanics for their distinctive identity is best understood
as a spirituality.[43] "A core spiritual issue facing each and every Hispanic,
whether he or she be of Mexican, Cuban, Puerto Rican, or of other Latin
American extraction, is how to relate to the dominant culture and to one's
culture of origin."[44] Juan-Lorenzo Hinojosa proposes four levels of acculturation and assimilation that move from the culture shock of the immigrant
through partial and stronger assimilation to the fully bicultural individual who
has achieved the new identity of *mestizaje.* He employs Paul Ricoeur's
understanding of the role of symbol as an important key to understanding the
faith development of U. S. Hispanics. The sense of the sacred evoked by the
symbols and stories on the level of the first naïveté must pass through the
"acids of modernity" (critical reflection) in order to arrive at the level of the
second naïveté, which is a new appropriation of the symbols and stories at a
deeper, post-critical level. He concludes in opposition to either capitulation to
the dominant culture or a "ghetto" separation from it as follows: "Those,
however, who want to engage the dominant culture and at the same time be
faithful to their roots will need to make the journey which honors the truth in
both realities. It is these who will make the most significant contribution to the
church and to society."[45]

Indispensable to such a contribution, then, is the critical appropriation from
within the contemporary U. S. Hispanic social context of the symbols, rituals,
dramas, and stories that have formed the heritage of the Hispanic/Latino
people. We are limiting this essay to the Mexican American experience but
obviously there are analogous experiences among Cuban Americans, Puerto
Rican Americans, and others. Central to all such experiences is narrative, the
telling of stories that have metaphoric impact. Hence at the outset it is well to
recall the dynamics of the narrative quest as outlined in the Introduction: (1)
the crisis for Mexican Americans is that of conquest and colonization, first in
Mexico and then in the United States, that has called forth, as is true of all
liberation theologians, a move from the intelligibility of creed and system to
the credibility of societal witness; (2) the concretely lived experience is one of
solidarity that gives rise to both individual and communal identity as *mestizaje,* the struggle to survive, especially among poor women of color *(la
mestiza)* in a praxis that is inherently communal and aesthetic; (3) the decisive
orientation is service to the reign of God through a transformative and liberating praxis that heralds the arrival of a new humanity: *la raza cósmica.* Let
us now examine the two central stories that embody this narrative quest for
Mexican Americans.

2. The Mexican American Experience

"To be a Hispanic living in the United States is to be a child of conflict and, at the same time, a prophet of reconciliation. In a world where national borders are becoming increasingly fluid and porous, where communications can be virtually instantaneous, where 'globalization' is no longer perceived as merely an option but as a necessity for the survival of any economic or political enterprise, the U. S. Hispanic stands as a living reminder that, in the face of the ever-present conflicts, human reconciliation is not an illusory ideal but an attainable goal, not a threat to be feared but a promise to be fulfilled."[46] For Mexican Americans to arrive at such an affirmation of their identity and their role as a people who embody the hope of true human reconciliation it has been necessary "to retell our story—the story of the great pilgrimage of our ancestors that has led us to be who we are today."[47] That story is primarily a story by and about women. It is *by* women because Hispanic women, through their stories and prayers and healing ministries, have been "the real teachers of values and evangelizers of the people."[48] It is *about* women because the most powerful images that embody the story include *La Malinche* (and the associated legend of *La Llorona), La Morenita del Tepeyac,* and *La Mestiza* (Chicana) of contemporary times. We will divide her story, as does Elizondo, into the first *mestizaje* represented by the Spanish-Catholic conquest of Mexico, the second *mestizaje* represented by the Nordic-Protestant conquest of Mexico, and the ongoing struggle for identity and maturity represented by the new *mestiza* in the United States.

A. *From La Malinche to La Morenita del Tepeyac.* Justo González calls us to move beyond "the myth of innocence" in remembering our past. An "innocent reading" of history, whether biblical history or Hispanic history or Anglo history, is simply "a selective forgetfulness" that allows us to avoid the consequences of a more realistic and responsible memory. "Reading the Bible in Spanish" involves a non-innocent reading that has its correlates in Hispanic history and its consequences for U. S. history.

> We know that we are born out of an act of violence of cosmic proportions in which our Spanish forefathers raped our Indian foremothers. We have no skeletons in our closet. Our skeletons are at the very heart of our history and our reality as a people. Therefore, we are comforted when we read the genealogy of Jesus and find there not only a Gentile like ourselves but also incest and what amounts to David's rape of Bathsheba. The Gospel writer did not hide the skeletons in Jesus' closet but listed them, so that we may know that the Savior has really come to be one of us—not just one of the high and mighty, the aristocratic with impeccable blood lines, but one of *us.*[49]

The story to be told is primarily parabolic insofar as it challenges the myth of dominance, whether Spanish-Catholic or Nordic-Protestant. Yet insofar as the tragedy of La Malinche has its mythic resolution in the victory over the powers of death imaged in La Morenita del Tepeyac the genre is more like Elizabeth Struthers Malbon's characterization of the Gospel of Mark, that of myth-parable or parable-myth. To understand this is integral and indispensable to any narrative quest for personal and communal identity. "Thus, to the question 'Who are we?' we respond: We are those who from the beginning have had to live beyond the myth of innocence."[50]

The story begins with the arrival of Hernan Cortés on the shores of Mexico, April 22, 1519. It is a well known story of conquest (by August 13, 1521) and subsequent colonization that, born out of the violence of greed and racism, devastated the Aztec-Nahuatl society of pre-Columbian times. Symbolic of the extreme degradation and exploitation to which the native peoples were subject and yet—somewhat ambiguously—of the beginnings of the new reality of *mestizaje,* is La Malinche, also known as Doña Marina. She became the translator and interpreter of Cortés as well as his mistress who bore him sons. Thus she has become "the symbol of violated womanhood out of which the new Mexicans were to be born—it was the conquistador father who violated our woman-mother and out of whose violent union we were born—Hijos de la Chingada (children of the violated one)."[51] Yet Elizondo seeks to retrieve her image as one of strength and power:

> Malinche, Guadalupe, Chicana! What do these three great women have in common? They have brought new life out of a situation of devastating chaos. For too long we have seen Doña Marina as the traitor who is responsible for the conquest. What nonsense. The victim is made into the villain. . . . She was a woman of silent strength who endured without despair what she could not change or control. She survived and her children prospered—they have become a numerous people. She is the prototype of Mexican-American women: even when abused or insulted, their inner selves cannot be touched or soiled. We have made the mother of *mestizaje* the villain of the conquest so that we could easily ignore and even despise the face of our Indian mothers, who even when raped, abused, and abandoned gave their lives of hard work and suffering for us, their mestizo children.[52]

The story of Guadalupe and the power of her image cannot be understood apart from the cries and suffering of the Indians: not just the physical death caused by wars and disease nor the destruction of their temples and monuments at Tlatelolco (August 13, 1521) nor even the abuse and violation of the women but the utter destruction of their "cosmovision," of their religio-cultural understanding of themselves in the world. As Elizondo has pointed out, the missioners, perhaps more than the conquistadors, posed an insidious threat to the natives for they sought to destroy not just external, physical things but the very core of their spirituality: "Seeing they did not see and hearing they did not hear" (cf. Mark 4:10-12).[53] But a suppressed and demeaned culture will survive in the ironic imagination of the people as manifest especially in popular religiosity. "Popular religiosity is, in effect, to a certain degree, the protest of the indigenous and mestizo consciousness submitted to a foreign culture, religion, and morality, which reconstitutes under their [foreign] names and forms the elements of its own proper religious and cultural identity."[54] This is especially true of *Tlecuauhtlacupeuh* ("she who comes flying from the region of light like an eagle of fire") whom the Spaniards understood in reference to the shrine of Guadalupe in Estremadura of their Spanish homeland.[55]

The story of La Malinche has survived in two forms. The one usually associated with her is the legend of "La Llorona, the 'Weeping Woman', who is condemned to forever look for her children whom she murdered in a rage against the father of her children. He, being Spanish and of a higher social class, did not marry her."[56] This is a tragic story of shame and defeat leading to despair. But as the contemporary rehabilitation of La Malinche suggests there is a redemptive side to her as the mother of the new Mexican race of *mestizos*.[57] The most striking feature of Guadalupe is that her hands are in a gesture of offering something to the world and her waist has a band *(cinta)* around it indicating that she is pregnant. What she is offering to the world is the birth of her son, who from her entire appearance can only be *mestizo*. This is a divine affirmation of the new reality that has come forth from a Spanish father and an Indian mother. The image of Guadalupe thus sublimates the image of Doña Marina, retaining what is true and good and lifegiving of her reality but elevating her and transforming her so that now, as La Morenita, she symbolically embodies a whole cultural ethos, a new people to be known henceforth as *la raza*.

To understand the image we must look at the story that gives it context and meaning. I will not reproduce the story here but simply focus on those elements that are most significant.[58] Jeanette Rodriguez, relying on the research of Clodomiro Siller-Acuña, highlights "the Nahuatl interpretation of the apparition" based on the full text of the *Nican Mopohua*.[59] The symbolic world of the Nahuatl-speaking people and its mythic expression was of course quite distinct from that of the Spaniards although there were some affinities on the religious level. As Elizondo notes well the Spaniards had a strong sense of individual dignity in relation first to their familial lineage and then to society; they considered themselves a chosen people called to defend the Church against infidels (Moors and Jews) and heretics and to conquer pagan peoples for the greater honor and glory of God; their language was strong and direct, employing abstract, conceptual, and syllogistic modes of expression to achieve exact meaning and self-evident truth. By way of contrast, "The indigenous world had a profound conviction of the integral unity of everything which is and everything which happens. Hence things could not be known in isolation—neither things, persons, nor celestial bodies. Everything was intimately interrelated."[60] Rather than reduce everything to its parts in order to grasp the whole they sought the whole picture first in order to understand the parts. *Flor y canto* (flower-song) combined with poetic narrative rather than discursive, philosophical speech is what communicates the deepest dimensions of reality for the Nahuatl-speaking people. They thought in terms of the union of dualities, employing *"disfrasismos"* (two words or symbols to express one meaning). Thus "heaven-earth" expresses the world, "flower-song" reveals the innermost reality of heaven, "face-heart" *(rostro y corazón)* the innermost depth of the human person, "night-wind" (invisible and untouchable) the innermost reality of the divine.[61] As Rodriguez points out, closely connected with this is the importance of numbers, especially "four" symbolizing "cosmic totality or completion" and "five" symbolizing "the center of the world."

"In the Nahuatl world all life was dual in nature. This principle of duality, which undergirded all existence, was called Ometeotl."[62] This was the originating male-female pair, also known as Ometecuhtli ("twice a man") and Omecihuatl ("twice a woman"). "According to Aztec myth, Ometecuhtli and Omecihuatl gave birth to four sons, each of whom became the principal god of a region: Tezcatlipoca, of the North; Quetzalcoatl, of the West; Huitzilopochtli, of the South; and Xipe Totec, of the East. . . ."[63] The North and South gods, associated with fire, were warrior gods. "Huitzilopochtli was the tribal patron of the Aztecs at Tenochtitlan. A diurnal counterpart of Tezcatlipoca and manifestation of the sun, he was a fearsome warrior, a killer of peoples and destroyer of towns who carried a fire-breathing dragon or serpent."[64] This was the god defeated by the Spaniards. The West and East gods, associated with water, were fertility gods. Quetzalcoatl is important to the story for two reasons: (1) he helped create "the race of commoners" along with the goddess Cihuacoatl-Tonantzin who combined both creative and destructive power and was revered as "Our Mother" (Tonantzin) on the hill of Tepeyac outside Mexico City, where Guadalupe appeared; (2) he was also defeated by Tezcatlipoca and forced to flee to the East in exile. He was expected to return from the East as a large white man with blond hair and a beard. The Aztecs, in the person of Montezuma II, and the other Nahuatl-speaking people opposed to them thought initially that Hernan Cortés was Quetzalcoatl returned! Finally the East god, Xipe Totec, representing maize, rain, and rejuvenation eventually was assimilated into the Christ child. According to Ingham the associated goddess of water, sustenance, and maize, Chalchuihtlicue, was assimilated into the Virgin Mary.[65] This corresponds to the expectation of salvation from the East though the expectation was for the return of Quetzalcoatl.

What, then, would the indigenous peoples have seen and heard in the image and story of Guadalupe? The language was Nahuatl. With regard to atmosphere, the place was on the top of the hill at Tepeyac, a shrine to "Our Mother" (Tonantzin). The time was "very early in the morning" on Saturday, December 9, 1531. Time and its exact measurement were very important to the

Nahuatl. Since the arrival of Cortés who turned out not to be the hoped-for Quetzalcoatl this had been a time of defeat and devastation at the hands of the Spaniards, fulfilling ancient prophecies of the end of their civilization. But now the moment of first light coming out of the darkness evokes the beginning of all time: "This meaningful time defined the Guadalupe event as fundamental, equal in significance to the origin of the world and the cosmos. . . ."[66] The atmosphere is further enhanced by imagery that evokes paradise: the story begins with music and ends with flowers, symbolic of the innermost reality of heaven; the Lady is surrounded by the radiance of the sun, symbolic of divinity; the flowers and ground glow like gold, symbolic of new life for the land as well as for the people.

With regard to characters, the persons of the drama include Cuauhtlatoatzin ("he who speaks like an eagle"), probably one of the elders or wise men who as an early Christian convert was known as Juan Diego.[67] His concern for the sacraments, his walking to early Mass "to hear about the divine things which are given and taught us by our priests, the delegates of Our Lord" and seeking a priest to confess his uncle and prepare him for death indicates that he has made a strong commitment to the new religion.

The second character identifies herself as "the ever holy Virgin Mary." Later, before the bishop, Juan Diego calls her "my Lady, the Lady of Heaven, Holy Mary, precious mother of God." Thus she is clearly the virgin Mary of Christian faith. But in the first encounter she proceeds to identify herself with five names of the Nahuatl gods ("five" symbolizes the center of the world). She is

> (1) the Mother of God, who is the God of truth; (2) the Mother of the Giver of life; (3) the Mother of the Creator or Inventor of men and women; (4) the Mother of the One who makes the sun and the earth; and (5) the Mother of the One who is far and close. In this passage, Our Lady of Guadalupe implies that she is the Mother of the ancient gods of the Mexicans by, in essence, stating the five names of the gods that were known to the Nahuatl, using Nahuatl duality and phrases. She gives the names of their gods: "the God of truth" and "the God who gives life." The third and fourth names are names that the Nahuatl understood to be the operative essence of God. The last one implied the cosmological and historical dimension of their God. . . .[68]

Thus there is a compenetration of Christian and Nahuatl symbolism in the person of the Virgin.

The third character is Fray Juan de Zumárraga, a Franciscan and bishop of Mexico who lives in a palace and can afford to keep a poor Indian like Juan Diego waiting and then put him off for another day, questioning him in detail on the second visit and finally demanding a sign as Juan Diego's word was not sufficient evidence. An atmosphere of hostility and disbelief is introduced by the servants in the bishop's household who, having been sent to follow him, lose track of him and when they return, tired and angry, try to convince the bishop not to believe him. When Juan Diego returns the final time they act as if he were not there and finally try to take the roses from him. For the Nahuatl the flower symbolizes "truth, beauty, and authenticity." "The history of how flower has become a symbol for truth in the Nahuatl culture emerges out of the myth that the truth of all things was brought by the god Quetzalcoatl in the form of a flower, so that humanity could live happily."[69] Now it is Juan Diego, a poor and discredited Indian, who brings the truth to the representatives of Spanish power, a truth that cannot be taken from him as representative of the indigenous people. "Symbolically, Siller sees this action [of trying to take the flowers away] as the dominant culture's attempt to take the truth away from the Indian. For Juan Diego, the conquerors and dominant culture have already taken his land, his goods, his city, his form of government, and his reasons for being and acting. Now they want to take away his truth, which is all he has left."[70]

With regard to plot the story unfolds around the numerical patterns of "four" and "five." There is a structure of four days precisely indicated by the beginning: "Early in the morning of Saturday, December 9, 1531" and the climactic ending: "Very early on the morning of Tuesday, December 12, 1531." There are four appearances, three to Juan Diego with the climactic fourth in the miracle of the *tilma* (cloak), Guadalupe's permanent presence among the people. (Some see a fifth appearance in the healing of Juan Diego's uncle, Juan Bernardino, but it is not related in the narrative directly.) There are other indicators: the word for song or music *(canto)* occurs five times; Juan Diego initially responds to the music by asking four questions; Guadalupe uses five names for Nahuatl divinities to identify herself; Juan Diego uses four descriptions of someone better suited for the mission: "important," "well known," "respected," "esteemed"; he describes himself with five terms: "nobody, a nothing, a coward, a pile of old sticks, just like a bunch of leaves"; she responds using five command words: "I beg you with great insistence . . . I sternly command you . . . greet him . . . make known my will to him . . . tell him . . ."; she responds to his concern about the sickness of his uncle with five rhetorical questions: "Am I not here, your Mother? Are you not under my shadow and protection? Am I not your foundation of life? Are you not in the folds of my mantle, in the crossing of my arms? Is there anything else that you need?"[71] Clearly the plot evokes the Nahuatl symbolic world of interrelatedness, of cosmic totality or completion, of being at the very center of the world.

The plot revolves around the symbolic importance of the new temple. When Juan Diego first hears the music he looks to the east, the place of the rising sun from which life came, to the top of the hill of Tepeyac, sacred site of Tonantzin from where "a lady of glowing beauty" with the sun radiating all around her and her face full of love and compassion speaks of her desire: "I have a living desire that there be built a temple, so that in it I can show and give forth all my love, compassion, help, and defense, because I am your loving mother: to you, all who are with you, to all the inhabitants of this land and to all who love me, call upon me, and trust in me. I will hear their lamentations and will remedy all their miseries, pains, and sufferings." The crisis around which the plot turns is whether she will be accepted or rejected through the agency of her messenger (prophet), a Nahuatl-speaking wise man. This receives its poignancy from the familiarity coupled with respect that exists between the two principal characters. They address each other in terms that are both familiar and respectful. She calls him "the smallest of my sons" and he calls her "the smallest of my daughters." Each recognizes the other as poor and insignificant simply by reason of their Indian features. She appears to him not seated in a position of dominance as an Aztec or Spanish noble but standing in an attitude of mutuality and dignity. She gives him a mission and will not accept his "victim mentality" of self-deprecia- tion but, as the sub-plot on the sickness of his uncle shows, respects his ability to choose. Like YHWH with the prophets, including Moses, Amos, and Jeremiah, she must insist that he is the one chosen and no other messenger will do. The irony, as with the prophetic tradition as a whole, including Jesus, is that the weak and powerless, the dominated and oppressed, are the ones chosen to speak truth to power. In choosing him she restores his dignity: "You are my ambas- sador and most worthy of trust." The most touching moment of the story comes when Juan Diego goes to the hill to cut and gather the roses of Castille, even though they were not in season and so should not have been in bloom, and brings them to her. She takes them in her hands and rearranges them in his *tilma*. Rodriguez cites the interpretation of Siller-Acuña: "Flowers, as explained above, were a sign to the Nahuatl people of truth and of the presence of divin- ity . . . Juan Diego brings truth (i. e., the flowers) to the 'Lady from Heaven'. She touches the flowers and makes herself present in them, remaining within the logical symbolic culture of the Indian."[72]

The roses of Tepeyac, celebrated even today with *las mañanitas* (songs sung very early in the morning in honor of Guadalupe), embody the truth of the Indian as he brings the flowers to her and the enduring presence of the divine as she arranges them with her own hands. At the same time, as Elizondo eloquently insists, "the feast of Our Lady of Guadalupe shouts out with joy the proclamation that a new dawn is breaking: the collective resurrection of a new people. Out of their own earth—Tepeyac—and in continuity with the life of their ancestors, a new mother emerges, pregnant with new life. She is not a goddess but the new woman from whom the new humanity will be born, *la raza cósmica de las Américas*. She is herself the prototype of the new creation. She is *la Mestiza*. She combines opposing forces so that in a creative way new life, not destruction, will emerge. On December 12 is celebrated the beginning of the new human-divine adventure." And further: "It is the roses of Tepeyac that take the place of the Easter lilies of western Christianity."[73]

In the course of her investigations Rodriguez asked some indigneous women in Mexico City what the significance of Guadalupe is, what makes her different from other Marys. One responded: *"Se quedó"* ("she stayed").[74] If the story gives context to the image, the image contains the story. With regard to tone the story is clearly told by an omniscient narrator who is invisibly present to all that happens and all that is said. But as with the Gospel of Mark the written account is dependent on prior oral traditions, in this case primarily a Nahuatl-speaking wise man. It is important to note that this tradition at the same time takes the form of pictorial codices familiar to the Nahuatl people. The icon that remains tells the story and embodies the experiences of generations. We will take a brief look at some of the more striking features.

The *face* is that of a young Indian maiden of olive-dark skin and dark hair. She is Indian but with a hint of white hue, so that she might already be considered *mestiza.* She communicates a sense of quiet dignity, of peace and joy, and above all of compassionate love. Her *eyes* are mature. They contain much as, deep within them, the *mestizo* world to come is anticipated in the four figures there: Cuauhtlatoatzin, the wise man known as Juan Diego; an Aztec "Cuacuacultin" priest in an attitude of prayer; the Spanish bishop; the indistinct form of a black woman. Thus there are four figures (symbolizing completion or totality): one white, one black, two Indian. Another aspect of her eyes is that unlike those of Indian gods who looked straight ahead they are looking down in an attitude of humility and simplicity.

The *hands,* as already mentioned, are in the traditional Indian manner of offering. The *band (cinta)* around her waist indicates that she is pregnant and so is offering to the world her son who embodies the new *mestizo* reality. The band itself may have been added later to make the fact of her pregnancy clearer to the Spaniards, for "below the tassel there is a small flower called *nagvioli.* To the Nahuatl this flower was a symbol of the sun god. . . . The flower's position on Our Lady of Guadalupe's womb verified for the Nahuatl that she was pregnant. . . ."[75]

One of the most striking aspects is her *robe* with its unusual luminosity. The rose color suggests the sun god Huitzilopochtli who both gave and preserved life and needed blood sacrifices to continue. Closely connected to this is her *mantle* whose turquoise color was reserved for the great mother goddess Omecihuatl. That Mary wears the colors of these gods indicates that she has displaced them by sublimating what is true, good, and lifegiving in them into herself. She is not herself a goddess yet she is greater than these gods. She unites in herself the opposing tensions that the four children of Ometecuhtli and Omecihuatl represent, tensions that had turned into a crisis with the defeat and conquest of Huitzilopochtli, the tribal patron of the Aztecs.

In addition to these features that are original to the image there are four features added later: the stars, the gold sun rays, the moon, and the angel. They have meanings within the Aztec-Nahuatl religious culture but also tend to move the image more in the direction of Spanish-Christian interpretation.[76] Thus they represent the compenetration of symbols necessary to a proper *mestizo* interpretation of both image and story.

The miracle of Guadalupe, La Morenita del Tepeyac, is the effect it produced among the Nahuatl-speaking people. She has given them the ability to interpret the devastating crisis of conquest and colonization in terms that embrace what was true and good and lifegiving in their pre-Columbian culture and yet as sublimated and transformed into this new religious symbolism of the Mother of God and her child, the Christ, whose rejection and death on the cross liberates them from the power of evil that has surrounded them. As such she responds to the deepest instincts of Mexicans: "obsession with legitimacy and the sentiment of being an orphan people."[77] Within six years of the appearance of Guadalupe millions of indigenous people had been baptized as Christians.[78] They had indeed found a new home, a new temple, a new image that gave them a new identity that could be called a "syncretic self" because of the compenetration of Indian and Spanish religious symbolism. "I contend that it [the Guadalupe story] is the first real anthropological translation and proclamation of the gospel to the people of the Americas."[79]

But for Mexican Americans this story and image is not just a cultural syncretism that was liberating for the indigenous population. It was at the same time the affirmation of the children of La Malinche as a new biological reality, *la raza,* born of a Spanish father and an Indian mother. "In *la Morenita* ('the brown Lady') the orphaned and illegitimate Mexican people discovered their true and legitimate mother. 'We are not the children of a violated woman, but children of the unsoiled Virgin Mother. In Guadalupe we pass from the shame and degradation of illegitimacy to the grandeur and pride of being *pure Mexican.'* " This affirmation of a new reality necessarily extends to all of Latin America. "Guadalupe is the key to understanding the Christianity of the New World, the self-image of Mexicans, of Mexican-Americans, and of all Latin Americans."[80]

B. *From La Morenita del Tepeyac to La Mestiza (Chicana).* "The Spanish-Indian confrontation gave birth to the Mexican people; the Anglo-American—Mexican confrontation gave birth to the Mexican-American people." Both have created the experience of *mestizaje:* "the origination of a new people from two ethnically disparate parent peoples."[81] But the two experiences are based on a radical difference. The Spanish-Catholic conquest of Mexico formed a new race through racial mixing; the Nordic-Protestant conquest sought to annihilate the native peoples (and eventually anyone else) if they were in the way of a new Anglo-Saxon Europe with the attendant expansionist mentality justified as "Manifest Destiny." Elizondo expresses the difference well: "Anglo-Americans started to move into the northern territories of what was then Mexican territory. Some came legally, but most were illegal immigrants who had no regard for Mexican laws. From the very first encounters, the Anglo-American immigrants looked upon the Mexicans (for them, all the Spanish-speaking) with disdain. The Mexican was brown, *mestizo,* Spanish-speaking, Roman Catholic. The North American was white, pure-blooded (racial admixture was contamination), English-speaking, Protestant."[82] Thus the first *mestizaje* was biological as well as cultural; the second was for the most part only cultural.

The ensuing history of the first war for independence from Mexico in Texas (the story of the Alamo in 1836) and the subsequent declaration of war on Mexico by President James Polk (May 1846) culminating in the treaty of Guadalupe Hidalgo (February 2, 1848) that ceded close to half of prewar Mexico to the United States (including Texas, the greater portion of the states of New Mexico, Arizona, California, and large parts of Colorado, Nevada, and Utah) is well known, although it has usually been told from the biased perspective of the victors.[83] I will not recount the history here but only point to the experiences that take on poignancy in the telling of the story, the many stories that must be told again and again lest we forget the reasons for so much anguish. It was not only an experience of conquest and colonization but in many ways one of attempted annihilation whether the instrument was murder, deportation, or cultural suicide through assimilation. The most important symbolic reality was the land, a land the conquerors sought to clear of indigenous inhabitants, be they Native Americans or Mexican Americans (also native), for their own greedy purposes. In this of course the provisions of the treaty of Guadalupe Hidalgo that guaranteed the property rights and political rights of those already living in the newly acquired territories, not to mention their right to retain their culture, language, religion, and traditions, were simply ignored or subverted. The history from that day to this has been one of unspeakable violence fueled especially by racist discrimination. The critical boundary was not the political one set up by the treaty but the social and cultural one set up in the hearts and minds of those who considered themselves to belong to a superior race.

Closely connected to the land, then, has been the symbol of the border. Mexican Americans are a border people in two senses. They have been forced to cross the border many times, either "repatriated" to Mexico or called back to supply cheap labor depending on the economic needs of the United States. But in another sense they are a people who by their very nature as *mestizo* can do no other than cross borders whether those borders be physical or cultural. As such they are as a people a living, symbolic embodiment of inclusivity that challenges the three constants of what Elizondo calls "the dynamics between an oppressor in-group and an oppressed out-group," namely group exclusivity or "purity," social distance at the individual, personal level, and elimination of anyone who threatens to diminish or destroy the group barriers. A *mestizo* group that understands itself as mediating a new reality, that takes what is best in each culture while rejecting what is evil without being assimilated into either, will be perceived as a serious threat to both parent cultures.[84]

The most fundamental experience symbolically, revealed in the despoliation of the land and the forced crossing of the border, is the experience of rejection *(rechazo)*. Mexican Americans are neither Mexican nor American but a new and unique ethnic strain born out of *mestizaje*. They have been rejected and demeaned by both Mexicans and Euro-Americans but the key to their future lies in ethnic pride. Elizondo maintains that they have passed through three phases: "survival efforts" that of course continue *(en la lucha)* but in a different way; "development efforts" that involved attempts to assimilate into the Anglo-American culture and so become "good Americans"; and "liberation movements" that utterly reject the preceding and seek to discover and affirm what is true, good, and lifegiving in their unique ethnic and cultural identity. This involves above all a keen remembrance of the past as it exists in their oral history: *cuentas* (stories), *leyendas* (legends), *corridos* (ballads), *bailes* (dances), *fiestas* (celebrations), *flor y canto* (all this combined with poetry and art). The term *Chicano,* a term of derision like "black" for African Americans, was chosen to symbolize the struggle to emerge with a new identity of ethnic pride. The recognition of being a *familia* as *la raza, el pueblo, la gente* is key to sustaining the process (especially *el movimiento* of the mid-1960s to the mid-1970s). "The *acceptance* of *mestizaje* is at the root of reversing the Mexican-American inferiority complex."[85] This means that sociopolitical and socioeconomic activity, as important as it is, is not enough and cannot sustain an ongoing process of liberation. The issue is one of cultural roots, remembered and passed on by *las abuelitas* especially in the form of popular religious practices.

Elizondo outlines the "ensemble of the yearly celebrations of the people," some symbolic of "ultimate identity and belonging," others of "struggle, suffering, and death," and still others of "new creation." Under this latter he places baptism (as rebirth and promise of new life) and the fiesta of Our Lady of Guadalupe. "Fiesta is the mystical celebration of a complex identity, the mystical affirmation that life is a gift and is worth living."[86] This is true of Guadalupe above all. In her we find a common mother for all the inhabitants of the Americas. She lives in all the grandmothers and mothers who have given us life, who have cared for us, and who have remained with us even when the fathers have abandoned us.

The importance of Jeanette Rodriguez's work is not simply the remembrance of the story of Guadalupe but her careful listening to the lived experience of Mexican American women to see how that story continues to live in their faith-experience and to empower them for the struggle. "The story of Our Lady of Guadalupe is a story about a caring God. The image, story, and experience of Our Lady of Guadalupe tell the people that God has not given up on them, affirms them, and is present for them. Moreover, Our Lady of Guadalupe herself is there for them, protects them, and loves them. Although the people's faith may appear uncritical, their faith is salvific because it helps give meaning to their lives. The image of Our Lady of Guadalupe is a symbol of power for a population in a seemingly powerless situation."[87] These women relate to Guadalupe as a person, a woman, a *mestiza,* a mother who listens and responds, heals and gives strength. They can be "intimate, honest, and frank" with her about what they are experiencing in their daily lives. She is a member of *la familia, la raza,* and she images God's unconditional love for them as a compassionate and powerful mother who is always present. Yet as Rodriguez concludes this strong personal relationship of affection and trust, to be liberative, must move one to embrace the prophetic mission as did Juan Diego. To do this each must know the story, not just the one handed on or the one selectively presented for pious purposes but the one that is grounded in Jesus' prophetic mission and reinterprets their own reality: they must know the *whole* story. This will produce tension with traditional expectations but it will be liberative and life-giving. "Bringing the image and devotion of Our Lady of Guadalupe in line with the new situation of Mexican-American women in the United States is akin to what Guadalupe calls upon Juan Diego to do: take the traditional religious symbol of flowers into a new situation, give it new meaning, and thus transform it."[88] Such a liberating interpretation must be related to the "gospel matrix" on the one hand and to the prophetic mission of *mestizaje* in the contemporary world on the other.

3. Gospel Matrix: Mark and the Mexican American Experience

How does the Mexican American experience as embodied in the story of Guadalupe correspond to the Gospel of Mark as we analyzed it in Chapter Two? Although Elizondo's analysis employs all the gospels as sources for what can be said about Jesus, Mark alone provides a sufficient gospel matrix. Mark's story is about the "faith of God" (Mark 11:22). If we have the fidelity of God we can move mountains; we can overcome the boundaries, perplexities, and intransigence that defeat the divine will in our world. Similarly Guadalupe has remained faithful *("se quedó").* Like Jesus in the early Christian communities she has remained alive and powerfully active in the community, the continuing presence of a personal, transcendent, and transforming power within the community. Her story has become intertwined with the story of subsequent generations, especially of *las abuelitas.* Indeed the community was born out of the resurrection experience celebrated as *las mañanitas.*

Here as with Mark "the poetics of narrativity" address "the aporias of time." Paul Ricoeur's threefold rubric applies here as well. First the "world behind the text" is the Amerindian experience of conquest and oppression, the destruction of their temples and the continuing threat to their cultural and spiritual identity. At the same time it is the good news of Jesus' death and resurrection as intended for and transformative of the Amerindian population. Second the "world of the text" is the configuration into a new synthesis of this world, a coherent narrative drawing on earlier oral and written sources that employs plot, character, atmosphere, and tone as already analyzed. As regards tone the "implied author" is clearly omniscient and reliable as narrator of the story. The point of view is God's point of view. The story is revelatory. God creates and affirms a new reality through the compenetration of religious symbolism. Third the "world before the text" involves the "implied reader" (or listener) who, caught up in the "dynamic" and "flow" of the narrative, will see new possibilities for his or her own contemporary reality. As such the genre, like the Gospel of Mark, is best described as "myth-parable" insofar as the story both establishes world and subverts world. The old world that imposes alien religious symbols is subverted but the new world of *mestizaje* is still structured by the paschal mystery of suffering, rejection, and death. All who hear this story will be drawn into the mystery of the reign of God, into the tension between life and death, myth and parable. This is a story that has metaphoric impact. It functions as "an instrument within a social process." The response of the reader/listener will reveal the depth of personal identities *(rostro y corazón)* and communal commitments.

We have already given a reading of both Mark and Guadalupe. Here it will be enough to point out some of the significant parallels. Will they respect this son born of an Indian maiden? It is a story told in the simple, rustic, yet eloquent language of Nahuatl. It is a story that redeems the Indians' dignity and importance for it is a story about their own, an Indian maiden and her child. The irony is that like Galilean Jews they were considered ignorant and insignificant and were despised by the rich and powerful as uneducated, lower class, rural. Jesus in Mark was from the obscure and insignificant Nazareth of Galilee, a contrast to all those from Judea and the Jerusalemites (Mark 1:5). From the very beginning of the gospel (1:1-13) something totally new and unexpected is happening. Whether at birth (Matthew and Luke) or at baptism (Mark) Jesus is identified as "the new human being" (eventually as the "Son of Man"), God's own beloved son, rejected by the world but chosen by God (1:10-11). Elizondo connects Galilee with *mestizaje:* "A natural, ongoing biological and cultural *mestizaje* was taking place [in Galilee] . . . a sign of impurity and a cause for rejection."[89] While the evidence for intermarriage is not strong he does make a more nuanced point about cultural *mestizaje:* "By growing up in Galilee, Jesus was a cultural *mestizo,* assuming unto himself the great traditions that flourished in his home territory. . . . Culturally and linguistically speaking, Jesus was a *mestizo.* And we dare say that to those of his time, he must have appeared to be a biological *mestizo*—the child of a

Jewish girl and a Roman father. . . . Jesus is thus the rejected one who becomes the source of solidarity among the rejected of society."[90]

For Mark, Jesus' proclamation of the reign of God and call for a radical change of mind and heart *(metanoia)* and for faith *(pistis)* is what leads to his rejection. This can be connected to *mestizaje* insofar as his message was universal and inclusive and so took the form of breaking social boundaries and purity maps in his actions of healing and table-fellowship. Such a challenge to the cultural, economic, and political codes both then and now carries with it rejection and the threat of death. The refusal on the part of those around Jesus is characterized as "hardness of heart," an inability to see and hear (Mark 4:10-12), so that even the new "insiders" have no guarantees that they will persevere. Openness to the "other" is a challenge to anyone who would be a disciple regardless of his or her social, cultural, and economic situation. Everything depends on what comes from the heart *(rostro y corazón)*. Elizondo puts it well: "Jesus became existential nothingness. He came that all might be one, and it is precisely by breaking all the barriers at the deepest level of human existence [death?] that he himself in his very person initiates the new existence. . . . Having suffered the pain of rejection, he rejects rejection and gives us the bases for the restructuring of all society. We are all invited to be children in the Reign of God."[91]

For Mark the only way to overcome the power of rejection and death is the way of the cross. For the new people born of *mestizaje* the crucified Jesus is no stranger. The "new human being" (Son of Man) must be handed over, tortured, rejected, killed. Jesus as the new human being was the only one who could free humankind from the captivity of sin, law, and death, but it is safe to say that only a truly *mestizo* people can, through participation in his way, free our world from the captivity of race, class, and gender, and so break the cycle of "sacred violence" especially in the form of sacrificial scapegoating. To do this requires a prophetic challenge to the symbols of established power, secular and sacred (city and temple). "Revitalized Christians are no longer afraid to die for what they believe in, for they know with the certitude of the faith-encounter that there is more to life than the threat of death, and that even torture and death cannot quench the Spirit. Because they have discovered life, they are no longer afraid to die. . . . In all this, prophecy is not just being spoken about; it is being lived out in ongoing confrontations by the previously powerless of society who now dare to go to the Jerusalems of today's society: city hall, transnational corporations, boards of education, ecclesiastical offices."[92]

Jesus' prophetic challenge to the power structure represented by the Temple and the authorities in Jerusalem would make no sense if it were not grounded in the Scriptures and the power of God (Mark 12:24), that is, the faith that God is a God of the living and not the dead. Thus the stone the builders have rejected (Ps 118:22, a favorite text of Elizondo) has become the foundation stone of a new reality. "The *mestizo* is the biblical stone, rejected by the builders of this world, that God has chosen to be the cornerstone of a new creation, not chosen for honor and privilege, but for a sacred mission."[93] Although it may appear that God has abandoned his beloved Son on the cross this parabolic openness is intertwined with mythic meaning, the final victory of God over the power of death. What was true of God, Jesus, and the disciples in our analysis of Mark is directly applicable to the experience of *mestizos*. First, God is a God of the living *who has power over death*. The circle of death is surrounded by the God of the living so that the final hope and ultimate confidence must be placed in this God, now revealed in *La Morenita*. Second, Jesus is the new human being, now *mestizo,* who *transforms the meaning of death.* He redeems us by being the man he was, a man who faced death already in this life (initially at his baptism) and defeated it on its own ground, who therefore is fully and completely free, who has broken through the boundaries of death (wilderness and tomb, sea and Temple) and so achieved a "reordering of power." Third, the new community of disciples *must be willing to face death.* This community, *la raza* as *una familia,* is inclusive, egalitarian, and grounded in the sole authority of Jesus' own free gift of his life for the sake of others, indeed of all humanity. This community is on a journey toward the end of history, the final and definitive liberation of all human beings as children of the same mother: *la raza cósmica.*[94]

4. The Rejected Prophet

It seems clear from all that has been said that the dominant image of Jesus, the root metaphor embodying the Mexican American experience is "rejected prophet." Jesus was a prophet sent to his people and rejected, but in his death and resurrection he has "rejected rejection" and enabled his followers to do likewise. "Jesus appears in the New Testament as the aggressive prophet of non-violent love who refuses to conform to the violence of the structures in full loyalty to the tradition of the God of his people. . . ."[95]

Elizondo formulates the new and emergent possibilities of *mestizaje* under three rubrics. "The first principle for the New Testament interpretation of the contemporary situation is the Galilee principle: *what human beings reject, God chooses as his very own.*"[96] For Mexican Americans this has been the experience of a double rejection by both parent cultures, Mexican and Anglo. But because this suffering and rejection has been so great Mexican Americans are uniquely fitted to be the mediators of *la nueva raza* that will unite the two Americas. Second there is "the Jerusalem principle: God chooses an oppressed people, not to bring them comfort in their oppression, but to enable them to confront, transcend, and transform whatever in the oppressor society diminishes and destroys the fundamental dignity of human nature."[97] For Mexican Americans this means that *mestizaje* is a prophetic mission to society that is both critical (including self-critical) and open to the "other." Such a mission invites violence and so demands a willingness to face death in order to defeat it on its own ground.

The "third principle of interpretation and re-creation" is "the *resurrection principle:* only love can triumph over evil, and no human power can prevail against the power of unlimited love."[98] For Mexican Americans this means that *mestizaje,* based in prophecy, must be festive. The *fiesta* is integral to the prophetic lifestyle for it is what keeps the Spirit alive and nourishes the life of the community. Of all the celebrations none is more central than *La Morenita del Tepeyac,* the foundational experience that gave birth to the Mexican American community as "local church." It is as significant as Pentecost for the "universal Church." "In the celebration of Our Lady of Guadalupe, we Mexican-Americans celebrate the common mother of all the inhabitants of the Americas. As it was the ones in greatest need, the despised and rejected Galileans, who first experienced the unlimited and compassionate love of the Father through Jesus, so it was the ones in greatest need at the time of the birth of the Americas, the conquered and despised Indians, who first experienced the unlimited and compassionate love of the mother of God."[99] The gift of her love is her child, Jesus—God's beloved Son, the rejected prophet, the *mestizo* who embraces all of humanity in the paschal experience of a new creation. And so it is that the story continues. . . .

Notes: Chapter Five

[1] Marcus J. Borg, *Meeting Jesus Again for the First Time. The Historical Jesus and the Heart of Contemporary Faith* (San Francisco: HarperSanFrancisco, 1994) 70.

[2] Borg offers a compelling analysis of "the centrality of 'story' in Jewish and Christian scriptures." (ibid., 120). This includes the narrative framework of the Bible as a whole, the many individual stories, and the "macrostories" among which he affirms three at the heart of Scripture: exodus, exile, and priestly. We need all three of these diverse metaphors that reflect the multiple and varied needs of the human condition: liberation from bondage (exodus), "coming home" from alienation and meaningless (exile), acceptance of ourselves as we are in our sin, guilt, shame, and negative self-image (priestly). These all affect our image of Jesus. Borg's point is to move beyond fideistic and moralistic images to a transformist understanding. "It is a vision of the Christian life as a journey of transformation, exemplified by the story of discipleship as well as by the exodus and exile stories. It leads from life under the lordship of culture to the life of companionship with God" (p. 136).

[3] John Shea, "Theology and Autobiography," *Commonweal* (June 16, 1978) reprinted in John Navone, S.J., *Seeking God in Story* (Collegeville: The Liturgical Press, 1990) 238.

[4] T. Richard Snyder, *Divided We Fall. Moving from Suspicion to Solidarity* (Louisville: Westminster/John Knox Press, 1992) 20.

[5] Ibid.

[6] Ibid., 121.

[7] Allan Figueroa Deck, "Latino Theology: The Year of the 'Boom,'" *JH/LT* 1/2 (February 1994) 51–63. Good review articles on the emergence of U. S. Hispanic/Latino theology include Fernando F. Segovia, "A New Manifest Destiny: The Emerging Theological Voice of Hispanic Americans," *RStR* 17/2 (April 1991) 101–109; Arturo Bañuelas, "U. S. Hispanic Theology," *Missiology: An International Review* 20/2 (April 1992) 275–300; Allan Figueroa Deck, S.J., "Introduction" in Deck, ed., *Frontiers of Hispanic Theology in the United States* (Maryknoll: Orbis Books, 1992) ix-xxvi; John P. Rossing, "Mestizaje and Marginality: A Hispanic American Theology," *Theology Today* 45/3 (October 1988) 293–304.

[8] There is much discussion over the best terminology to describe this movement as a group. Many authors use the terms "Latino" and "Hispanic" interchangeably. The unresolved tension is reflected in the title of the new *Journal of Hispanic/Latino Theology*. Some prefer to be more specific as in Cuban American, Mexican American, etc. With regard to the latter as an ethnic group Virgilio Elizondo distinguishes in terms of what people prefer to call themselves between *Mexicanos* who "still speak Spanish and maintain strong ties with old Mexico," Mexican Americans who "usually 'accept' their Mexican heritage, but linguistically, socially, and culturally . . . identify more with the U. S. mentality and lifestyle," and Chicanos who "are struggling to emerge with a new identity." Virgilio Elizondo, *Galilean Journey. The Mexican-American Promise* (Maryknoll: Orbis Books, 1983) 21. Mexican American has the advantage of offering parallels to African American, Native American, Euro-American, etc. We will retain that designation as does Elizondo, but understanding it now in terms of the Chicano struggle for a distinctive cultural identity that Elizondo calls *mestizaje*.

[9] Virgilio Elizondo, "Hispanic Theology and Popular Piety: From Inter-religious Encounter to a New Ecumenism," Catholic Theological Society of America, *Proceedings of the Forty-Eighth Annual Convention* (June 10–13, 1993) 13.

[10] Juan Luis Segundo, "Two Theologies of Liberation," *The Month* (October 1984) 321–327, cited in Phillip Berryman, *Liberation Theology. The Essential Facts About the Revolutionary Movement in Latin America and Beyond* (Bloomington: Meyer-Stone Books, 1987) 86–87.

[11] Berryman, *Liberation Theology* 5–6, offers these elements as an initial description of liberation theology.

[12] Jon Sobrino, *Jesus the Liberator. A Historical-Theological Reading of Jesus of Nazareth* (Maryknoll: Orbis Books, 1993) 28. See my review in *TS* 55 (September 1994) 565–567.

[13] This is the view especially of Gustavo Gutiérrez. See Michael L. Cook, S.J., "Jesus From the Other Side of History: Christology in Latin America," *TS* 44 (June 1983) 258–261.

[14] Ibid., 277.

[15] This point has been strongly emphasized by U. S. Hispanics. See Deck, "Latino Theology" and the references cited there.

[16] "In contrast with the antidialogical and non-communicative 'deposits' of the banking method of education, the program content of the problem-posing method— dialogical par excellence—is constituted and organized by the students' view of the

world, where their own generative themes are found." Paulo Freire, *Pedagogy of the Oppressed* (New York: The Seabury Press, 1970) 101. And further: "It is absolutely essential that the oppressed participate in the revolutionary process with an increasingly critical awareness of their role as Subjects of the transformation" (ibid., 121). A good summary of the method is in Berryman, *Liberation Theology* 34–42.

[17] Freire, *Pedagogy of the Oppressed* 31. In terms of the faith-images of Jesus we have proposed, an overemphasis on the suffering and abandonment of Jesus in Mark can lead to internalized impotence, the mystical and contemplative orientation in the Creed to a flight from this world, the academic and synthetic thrust of systematics to ideological dominance. Leonardo Boff summarizes some of the criticisms of "the traditional pictures of Christ" proposed by liberation christology: "The agonizing and dying Christ of Latin American tradition is what Assmann calls a 'Christ of the internalized impotence of the oppressed.' The Mother of Sorrows, with her pierced heart, personifies the passive submission and subjugation of the woman. Her tears are an expression of the pain that Latin American women endured as the colonizers' greed for power and gold massacred their children. But it is not merely the christology of resignation that is subjected to criticism. Equally under attack is the christology of active domination, with its imperial, monarchical Christ, covered with gold, like the Portuguese or Spanish kings, or with its images of a warlike Christ who knows only victories." Leonardo Boff, "The Contribution of Liberation Theology to a New Paradigm" in Hans Küng and David Tracy, eds., *Paradigm Change in Theology. A Symposium for the Future* (New York: Crossroad, 1989) 410–411. See José Míguez Bonino, ed., *Faces of Jesus. Latin American Christologies* (Maryknoll: Orbis Books, 1984), especially the articles by Saúl Trinidad, Pedro Negre Rigol, and Georges Casalis. These articles are also used as a resource in Cook, "Jesus From the Other Side of History," 279–280.

[18] Carlos Mesters, *Defenseless Flower. A New Reading of the Bible* (Maryknoll: Orbis Books, 1989) 24. The book "describes what has happened and what continues to happen among the poor when they use and interpret the Bible in the midst of their day-to-day lives" (p. viii). This involves a new way of seeing "from below" but the purpose is to integrate three forces that are in constant tension: the life of the people ("pre-text"), the faith of the Church ("con-text"), and the results of scientific exegesis ("text"). "Despite all its defects and failings, this reading of the Bible by the poor creates a new context which enables academic exegesis to rediscover its mission in the church" (p. 159).

[19] Gustavo Gutiérrez, "The Irruption of the Poor in Latin America and the Christian Communities of the Common People," in Sergio Torres and John Eagleson, eds., *The Challenge of Basic Christian Communities* (Maryknoll: Orbis Books, 1981) 107–123.

[20] "The social and political impact of base communities may be viewed in terms of (1) initial consciousness-raising, (2) their vision of life and motivation for involvement, (3) the sense of community and mutual aid and support they generate, (4) the experience of grass-roots democracy, (5) the direct actions they engage in, and (6) directly political effects." Berryman, *Liberation Theology* 72–73. While emphasizing the importance of base communities as qualitative, Berryman insists on maintaining a sense of proportion in quantitative terms. Only a small proportion of the population participates even where such communities are highly developed. "Despite the

considerable attention given to base communities in Nicaragua, far less than 1 percent of the population participates in them. Even in Brazil, where these communities are most developed, somewhat under 2 percent of the country participates actively in base communities" (p. 72).

[21] Cook, "Jesus From the Other Side of History," 278.

[22] Andrés G. Guerrero, *A Chicano Theology* (Maryknoll: Orbis Books, 1987) 129. I say "has become English" because the case can be and has been made that the southwestern United States was originally indigenous and Mexican and that the later predominance of English speakers represents an invasion and occupation. See Rodolfo Acuña, *Occupied America. A History of Chicanos* (3rd ed. New York: Harper Collins, 1988).

[23] Deck, "Latino Theology," 55–56. See Roberto Goizueta's discussion of "the shift from a Eurocentric to a polycentric Christianity" (J. B. Metz) in which there is no longer one center but many centers (David Tracy): "By definition, a genuine polycentrism rejects the existence of *a* center, the very center presupposed by the notion of marginalization." Roberto S. Goizueta, "United States Hispanic Theology and the Challenge of Pluralism" in Deck, ed., *Frontiers of Hispanic Theology* 14 (emphasis in original).

[24] Segovia brings out well the diversity and complexity of such umbrella terms in Fernando F. Segovia, "Hispanic American Theology and the Bible: Effective Weapon and Faithful Ally" in Roberto S. Goizueta, ed., *We Are A People! Initiatives in Hispanic American Theology* (Minneapolis: Fortress Press, 1992) 25–30.

[25] Segovia's article (ibid.) offers a fine analysis of the several positions by using a Hispanic theologian as representative of each: Ada María Isasi-Díaz, a Cuban American and Roman Catholic for *mujerista* theology (see her more recent work *En la Lucha. In the Struggle. A Hispanic Women's Liberation Theology* [Minneapolis: Fortress Press, 1993]); Harold J. Recinos, a Puerto Rican American and a United Methodist minister for *barrio* theology (see his *Hear the Cry! A Latino Pastor Challenges the Church* [Louisville: Westminster/John Knox Press, 1989]); Virgilio Elizondo, a Mexican American and Roman Catholic priest for *mestizaje* theology (see his *The Future Is Mestizo* [New York: Crossroad, 1988]); Justo L. González, a Cuban American and United Methodist minister for *mañana* theology (see his *Mañana. Christian Theology from a Hispanic Perspective* [Nashville: Abingdon Press, 1990]).

[26] Roberto S. Goizueta, "Rediscovering Praxis: The Significance of U. S. Hispanic Experience for Theological Method" in Goizueta, ed., *We Are A People!* 57. The citation is from Aristotle, *Politics* 1.4.1254.

[27] Ibid., 63.

[28] Ibid., 67.

[29] Ibid., 68. The importance and centrality of popular religiosity is a common theme among U. S. Hispanic/Latino theologians. See, for example, Orlando O. Espín, "Tradition and Popular Religion: An Understanding of the *Sensus Fidelium*" in Deck, ed., *Frontiers of Hispanic Theology* 62–87; idem, "Trinitarian Monotheism and the Birth of Popular Catholicism: The Case of Sixteenth-Century Mexico," *Missiology* 20/2 (April 1992) 177–204; idem, "Grace and Humanness: A Hispanic Perspective" in Goizueta, ed., *We Are A People!* 133–164; Juan José Huitrado-Rizo, M.C.C.J., "Hispanic Popular Religiosity: The Expression of a People Coming to Life," *NTR* 3/4

(November 1990) 43–55; Rosa María Icaza, C.C.V.I., "Prayer, Worship, and Liturgy in a United States Hispanic Key" in Deck, ed., *Frontiers of Hispanic Theology* 134–153; C. Gilbert Romero, *Hispanic Devotional Piety: Tracing the Biblical Roots* (Maryknoll: Orbis Books, 1991). Recently, Robert E. Wright has offered a telling critique of the term "popular religiosity," which *may* be fleeting and transitory. He prefers "folk religiosity," which includes popular religiosity but is transgenerational and people-forming-and-sustaining. "Precisely because of its 'staying power' and the identification of the folk with it, folk religiosity gives the student a more profound entry into the religious life of a cultural group." Robert E. Wright, "If It's Official, It Can't Be Popular? Reflections on Popular and Folk Religion," *JH/LT* 1/3 (May 1994) 61. For an interesting example of such a study see John M. Ingham, *Mary, Michael, and Lucifer. Folk Catholicism in Central Mexico* (Austin: University of Texas Press, 1986).

[30] For a vivid portrayal of the importance of *abuelitas* in the culture, see Rudolfo A. Añaya, *Bless Me, Ultima* (Berkeley: Tonatiuh-Quinto Sol, 1972); also Victor Villaseñor, *Rain of Gold* (New York: Laurel [Dell], 1991). It is equally important, however, to recognize the reality (*la realidad*) of "the new *mestiza*" (Gloria Anzuldúa, *Borderlands: The New Mestiza* [San Francisco: Aunt Lute Book Co., 1987]). U. S. Chicanas have been categorized as "the elder generation," "contemporary urban women," and "young women" (Irene I. Blea, *La Chicana and the Intersection of Race, Class, and Gender* [NewYork: Praeger Books, 1992]). Yolanda Tarango makes a similar distinction in relation to the Church between *viejitas* who foster popular religiosity in the *home*; the mothers of the present generation who perform voluntary service in the *parish*; and today's women who are rediscovering community *outside the Church* and so "are 'recreating' church" (Yolanda Tarango, C.C.V.I., "The Hispanic Woman and Her Role in the Church," *NTR* 3/4 [November 1990] 61). Jeanette Rodriguez, "Experience as a Resource for Feminist Thought," *JH/LT* (November 1993) 68–76, employs these resources and concludes that "the struggle of the *mestiza*, above all, is a feminist one" (p. 74).

[31] Goizueta, "Rediscovering Praxis," 69–74.

[32] Ada María Isasi-Díaz and Yolanda Tarango, *Hispanic Women. Prophetic Voice in the Church* (Minneapolis: Fortress Press, 1988) 94–103 describe the method as critical reflection on action that involves dialogue and conscientization: (1) "telling our stories," which brings lived experience into common awareness for the sake of self-determination; (2) "analysis," which must be born out of the lived experience and explore causes and structures; (3) "liturgizing," the aesthetic as an expression of feeling/reason that frees and encourages the religious imagination; and (4) "strategizing," which is an ongoing communal process to change oppressive structures (whether internal to oneself, familial, or societal) through education, advocacy, and witness. The task and goal is liberation as an ongoing process. For further developments and refinements, see Isasi-Díaz, *En la Lucha*. Guerrero, *A Chicano Theology*, employs a similar method of listening to the story to allow shared themes to emerge and questioning to clarify and remove doubts. In all of this there is heavy reliance on oral tradition.

[33] Isasi-Díaz and Tarango, *Hispanic Women* 3–4. This book, along with Isasi-Díaz's *En la Lucha*, represents an attempt to put into practice the basic methodological principle of Gustavo Gutiérrez, namely that the poor and oppressed must become "the active, historical subjects of a new understanding of faith and theology." Hence both

books insist that the true theologians are the community of Hispanic women, including the grass roots, the pastoral agents, and the professionals. This is grounded in the fact that the source of *mujerista* theology is "the lived experience of Hispanic women" (*En la Lucha* 73, 173–179).

[34] Ada María Isasi-Díaz, "Praxis: The Heart of *Mujerista* Theology," *JH/LT* 1/1 (November 1993) 44–55.

[35] Isasi-Díaz and Tarango, *Hispanic Women* 4–6. The same themes are developed by Isasi-Díaz in her article "Praxis" and her book *En la Lucha*.

[36] Jeffrey Carlson, "Crossan's Jesus and Christian Identity" in Jeffrey Carlson and Robert A. Ludwig, eds., *Jesus and Faith. A Conversation on the Work of John Dominic Crossan* (Maryknoll: Orbis Books, 1994) 38.

[37] Isasi-Díaz and Tarango, *Hispanic Women* 66–70; Isasi-Díaz, *En la Lucha* 45–52.

[38] Isasi-Díaz, *En la Lucha* 11. Chapter One describes three main elements of Hispanic women's ethnicity: *mestizaje,* survival, and socioeconomic reality. Chapter Two describes three more: Latinas' preferred future (*proyecto historico*), popular religiosity, and Spanish. The rest of the book unfolds an "ethnomethodology" that learns from people by dialoguing with them and seeks a "knowledge synthesis" that is inductive and interpretive, holistic and open to diversity, and engages in comparative analysis to beget "generative words." Therefore ethnography and meta-ethnography help "to discover, organize, present, and interpret the source of *mujerista* theology: the lived-experience of Hispanic Women" (p. 73).

[39] Ibid., 167.

[40] Ibid., 168.

[41] Guerrero, *A Chicano Theology* 95.

[42] Allan Figueroa Deck, S.J., "Introduction" in Deck, ed., *Frontiers of Hispanic Theology* xv. The summary articles referred to in n. 7 make the same point. Rossing, "*Mestizaje* and Marginality," 297 puts it well: "The bilingual, bicultural identity weaves Latin American and North American cultural traditions together into a new fabric."

[43] Deck, "Latino Theology," 62–63. Compare Arthur F. McGovern, *Liberation Theology and Its Critics* (Maryknoll: Orbis Books, 1989) 83: "I would clearly designate spirituality as *the* dominant theme of contemporary liberation theology" (emphasis in original).

[44] Juan-Lorenzo Hinojosa, "Culture, Spirituality, and United States Hispanics" in Deck, ed., *Frontiers of Hispanic Theology* 155.

[45] Ibid., 163.

[46] Roberto S. Goizueta, "Preface," in Goizueta, ed., *We Are A People!* viii.

[47] Elizondo, *The Future is Mestizo* 39.

[48] Gloria Iñes Loya, P.B.V.M., "The Hispanic Woman: *Pasionaria* and *Pastora* of the Hispanic Community" in Deck, ed., *Frontiers of Hispanic Theology* 128. Virgilio Elizondo in his "Foreword" to Jeanette Rodriguez, *Our Lady of Guadalupe. Faith and Empowerment among Mexican-American Women* (Austin: University of Texas Press, 1994) x, makes the same point very strongly: "As theologians are supposed to be the interpreters of our faith experience, so the Mexican-American women have been the main interpreters and transmitters of our dynamic faith experience. Our *abuelitas, viejitas,* and *madrecitas* have been the functional priestesses and theologians of our *iglesia del pueblo.*"

[49] Gonzalez, *Mañana* 77–78 (emphasis in original). This has consequences for U. S. history: "Therefore, part of our responsibility as Hispanics, not only for our own sake but also for the sake of other minorities as well as for the sake of the dominant group, is constantly to remind that group of their immigrant beginnings, of the Indian massacres, of the rape of the land, of the war with Mexico, of riches drawn from slave labor, of neocolonial exploitation, and of any other guilty items that one may be inclined to forget in an innocent reading of history" (pp. 79–80).

[50] Ibid., 41.

[51] Virgilio P. Elizondo, *La Morenita. Evangelizer of the Americas* (San Antonio: Mexican American Cultural Center, 1980) 45. In a similar vein Guerrero (*A Chicano Theology* 113–115), under the heading "Guadalupe as a Symbol of Woman Against *Machismo*" avers that the *macho* must contend with the fact that "we are the '*hijos de la chingada*,' the sons of the Violated One" not to scapegoat her and maltreat her but to defend her and protect her, as does Guadalupe. A full explanation of the term can be found in Octavio Paz, *The Labyrinth of Solitude and Other Writings* (New York: Grove Weidenfeld, 1985) in the chapter entitled "The Sons of La Malinche," 65–88.

[52] Elizondo, "Foreword" in Rodriguez, *Our Lady of Guadalupe* xiii. Rodriguez herself under the heading "Malinche: The Archetype of the Feminine" (pp. 73–76) discusses the traditional view and an alternative view: "In summary, the Mexican woman historically has been depicted as treacherous, passive, and willingly violated (i. e., Malinche). An alternative view is a young woman who was able to assess her situation and able to act according to a value system that acknowledges and honors her understanding and worldview as well as concern and compassion for the people around her" (p. 75).

[53] Elizondo, *La Morenita* 60ff. He offers a good analysis of the "cosmovision" of indigenous America (ch. 1), then of Spain (ch. 2), and brings the conquest into focus from the viewpoint of the conquered (ch. 3). Jeanette Rodriguez has a good summary in ch. 1, "Historical Context: The Spanish Conquest" in *Our Lady of Guadalupe* 1–15. Ana María Pineda, R.S.M., "Evangelization of the New World: A New World Perspective," *Missiology* 20/2 (April 1992) 151–161 makes the important point that the Mesoamerican world had an oral system of communication whereas Spain was a literate culture. Thus the destruction of the Aztec-Nahuatl wise men and their painted codices incapacitated the people and removed the sources necessary to understand the culture and so evangelize effectively. "Instead of building on the perspective of oral culture, the original evangelizers assumed that literacy was the medium characteristic of all human beings" (p. 160). In the same issue of *Missiology* Orlando Espín, "Trinitarian Monotheism" 177–204 analyzes colonial Mexican "popular religious constellations," i. e., Amerindian pictorial catechisms, religious art, and popular devotions, and concludes: "These European Christians were so bound to the philosophical language of their theologies that they could not inculturate trinitarian doctrine" (p. 199). See also Robert Ricard, *The Spiritual Conquest of Mexico* (Berkeley: University of California Press, 1966).

[54] José Míguez Bonino, "La piedad popular en América Latina," *Concilium* 96 (1974) 442 (translation mine from "Jesus From the Other Side of History" 278; there follows a discussion of "the ironic sense of popular culture which expresses both the originality of the people and a subliminal protest that is potentially subversive").

[55] Rodriguez, *Our Lady of Guadalupe* 45–46.

⁵⁶ Loya, "The Hispanic Woman," 129. She refers to John West, *Mexican American Folklore* (Little Rock: August House, 1988) for more background and variants to the legend.

⁵⁷ Ingham, *Folk Catholicism in Central Mexico*, makes a similar correlation through the image of "two Eves: the innocent Eve and the Eve of the Fall, although both are one. These considerations may explain why young girls dress as Malinches for the fiesta of the Virgen de Guadalupe. La Malinche evokes the negative side of Eve inasmuch as she is associated with the Llorona, but she is also connected, through her association with Eve, to Mary. The practice implies that Malinche is identified with the Virgin, and indeed 'Malinche' is a diminutive form of 'Mary'. Young girls are asexual, like Eve before the Fall. Interestingly, even the Llorona wears a wedding dress, a symbol of virginal purity" (p. 183).

⁵⁸ Elizondo, *La Morenita* 75–81, gives an abbreviated version that is reproduced in Rodriguez, *Our Lady of Guadalupe* 31–36. Direct quotations in English are taken from the latter unless otherwise noted. Both authors are not so much interested in the scientific "history" (that, Elizondo says, is a concern of the powerful) but in the story as a story of the powerless in their struggle for survival and liberation. Jacques Lafaye, *Quetzalcoatl and Guadalupe. The Formation of Mexican National Consciousness 1531–1813* (Chicago: University of Chicago Press, 1976) sees her primarily as a sociopolitical tool of Mexican creoles (Spaniards born in Mexico) striving for national unity and liberation against the "*gachupines*" (Spaniards). For him the image has no historical basis but was painted by an unknown Indian ca. 1556 and the cult was "invented" by Miguel Sánchez in 1648: "Allegorical exegesis was a springboard from which Miguel Sánchez vaulted to the peaks of creole syncretic spirituality. . . . Through the metamorphosis of beliefs the Mexicans rediscovered their solar emblem, obscured by the Conquest. There, perhaps, is one of the secrets of the enigmatic figure of Tepeyac" (p. 261). And further: "The importance of the cult of Our Lady of Guadalupe in Mexican spiritual life, with its numerous intellectual and artistic repercussions, was only equalled by the weakness of the pious tradition's historical foundations" (p. 262). The prejudice of a print culture comes to the fore in the following: "Modern methods of historical inquiry do not consider oral tradition admissible evidence when it comes to establishing facts" (p. 290). In the final analysis, however, he does recognize that "the question is not whether the image of Our Lady of Guadalupe, venerated on Mount Tepeyac, is the result of a miracle or the work of a native artist. 'The problem is to understand how it happened that so many men believed and still believe . . .'" (p. 299, citing Marc Bloch). Indeed the originality of this new mythical image is "the birth certificate of a new culture" (p. 301).

⁵⁹ Rodriguez, *Our Lady of Guadalupe* 36–44. See Clodomiro L. Siller-Acuña, *Flor y canto del Tepeyac: Historia de las apariciones de Sta. Ma. de Guadalupe; Texto y comentario* (Mexico: Servir, 1981) and his other articles noted by Rodriguez. The comments that follow frequently depend on this fuller version as the abbreviated version too often leaves out just those elements vital to the Nahuatl interpretation. The original language of the *Nican Mopohua* ("Here it is told" or "In good order and careful arrangement"), published in 1649 by Luis Lasso de la Vega, is Nahuatl. Some scholars believe it contains a much earlier document written around 1560–1570 by an Indian who was a writer and scholar, Don Antonio Valeriano. It would be based on earlier oral tradition (and an early written summary). Thus as in the case of the gospels

there would be a period of oral tradition, a first and second redaction in written form, and a final edition. See Rodriguez, *Our Lady of Guadalupe* 17–19.

[60] Elizondo, *La Morenita* 12.

[61] Rodriguez, *Our Lady of Guadalupe* 6–10, gives a good account of "the clash of cultures," following Elizondo's themes: "land, the soul, the greatest sins, the nature of the person, truth, and the understanding of reality, time, and death" (p. 7).

[62] Ibid., 9.

[63] Ingham, *Folk Catholicism in Central Mexico* 26.

[64] Ibid., 28.

[65] Ibid., 180–185. In his study of syncretism in Tlayacapan (a small village in the northern uplands of Morelos in Central Mexico) he sees the gods of pre-Hispanic times being replaced by and assimilated into Christian figures as follows: North into devils and demons; West into Adamic figures; South into agents of the devil; and East into holy figures including Christ, Mary, St. Michael the Archangel, and St. John the Baptist. He affirms "a measure of symbolic sense" in associating Mary with Tonantzin-Cihuacoatl insofar as she is the second Eve who overcomes the evil of the first Eve (also represented by La Malinche and La Llorona), but he feels there was "a stronger basis" for identifying Mary with Chalchuihtlicue, namely her blue dress, her virginity, her symbolism of fertility and rejuvenation.

[66] Rodriguez, *Our Lady of Guadalupe* 38, citing Siller-Acuña.

[67] Ibid., 52.

[68] Ibid., 40, citing Siller-Acuña.

[69] Ibid., 37.

[70] Ibid., 44.

[71] Ibid., 43, following the text of Siller-Acuña.

[72] Ibid., 44.

[73] Elizondo, *Galilean Journey* 43–44.

[74] Rodriguez, *Our Lady of Guadalupe* 127–128.

[75] Ibid., 29.

[76] *Stars* = the "luminous skirt" of Omecihuatl and the Christian "Queen of heaven"; *sun-rays* = the sun god, Quetzalcoatl, and Christian glory surrounding one assumed into heaven; *moon* = the god of night, the moon god, and the Christian image of the woman in Revelation; *angel* = being carried by others as a sign of royalty/divinity and the Christian image of Mary as "Queen of Angels," the mediatrix of all graces. Lafaye, *Quetzalcoatl and Guadalupe* 241ff. suggests that the cult as "invented" by Miguel Sánchez in 1648 was based on Rev 12:1-2: "A great portent appeared in heaven: a woman clothed with the sun, with the moon under her feet, and on her head a crown of twelve stars. She was pregnant and was crying out in birthpangs, in the agony of giving birth" (NRSV).

[77] Elizondo, *La Morenita* 90.

[78] Rodriguez, *Our Lady of Guadalupe* 45 says "nine million" citing Elizondo, *La Morenita* and William Madsen, "Religious Syncretism" in Manning Nash, ed., *Social Anthropology*. Vol. 6: *Handbook of Middle American Indians* (Austin: University of Texas Press, 1967) 369–391.

[79] Elizondo, *The Future is Mestizo* 60.

[80] Elizondo, *Galilean Journey* 12 (emphasis in original).

[81] Ibid., 5.

⁸² Ibid., 14.

⁸³ For the Latino/Hispanic viewpoint there are brief summaries in Elizondo, *Galilean Journey* 1–46; idem, *The Future Is Mestizo*; Guerrero, *A Chicano Theology* 5–30; Allan Figueroa Deck, S.J., *The Second Wave: Hispanic Ministry and the Evangelization of Cultures* (Mahwah, N.J.: Paulist Press, 1989) 26–52. For fuller accounts (1) with a more political and economic emphasis see Acuña, *Occupied America*; Carey McWilliams, *North From Mexico. The Spanish-Speaking People of the United States* (Philadelphia: J. B. Lippincott, 1949; repr. New York: Greenwood Press, 1968); (2) with a more ecclesial emphasis Moises Sandoval, ed., *Fronteras: A History of the Latin American Church in the USA Since 1513* (San Antonio: Mexican American Cultural Center, 1983); idem, *On the Move. A History of the Hispanic Church in the United States* (Maryknoll: Orbis Books, 1990); (3) for a collection that includes selections on liturgy, catechetics, history, poetry, politics, and culture see Antonio M. Stevens Arroyo, *Prophets Denied Honor. An Anthology on the Hispanic Church in the United States* (Maryknoll: Orbis Books, 1980); for a similar collection with more emphasis on literature see Luis Valdez and Stan Steiner, eds., *Aztlan. An Anthology of Mexican American Literature* (New York: Alfred A. Knopf, 1972) as well as the novels cited in n. 30.

⁸⁴ Elizondo, *Galilean Journey* 16–18. This entails a sense of rejection that flows from the double alienation and margination of the *mestizo* who "is not allowed to feel at home anywhere" (p. 99). "As Mestizos, our flesh and blood identity has consistently margined us from both parent groups. We have been too Spanish for the Indians and too Indian for the Spaniards, too Mexican for the United States, and too 'Gringo' for our Mexican brothers and sisters. Our nonbeing has been our being!" Elizondo, "Hispanic Theology and Popular Piety," 5.

⁸⁵ Elizondo, *Galilean Journey* 23.

⁸⁶ Ibid., 43.

⁸⁷ Rodriguez, *Our Lady of Guadalupe* 120–121. Ada María Isasi-Díaz and Yolanda Tarango also employ the method of listening to the voices of Latinas at the grass-roots level.

⁸⁸ Ibid., 164.

⁸⁹ Elizondo, *Galilean Journey* 51.

⁹⁰ Elizondo, *The Future is Mestizo* 79.

⁹¹ Ibid., 82–83.

⁹² Elizondo, *Galilean Journey* 118.

⁹³ Elizondo, *The Future is Mestizo* 84.

⁹⁴ Roberto S. Goizueta, "La Raza Cósmica? The Vision of José Vasconcelos," *JH/LT* 1/2 (February 1994) 5–27 offers a very fine analysis of Vasconcelos's view of "cultural-racial aesthetics" but also warns against its ambiguity and insufficiency if it remains on the level of a romantic, idealist abstraction that is not sufficiently attendant to the material, historical realities (social, cultural, political, and economic practices, institutions, and structures). "An idealist aesthetics would sever the connection between those beautiful cultural expressions and the histories of suffering and conquest in which they were born. Uprooted from their integral and historical link to the oppressed communities' struggle for liberation, that is, ethical-political praxis, those aesthetic expressions can readily become mere commodities to be consumed in the search for multiculturalism. Our solidarity with the poor would then no longer de-

mand a commitment to social justice but merely sympathetic feelings for 'the other'"
(p. 26).

[95] Virgil P. Elizondo, "*Mestizaje* as a Locus of Theological Reflection" in Deck, ed.,
Frontiers of Hispanic Theology 117.

[96] Elizondo, *Galilean Journey* 91 (emphasis in original).

[97] Ibid., 103.

[98] Ibid., 115 (emphasis in original).

[99] Ibid., 123.

Conclusion: Does the Story Have an Ending?

The thesis of this book is the centrality of narrative in communicating the significance of Jesus. Stories that have metaphoric impact as exemplified in the parables of Jesus, the Gospel of Mark, and the *tilma* of Guadalupe are the primary means of divine revelation. More conceptual kinds of language as exemplified in the Nicene-Constantinopolitan Creed and the *Summa theologiae* of Thomas Aquinas are legitimate and necessary but always subordinate to the primacy of the story that is the foundation and only adequate context for such language. This is similar to Paul Ricoeur's notion of the primacy of the symbol in that we always experience symbols with a kind of first naïveté, then go through a process of critical appropriation of the symbol through asking questions, be they historical, philosophical, personal, etcetera, so that we then experience the symbol anew with a second, postcritical naïveté. This is an ongoing process that, imaged as a spiral, is never-ending. Ricoeur maintains that symbols, which are deeply rooted in life, come to expression as metaphors. I maintain that what give metaphors their primary context and meaning are the stories we tell, specifically those kinds of stories that have metaphoric impact.

To emphasize the metaphoric impact or potential of stories is to emphasize their radical openness to the future. As set forth in Chapter One a narrative-centered christology would seek to maintain the validity and necessity of particular, concrete experience within a given sociohistorical and cultural context (first-century Palestine) precisely in order to sustain the truly catholic (in the sense of inclusivity of all cultural experience in its diversity) and universal (in the sense of transcultural unity) character of the mystery that is Jesus. True universality and intense particularity are inseparably connected in stories that have metaphoric impact. In our analysis of the four faith-images of Jesus we have sought to maintain this catholic instinct of openness to all truth and every value. This does not mean, however, an uncritical acceptance of every claim. As Justo González makes clear there are no innocent stories. Even Aquinas had to struggle with the meaning of Jesus' death on the cross. And struggle in the face of crisis, for many the struggle just to survive, is the basic impulse for every story as a journey that takes shape in concretely lived experience and moves toward a desired outcome (personal and communal identity).

To be effective stories must embody true solidarity with the lived experience of alienation and oppression, and so must have practical, ethically responsible consequences for those who hear and read them. Addressing the challenges to contemporary theology both within the Church and in relation to society, Johann Metz affirms the thesis of this book:

> The idea of God to which Christian orthodoxy binds us is itself a practical idea. The stories of exodus, of conversion, of resistance and suffering belong to its *doctrinal* expression. The pure idea of God is, in reality, an abbreviation, a shorthand for stories without which there is no Christian truth in this idea of God. This also applies to christological orthodoxy. At its core is once again practical knowledge. At its center is not an idea to which one must assent, but a story, not an entertaining story but rather a dangerous one, a story not only to be told but to be lived. Its saving truth is revealed only in this living practice.[1]

The ultimate goal of this book has been to affirm the legitimacy of each faith-image of Jesus within its particular cultural and historical conditions while freeing the normative and authoritative tradition from any form of cultural and/or intellectual imperialism. This means that the very telling of the stories must be done in a way that is truly liberating and not alienating. While Mark's turn to narrative in written form represents a certain distancing of the story from oral immediacy, an overemphasis on the suffering and abandonment of Jesus has led to a kind of internalized impotence on the part of the suffering poor. While the Creed's engagement of a new and different cultural and linguistic environment represents a legitimate attempt to maintain the continuity of the story, an overemphasis on the mystical/contemplative journey into the supra-terrestrial reality of the divine has led to a flight from and denigration of this world. While Aquinas's employment of the new "science" of Aristotelian bent represents an admirable attempt to maintain the consistency of the story, an overemphasis on the purely academic and intellectual has led to ideological dominance that assumes the cultural superiority of the West. And finally, while liberation theology in its return to narrative represents a certain fusing of the story with the contemporary experience of oppression, an overemphasis on the legitimacy of diverse cultures has led to an uncritical romanticizing of one's own culture and a consequent cultural relativism.

In Metz's terms the story of Jesus is a dangerous story. He proposes that theology, in opposition to late modernity, "has to mobilize that dangerous memory which has its source primarily in the proscribed or misunderstood apocalyptic tradition."[2] This involves a hermeneutic of memory that is a critical appropriation of the past through the power of imagination. That creative imagination expresses itself in the power of story for, as Ricoeur says, it is only in narrative that we can overcome the aporias of time. Does the story have an ending? The future is opened up to us insofar as we remember the past not simply as past but as having living and vital consequences in the present that in turn carry us forward into the future. The purpose of handing on apocalyptic texts and symbols is "to discover the sources of our modern fear . . . a fear that there will be no end at all, that our life and our history is pulled into the surging of a faceless evolution which finally rolls over us all, as over grains of sand on the beach."[3]

The story of Jesus is the story of a God who walks in solidarity with those who, as Metz says, should have no history and no future according to the selective process of endless evolution and the dominance of those who would claim to be more fit for survival. Beyond Jonathan Schell's concern for the fate of the earth and Stephen Hawking's proposal of a finite cosmos with no boundaries there lies the free, creative, ironic imagination that Sandra Schneiders calls "the paschal imagination." Whether it is imagined as an apocalyptic cataclysm or a gradual transformation, the important thing is that the story does have an end. It is this hope, this expectation that energizes the imagination and finally constitutes Christian identity. It is this that drives us *into*—not away from—history as the place of God's self-communication and as the place where the powers of evil and death must be confronted and overcome. So it was with Jesus and so it must be with us if we are his followers. The story, finally, is God's own story and it is God who is the teller of the tale.

To return in conclusion to the question with which we began: has our image of Jesus, the way we experience and imagine him, shifted?[4] Indeed it has and must continue to do so if he is to remain alive, active, and present in the midst of our human lives and histories. Thus it is that we continue to re-tell the story of Jesus in our own lives until the master of the house comes (Mark 13:35) and wipes away every tear (Rev 21:4).

Notes: Conclusion

[1] Johann Baptist Metz, "Theology Today: New Crises and New Visions," Catholic Theological Society of America *Proceedings* 40 (1985) 7 (emphasis in original). In the course of his argument he advocates "a narrative-practical expression" of Christian universality "which avoids the dangers of intellectual imperialism" (p. 5).

[2] Ibid., 11.

[3] Ibid., 13.

[4] Rudolf Schnackenburg, *Jesus in the Gospels. A Biblical Christology* (Louisville: Westminster/John Knox Press, 1995) reviews the "faith-picture" of Jesus in each of the

four gospels and concludes that while the picture is varied there is a "unified faith-picture" of Jesus that underlies the various sketches. This is true, but the differences—especially in the move from Mark to John—remain striking and represent a shift conditioned by changing historical, cultural, and theological circumstances.

Index of Modern Authors

This index is intended as a bibliographical aid. Ancient authors are pretty well limited to the chapters that treat of their period in history. Only modern authors are indicated where the name actually appears. Some names are omitted if they are not cited in a substantive way.

216